Social Capital and Institutional Constraints

The sociological concept of social capital has grown in popularity in recent years and research programs in North America, Europe and East Asia have demonstrated how social capital has a significant impact on occupational mobility, community building, social movement and economic development.

This book uses new empirical data to test how social capital works in different societies with diverse political-economic and cultural institutions. Taking a comparative approach, this study focuses on data from three different societies, China, Taiwan and the US, in order to reveal the international commonalities and disparities in access to and activation of social capital in labor markets. In particular, this book tests whether political economic and cultural differences between capitalist and socialist economic systems and between Western and Confucian cultures create different types of individual social networks and usages. This comparison leads to Joonmo Son's fundamental argument that the institutional constraints of a society's political economy on the one hand, and culture on the other, profoundly impact on both the composition and utilization of social capital.

Based on rigorous statistical analysis, this book will be essential reading for students and scholars of economic sociology and comparative politics.

Joonmo Son is Assistant Professor of Sociology at the National University of Singapore.

Routledge Contemporary China Series

Social Capital and Institutional Constraints

A comparative analysis of China, Taiwan and the US

Joonmo Son

LONDON AND NEW YORK

First published 2013
by Routledge
2 Park Square, Milton Park, Abingdon, Oxon OX14 4RN

Simultaneously published in the USA and Canada
by Routledge
711 Third Avenue, New York, NY 10017

Routledge is an imprint of the Taylor & Francis Group, an informa business

© 2013 Joonmo Son

British Library Cataloguing in Publication Data
A catalogue record for this book is available from the British Library

Library of Congress Cataloging in Publication Data
Son, Joonmo.
  Social capital and institutional constraints : a comparative analysis of
China, Taiwan and the US / Joonmo Son.
    p. cm. – (Routledge contemporary China series)
  Includes bibliographical references and index.
  1. Social networks – Cross-cultural studies. 2. Economics – Sociological
aspects – Cross-cultural studies. 3. Social capital (Sociology) – China.
4. Social capital (Sociology) – Taiwan. 5. Social capital (Sociology) –
United States. I. Title.
  HM741.S64 2012
  302.3 – dc23

                                                                    2012004415

ISBN: 978-0-415-59522-3 (hbk)
ISBN: 978-0-203-10474-3 (ebk)

Typeset in Times New Roman
by RefineCatch Limited, Bungay, Suffolk

Printed and bound in the United States of America by Publishers Graphics,
LLC on sustainably sourced paper.

For Mi-Kyeong

Contents

Tables

Figures

Preface

I first became interested in the relationship between social capital and institutional constraints when I worked as a second-year reporter at YTN, a twenty-four-hour news channel in South Korea in 1996. It was September 18, another seemingly normal day. At dawn I made the rounds of several major police stations in Seoul to check if there were any significant events to report on air. Nothing unusual occurred until I got a call from a senior reporter who told me to go quickly to the Ministry of Defense in Yong-san. When I arrived at the pressroom of the ministry, I could feel that something had gone seriously wrong. I received another call informing me that a car with a camera crew had been sent to pick me up at the ministry. Its destination was An-in-jin Ri – the name was unfamiliar to me then – in Gang-neung city, a small northeastern fishing village about seventy kilometers from the borderline between North and South Korea. As we rode in the car I at last became fully aware that North Korean armed spies had come onshore from a submarine – a submarine that had malfunctioned so they were forced to land.

As soon as the dozens of reporters from newspapers and broadcasting companies arrived at the spot in the afternoon, we were led by a group of South Korean soldiers to a nearby mountain called Cheong-hak. There was no explanation of why we had to hurriedly climb the mountain. Halfway up the mountain the soldiers at the head stopped suddenly; on the hillside a yellow photo line had been placed around a vacant area. At first I could not tell what was inside the line because a thick forest darkened the area. I became aware of a bad smell and some of reporters began vomiting. I realized that the corpses of eleven North Korean soldiers lay in a row on the ground covered with fallen leaves. They had all been shot in the head. Later it was revealed that they were crew members of the submarine who were supposedly untrained for survival as armed spies. However, it was not clear if they had committed suicide voluntarily or had been killed by the armed spies, their own colleagues. One thing was clear – there was no sign of a fight between the crew members and the armed spies. It thus appeared that their rules of engagement prescribed that the crew members should be terminated first if they were pursued by enemies.

A mop-up operation in search of the North Korean armed spies went on for forty-nine days until early November, requiring over a million man-days in the region, and leaving seventeen South Korean soldiers and civilians dead and over thirty wounded. In the days following the incident thirteen of the remaining armed spies were killed in action. Only one remained missing and was assumed to have crossed the border successfully. Thus they either died or fled. However, there was an outlier. One spy, Kwang-soo Lee, managed to separate from his colleagues and surrendered on the first day. I recall his recorded message to his colleagues resounding throughout the mountainous areas in eastern Gang-neung through megaphones mounted on numerous military trucks: "Comrades, surrender. They will not kill you. I am treated well." In late October, at a nationally televised press conference held in Seoul, I was able to ask him the question that had haunted me: had the crew members at the Cheong-hak Mountain killed themselves, or had they been killed? He stared at me for a while, then slowly lowered his head. Mr Lee is now in his late forties and gives special lectures to South Korean soldiers on security threats from the North.

In my over seven years as a reporter I experienced not a few impressive social and political incidents. Nonetheless, the tragic scene of the dead North Koreans who were indoctrinated to be killed or commit suicide in certain situations was the most persistent one in my memory. Given that it is likely that the crew members were killed by their comrades – or at least that the armed spies did not prevent them from shooting themselves – it appeared that their social relations were shattered by institutional directives. From a sociological viewpoint these men had been oversocialized to give up their lives, even though the term, oversocialization, has been criticized as a simplified concept that stresses too heavily the power of social structure. Yet not all the North Koreans who landed on An-in-jin Ri succumbed to the power of structural indoctrination. One deviated from it and tried, though unsuccessfully, to persuade his comrades to desert the unconditionally robotic behavioral pattern.

In 2002 I made the transition from reporter to doctoral student in sociology in the United States. While taking a course on social capital from Professor Nan Lin in my first semester at Duke, I made up my mind to conduct research on how institutional constraints moderate the effect of social capital crossnationally. Of course, I had North and South Korea in mind. However, gathering data from the North was – and is – impossible. I therefore decided to compare China, Taiwan, and the United States because Professor Lin planned to administer surveys composed of the same social capital module in these three countries. The two most important comparative axes I adopted were political economy and culture; political economy divides the three countries into a capitalist (the United States and Taiwan) vs. socialist (China) dichotomy, while the collective Confucian culture joins the two East Asian countries against the United States with its individualistic culture. The main focus was placed on China. I found that compared to Taiwan and the United States, the effect of social capital in China was smaller, presumably affected by the dual constraints of socialism and Confucianism; nevertheless, its effect remained significant on status attainment outcome, indicating the resilience of individual social capital. Therefore the study found that individual choice in forming and utilizing social capital still takes its portion in explicating labor market outcomes even under rigid institutional constraints, as Mr Lee's choice went against inhumane directives even though he could only save his life alone. Helped greatly by the mentorship of Professor Lin, I defended my dissertation on this topic in 2008. This monograph is a thorough revision of the dissertation, undertaken over the past three years since my arrival at the National University of Singapore.

I am indebted to many persons for their help with this book. I thank Professors Nan Lin, Edward Tiryakian, John Wilson, Linda George, Lynn Smith-Lovin, and Angie O'Rand. Without their critical advice I could not have developed this comparative research on social capital. Dr Qiushi Feng, my long-time friend from Duke years and now also a departmental colleague at the NUS, contributed insights and instrumental assistance on Chinese socialist institutional constraints found in Chapter 3. In regard to Taiwanese institutional constraints, Professors Nan Lin and Chih-joy Jay Chen at the Academia Sinica read the manuscript and gave helpful comments.

The Faculty of Arts and Social Sciences and the Department of Sociology at the NUS allowed me to have a sabbatical semester without which I could not have finished the manuscript. In particular, I am thankful for the collegial support of Professors Chua Beng Huat, Paulin Straughan, Vineeta Sinha, Jean Yeung, Ho Kong Chong, Lian Kwen Fee, and Tan Ern Ser at the NUS Sociology. My student Fadzli Baharom did an excellent job in helping the literature review of the institutional constraints in the labor markets of the three focal countries. Cyndy Brown, my copyeditor, went the extra mile to improve the quality of the manuscript. Hannah Mack and Ed Needle at Routledge patiently provided editorial support.

I give special thanks to the late Mr Tae-Joon Park, the president of the POSCO TJ Park Foundation, from which I was awarded a research grant for this monograph. He passed on when the manuscript was about to be completed.

I am truly grateful for the sacrificial love and support of my wife, Mi-Kyeong Kam, through the years when I was a reporter, a doctoral student, and a professional sociologist in Korea, the United States, and Singapore. This book is dedicated to her. My two adorable children, Hahae and Hajin, could not play with their father as much as they wished because this project and others occupied his time. I am sorry about this and want to spend more time with them to show how much I love them. My parents in Seoul, Yeong-Gu Son and Sam-Nam Kim, consistently prayed for me and my family, allowing me to break out of my own personal "constraints" and reach significant goals that were almost unimaginable in the past.

Lastly, I want to make clear that the goal of all my work, including this book, is to try to fulfill God's justice in the social world, particularly for those who are under the shackles of inhumane institutional constraints.

Then you will know the truth, and the truth will set you free (John 8:32).

Acknowledgments

Data used in this monograph were drawn from the thematic research project "Social Capital: Its Origins and Consequences," sponsored by Academia Sinica, Taiwan, through its Research Center for Humanities and Social Sciences, and the Institute of Sociology. The principal investigators of the project are Nan Lin, Yang-Chih Fu, and Chih-Jou Jay Chen. I also gratefully acknowledge receipt of a Research Grant for Asian Studies awarded by the POSCO TJ Park Foundation in Seoul, Korea.

1   A comparative study of social capital

The essential building blocks of the social world are relations among human beings. Like it or not, a significant part of one's social life is composed of ties with others who are either immediately or indirectly related. Figuratively speaking, humans are not isolated islands floating around an infinite ocean (Flap 2002); rather, people usually form specific relations with others in structurally arranged and, to some significant extent, confined areas of social life. This means that there are structural forces that prearrange the general settings of social relationships even before actors appear on the scene and choose their social contacts out of the seemingly countless people around them. In other words, the choices of social relations are far from a random selection.

For example, it is not likely that a five-year-old boy in Abu Dhabi in the United Arab Emirates could befriend another five-year-old boy in Seattle, Washington in the United States. If this geographic barrier sounds too obvious, it may be that a temporary Mexican migrant construction worker in the United States cannot make regular contact with a local white-collar manager in the IT industry, even when geographic distance is removed. Further, it is well known that even in a single society, racial/ethnic groups, if any, have a strong tendency to maintain predominantly homogeneous in-group ties; as a result, interracial or interethnic ties are significantly fewer. In addition, ethnic differentiation even within a race can hardly be ignored, as in the tragic "ethnic cleansing" of Tutsi by Hutu in Rwanda in the mid-1990s, even though the deadly antagonism between these two ethnic groups was much affected by the Rwandan postcolonial legacy. Even when visible cues of collective differentiation do not exist in racially and ethnically homogeneous societies, dialects may instead work as verbal signals of regional origin, and minute linguistic differences among regions may form invisible but effectively exclusive structural boundaries among social groups, as we see from the long-standing conflict between the Young-nam and Ho-nam regions in South Korea. Religion should not be omitted from the list of possible structural barriers of social relations, as the history and current affairs of Europe, Africa, and Asia have shown; it is perceived to be the core pillar in the clash of civilizations in the post-Cold War era (Huntington 1996). Of course, the existence of structural barriers does not mean that all social relations are predetermined and actors accept them unconditionally. Nonetheless, one cannot deny that the pattern of social relations is strongly associated with social structure. Therefore it is necessary to understand macrostructural or institutional constraints that affect how the pattern of social relations is formulated. These constraints can be composed of a variety of factors such as race and/or ethnicity, gender, or types of political economy in accordance with the set of unique contextual factors of a given society.

Structuring of social relations

According to Breiger (2004), who tracked down the metaphoric use of networks to several key figures in sociology, Marx stated, "Society is not merely an aggregate of individuals; it is the sum of the relations in which these individuals stand to one another" (Marx [1857] 1956: 96, cited in Breiger 2004: 505). Thus interest in social relations is as old as the history of sociological enterprise itself. In particular, from its incipient period sociological enterprise has had much stake in the relationship and interaction between social relations and macrostructural factors (Durkheim [1895] 1964; Simmel [1922] 1955). For instance, Durkheim proposed the idea that individual identity and behavior are affected by the social location of an actor, and social networks among actors are conduits of new economic rules formed among occupational categories in modern and industrialized society (Durkheim [1893] 1984; Dobbin 2004). Thus individuals are not individuals per se in sociological research; they are enclosed within and interacting with the social structure in which they are embedded. This is the basis of the Durkheimian argument that self-interest-seeking behavior of each actor based on egoism does not guarantee social integration but could instead be deleterious to both individuals and community (Tiryakian 2008). In an extreme case of strong embeddedness, social structure and societal force may sometimes generate indirect cause of altruistic suicides committed by those who believe they should do so for the benefit of moral commitment and social integration (Durkheim [1897] 1951). Again, it is notable that social networks exist between a macrosocial structure and individual actors, and it is through networks composed of people as their nodes that specific behavioral patterns in accordance with the structural arrangement are shared, interpreted, enforced in varying degrees, reorganized, or sometimes refuted.

Thus, over the long run, different social structures give rise to their own brands of social networks – largely affected by the distinct history and culture of each society. For instance, the social networks coined by the medieval Catholic Church that condemned wealth and exalted poverty were different from those introduced by Protestant ethics in the industrialization era in which accumulation of wealth was taken as a sign of God's elects (Weber [1905] 1998; Freund 1968). Likewise, the Chinese dynasties under Confucian ideology organized a unique set of rules and regulations, including tacit

2 Dimensions (1) Access (2) Mobilization (Activation)

knowledge regarding how to relate to each other by considering age, gender, or social positions, that differ to a significant extent from the principles of social relations in socialist China (Tu 1991, 1993). Further, to mention a specific dimension of demographic features, social networks of the American people in terms of their racial proportion differ before and after slavery and racial segregation, even though racial homogeneity is still a dominant tendency for both whites and nonwhites (Franklin and Moss 1994; Moody 2001).

Social capital and institutions

In particular, this monograph tests whether political, economic, and cultural differences between capitalist and socialist systems and between Western and Confucian cultures yield different types of individual social networks and usages (Hall and Soskice 2001).

In other words, the intrinsic principles of network composition and utilization can be dissimilar in different political economic and cultural institutions. The specific macrostructural contexts in this book take three different societal entities, China, Taiwan, and the United States. The fundamental argument is that the institutional constraints of the political economy and culture affect the composition and utilization of social capital, or social resources, in the three countries.

To delimit the scope of the study, in this book "social capital," defined as "the resources embedded in social networks accessed and utilized by actors" (Lin 2001: 25), is the main variable of interest accounted for by the effects of the two macroinstitutional arrangements – political economy and culture. As implied by the definition, social capital lies in social networks at the individual level, and its volume is determined by how resourceful each node (i.e., a friend or a work colleague) of a social network is. Social capital has two dimensions: one is access (or accessibility) to the nodes and their embedded resources; and the other is activation (or mobilization) of the resources when certain instrumental or emotional needs must be fulfilled. Access is the necessary condition for activation, but it is not a sufficient condition because access may not guarantee activation all the time, and we know that in reality some ties exist that are not utilizable although they are resourceful. It is undeniable, though, that there is a strong correlation between access and activation; in other words, those who have better access to social capital are more likely to activate pertinent social resources when needed. In sum, the access dimension is related to the whole volume of social capital, while the activation dimension is associated with the efficacy of social capital by which an instrumental or expressive goal can be achieved.

Regarding the comparative study of social capital in varied social contexts, I propose that to a large extent the access dimension is formed by the effects of macroinstitutions in each given country because institutions provide different chances of creating social ties between individuals, organizations, and social groups. How are institutions related to networks in the first place? As

Social networks (not differentiated from S.C.)

KEY Proposition

Def. of S.C.

2 inst. arrangements (1) pol. econ. (2) culture.

insts / networks

A in m

→ SC. resides at indiv. level. necessary + sufficient.
(1) accessibility.
(2) mobilization

Nee and Ingram (1998) point out, institutions exert their powers over social networks. In other words, institutions provide general principles of social relations. This is shown vividly in their definition of an institution: "An institution is *a web of interrelated norms* – formal and informal – governing social relationships. It is by structuring social interactions that institutions produce group performance, in such primary groups as families and work units as well as in social units as large as organizations and even entire economies [emphasis in the original]" (Nee and Ingram 1998: 19). Nee and Ingram also note that it is like seeking a missing link between network embeddedness and new institutionalism perspectives so that an integrative and balanced theoretical view of "a choice-within-institutional-constraints approach" can be generated. The present study presents an empirical trial to seek such a missing link by testing the interaction between social capital and institutional constraints.

Accessed and activated social capital

Institutions stipulate by formal and informal norms what kind of social relations are duly accessible and which are not. This structuring of social interactions at the individual level adds up to a generalized pattern of network composition at the national level, which can be compared to those from other countries.

As depicted in Figure 1.1, the key interest of the present study lies in the differential effects of macroinstitutional arrangements such as capitalist vs. socialist political economy and Western vs. Confucian cultures. Specifically, I propose that the advanced capitalist United States, state socialist China, and developmental Taiwan have formed unique sets of accessed social capital due to the institutional differences. I propose that differences, if any, in accessed social capital across the three countries can be explained at least in part by the political economic institutions (capitalist vs. state socialist) and/or cultural institutions (Western vs. Confucian) among them. My first aim is to identify variances in the compositions of accessed social capital among the countries. Above all, a uniform set of measures of accessed social capital is essential for the purpose of comparative study among different countries. A consistent comparison of the United States, China, and Taiwan in terms of their access dimensions of social capital is plausible with the help of identical measures of social capital based on the network alters' positions in the occupational hierarchies in the three societies. I conduct the comparative study of social capital among the three case societies employing the position generator method (Lin 2001; Lin and Dumin 1986; Lin, Fu, and Hsung 2001). This approach makes it possible to launch a systematic comparative study on social capital in the labor markets of different countries.

Once the possible institutional effects on the formation of social capital are identified, the second goal of the present study is to check the effect of activation and utilization of social contacts in the status attainment process. The efficacy of activating social resources to produce beneficial returns in the

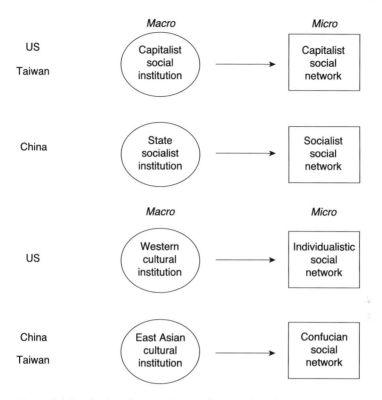

Figure 1.1 Institutional constraints and types of social networks

labor market has been supported empirically in the literature (Lin, Dayton, and Greenwald 1978; Lin, Ensel, and Vaughn 1981; Marsden and Hurlbert 1988; Smith 2005; Wegener 1991). In line with the present study, De Graaf and Flap (1988) conducted a comparative study on the activation of social capital in the labor markets of several Western countries. They found that Americans were more likely to use social contacts than Germans or Dutch, though the data they used were neither nationally representative nor from the same survey module. Likewise, the main thrust related to the issue of activated social capital in the present study is to (1) check if the patterns in activating social resources vary in the three countries, (2) identify which people are more prone to using social contacts in the job search, and (3) test if the use of social contacts is positively related to better returns in the three labor markets and which people get the strongest effect of social resources. The analysis of whether and to what extent social resources affect social mobility may shed light on the possible variation in the role of social resources in the labor markets of the three countries.

Specifically, in each society I analyze two types of variations: demographic variation in the access and utility of social resources; and the relationship between tie strength and social resources. By utilizing sociodemographic categories such as gender and race, the intrasociety variation of social capital across different social groups is investigated. Females and racial minorities are expected to have less access to and activation of social capital compared with males and the racial majority. The analysis of race provides a chance to delve into the unequal distribution of social resources between whites and nonwhites, which is found only in the United States. Gender analysis generates much information on inter- and intrasocietal comparisons of accessed and activated social capital since almost every society suffers from gender inequality.

I then check whether Granovetter's strength-of-weak-ties proposition holds in different institutional milieus related to the activation of social contacts. Granovetter states that "the strength of a tie is a (probably linear) combination of the amount of time, the emotional intensity, the intimacy (mutual confiding), and the reciprocal services which characterize the tie" (1973: 1361). He then shows that work contacts (weak ties) of male professional, technical, and managerial workers are more likely to provide matches with better jobs in the job market than family-social ties (strong ties) ([1974] 1995: 45). However, the strength-of-weak-ties proposition has produced inconsistent results in empirical studies (Approval: Granovetter 1974; Lin, Dayton, and Greenwald 1978; Lin, Ensel, and Vaughn 1981 vs. Denial: Bian 1997; Bridges and Villemez 1986; Marsden and Hurlburt 1988). It is notable that Bian found that strong ties were essential bridges between job seekers and their helpers in administrative positions of job allocation in state socialist China. This case study hints at the strong possibility that patterns of tie utilization differ between capitalist and socialist countries. Furthermore, since the study tests the primacy of family ties in China, it suggests cultural differences between East Asian societies and their Western counterparts, thereby implying a possible reason for the inconsistent results of the strength-of-weak-ties proposition. In the literature role relations (families, neighbors, friends, or work contacts) of respondents have been inconsistently used to indicate strong or weak tie strength. For instance, some researchers include the role category of "friends" in strong ties (e.g., Völker and Flap 1999), whereas others include it with weak ties (e.g., Lin and Dumin 1986). Even though the strength of tie may form a continuum, the way it is measured depends on the dichotomous concept of strong vs. weak ties based on the presence or absence of ties of a specific role relation.

In order to avoid this perplexing problem of gauging the relational distance between a person and his/her contact, I introduce three structural layers of social relations: binding (family-oriented ties), bonding (daily contacts), and belonging (participation in formal organizations) (Lin, Ye, and Ensel 1999; Son, Lin, and George 2008). I propose that the structural layers of social relations function as the seedbeds of social resources. According to this schema, social relations are categorized into three hierarchical structures in which (1) binding (family-oriented ties) takes the innermost layer where human relations are initially formed; (2) belonging (participation in formal organizations) generates the outermost layer where secondary associational motivations such as political, social, economic, or religious causes, apart from primary social relations, relate social actors to one another through organizational fields; and (3) bonding (daily contacts) makes up the middle space between the informal binding layer and the formal belonging layer. In some sense, the binding layer works as a proxy for strong ties, while the belonging layer serves as a proxy for weak ties. That said, I suspect that the binding layer will be the main source of social resources in East Asian societies due to the Confucian social order of family orientation, whereas the belonging layer will produce the most social resources in the United States because it has been a country of associations from its incipient period of nation building (Tocqueville [1840] 2003). The bonding layer in between the innermost and outermost layers is conceptualized as a buffer zone in which a person interacts with network alters regardless of role relations. Logically, this layer may thus include diverse social contacts of family members, work colleagues, or comembers of a voluntary association. Nevertheless, the basic assumption is that the richer the bonding layer the better returns one may expect in labor market outcomes because the layer is an indicator of accessed social capital capacity.

As explained, it is assumed that retaining greater accessed social capital will provide a higher chance of activating it, which in turn may bring forth instrumental or expressive outcomes that were otherwise not obtainable. From the procedural perspective, the bipartite dimensions of social capital produce a dynamic process wherein the access and activation of social resources develop concurrently in multifaceted informal and formal domains of family, school, religion, voluntary associations, or the labor market, as a result of which its holders may experience higher likelihood of achieving their goals. If such individual outcomes are aggregated at the national level it is then expected that societies rich in accessed social capital will see greater returns from activated social capital on average than those that are poor in accessed social capital. Without accessed social capital or social capital capacity one is less likely to activate social capital; thus accessed social capital precedes activated social capital. In general, it is expected that the amount of accessed social capital is related to the higher chance of its being activated. However, actors with the same amount of accessed social capital do not always achieve the same outcomes; it depends on how skillfully one deploys and activates social capital for a purposive action. Likewise, activation of social capital by actors is proposed to produce a variation in outcomes in the labor market. Strategic use of the right kind of contacts can help increase the success rate of purposive actions. Thus in terms of the theoretical framework I emphasize the constraints of social institutions on the formation of accessed social capital; however, even under such constraints and the resultant limited degree of freedom, actors react to the constraints and exert their power of agency by activating social capital so that social mobility, however restricted, finds its portion in the structure, as depicted in Figure 1.2.

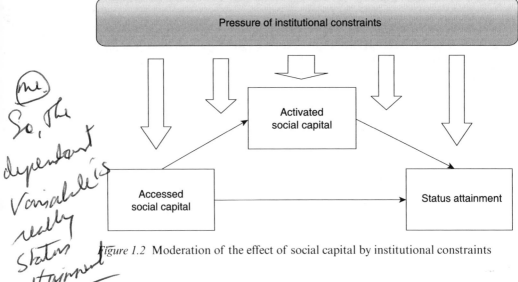

Figure 1.2 Moderation of the effect of social capital by institutional constraints

[handwritten margin notes: "(me) So, the dependent variable is really Status attainment"; "(we) How does this follow?"; "Causal Sequence"]

Therefore, activated social capital performs two major roles. First, it becomes an indicator of the power of agency. If we suppose an extreme case where activated social capital does not carry any significant effect on status attainment, we conclude that institutions nullify the choice of agency. I propose that even when institutional constraints are rigid, activated social capital still has a share in explaining the variance of status attainment. Second, the comparison of activated social capital among societies thus shows which society has stronger agency. The effects of activated social capital may vary across societies. I propose that societies with less institutional constraints are likely to have a stronger effect of activated social capital than those with more.

Independently from the access–activation–achievement causal sequence, accessed social capital by itself may exert direct impact on achievement (see Figure 1.2). The reasons vary. First, it is possible that social capital works though the invisible hand; for instance, routine job information flows in without activation of social contacts. Using the same US data as the present study, Lin and Ao (2008) found that greater accessed social capital is associated with higher likelihood of receiving job information in routine situations. In turn, getting routine job information is related to better returns in the labor market in terms of wage and occupational status. Other studies also report that unsolicited job information is related to attainment of better jobs, especially among mid-career male workers (McDonald 2005; McDonald and Elder 2006). It is likely that workers with a good reputation and more accessed social capital tend to get job information when they are not actually searching for new positions. Second, it is also possible that the effect of accessed social capital (or social capital capacity) is not fully captured (or mediated) by activated social capital or routine job information measures; in other words, there could be "unmeasured" and "undetected" portions of accessed social capital (Lin and Ao 2008: 131). Therefore it is not unusual that accessed social capital maintains its direct effect on labor market outcomes after its power is partially mediated by activated social capital specifically invoked to help attain the outcomes. Considering that in general the empirical findings from the United States report that accessed and activated social capital are effective in the status attainment process *ceteris paribus*, the main question is whether they also carry significant explanatory power of status attainment in China and Taiwan; a greater concern applies to China because the job assignment system enforced by the socialist state officially prohibited the use of social contacts up until the early 1990s.

Overview

Having described the conceptual frame of the study thus far, the relevant literature on accessed and activated social capital is reviewed in Chapter 2. As bipartite indicators of the social resources, understanding of accessed and activated social capital is crucial for developing a mediatory relation between social capital and status attainment. In Chapter 3 I discuss institutions and their plausible constraints on individual choices. In particular, political economy and culture comprise the two institutions that provide typologies for the three case countries that I employ in the monograph. How was accessed social capital formed under the plausible influence of institutional constraints in each country? Further, how likely is it that activated social capital affects status attainment outcomes under different institutional environments? With these two questions in mind, we need to identify some specific institutional conditions and constraints that possibly mark the structural boundaries of social capital and its use in each selected country.

In Chapter 4 I introduce specific institutional models of the three countries, the measurement of social capital, and two sets of hypotheses to be tested in the empirical part of the book – the two sets of hypotheses deal with accessed and activated social capital respectively. In particular, the position generators are presented as the method to measure accessed social capital embedded in social relations based on the positions taken by network alters in labor markets. This measurement is the backbone of this study because its assumption is that accessed social capital can be compared across societies using the same module of position generators. The hypotheses deal with the relationship among accessed and activated social capital and status attainment, controlling for other plausible confounders of the causal relation. The data, measures, and methods are described in Chapter 5. The data are from the same module of the survey in the three countries. Thus the measures, including position generators, the items on activated social capital, and other control variables are comparable among the cases. I employ both regression and structural equation modeling as methods. The reason for utilizing structural equation modeling is largely because (1) it is fitted to the path model framework in which accessed and activated social capital are proposed to affect status attainment, other things being equal; and (2) the modeling technique also allows systematic comparison of structural coefficients across the three countries.

Chapter 6 tests if the structural layers of binding, bonding, and belonging are related to the three indicators of accessed social capital, extensity, upper reachability, and range of prestige. The amounts of accessed social capital are also compared across the three societies on the basis of the latent means of accessed social capital indicators measured by a structural equation model. The path analytic sequence from accessed social capital through activated social capital to status attainment is tested in Chapter 7. I first identify whether accessed social capital based on the position generators is related to several indicators of activated social capital, namely presence of contact, chain length of the contacts, contact status, and routine job information. Among these, contact status should be the most pertinent indicator of activated social capital because it captures the quality of utilized social resources; however, other items are also relevant in testing some plausible variation in activated social capital across the focal case societies. For instance, it is worth testing if routine job information turns out to be an efficacious predictor of status attainment in the three societies. In addition, the length of contact chain is expected to be longer in China because job searchers tended to depend mainly on trustable strong ties due to the illegal nature of the use of personal contacts under the job assignment system up until the early 1990s (Bian 1997). I next test if either accessed or activated social capital is related to the outcomes in the labor markets, that is, occupational class and income. Lastly, I present multigroup (composed of the three countries) path analysis results of the aforementioned sequence from accessed, activated social capital to status attainment, after which the test of parameter invariance is employed to identify whether the effects of social capital vary among the three countries. In Chapter 8 the hypotheses presented in Chapter 4 are recalled to clarify whether each is supported in light of relevant statistical test results. The concluding chapter also discusses the resilience or counterreaction of individual choice against institutional constraints. I conclude that due to differential degrees in interactions between individual social capital and institutional constraints, variation exists in both accessed and activated social capital and their effects on status attainment across the three societies. Although restricted in its generalizability in the sense that the study has a limited number of cases, the results point to the possibility that multinational variation in social capital and its effect on status attainment may be at work in varied societies of different institutional composition and constraints, and cultural and historical legacies.

2 Accessed and activated social capital

The term "social capital" has been widely used in a variety of areas such as sociology, management studies, economics, health and illness, development studies, and political science (e.g., Adler and Kwon 2002; Evans 1996; Fukuyama 2001; Kawachi et al. 1997; Knack 2002; Knack and Keefer 1997; Nahapiet and Ghoshal 1998; Putnam 1993, 2000; Wilson and Musick 1998; Woolcock 1998). In terms of its conceptualization, various indices were used in forming the concept of and measuring social capital, including trust, civic participation, social cohesion, norms of reciprocity, participatory democracy, social development, and even census response (Bebbington and Perreault 1999; McClenaghan 2000; Paxton 2002; Putnam 1993, 2000; Putnam, Leonardi, and Nanetti 1993; Schafft and Brown 2000). In regard to the level of analysis, some argue that social capital is collective resources at the community level, while social networks are relational assets at the individual level (e.g., Kawachi et al. 1997). Considering such a lack of unity in conceptualizing and measuring social capital, it is necessary to clarify what kind of social capital concept I follow in this book.

As made clear in the previous chapter, I take the view that social capital is social resources in the sense that it refers to embedded resources in social relations. This view has been employed mostly in the literature of status attainment at the individual level (Lin 2001; Lin and Dumin 1986; Mouw 2003); however, it also has potential to be utilized at the organizational level (Son and Lin 2008). In regard to this particular line of social capital theory that presupposes network embeddedness, we can begin the discussion with Coleman and Bourdieu because both of them conceived social capital as collective resources exclusively available among actors who share networks.

It should be noted that Coleman and Bourdieu were among the first to introduce the notion of social capital. Coleman (1988, 1990) offers a general theoretical framework of social capital characterized as human capital embedded in or available through social networks. According to him, social networks function to link individuals with resources in closed communities. His concept of social capital thus stems from the traditional structural-functional approach:

> Social capital is defined by its function. It is not a single entity but a variety of different entities, with two elements in common: they all consist of some aspect of social structures, and they facilitate certain actions of actors – whether persons or corporate actors – within the structure. Like other forms of capital, social capital is productive, making possible the achievement of certain ends that in its absence would not be possible. Like physical capital and human capital, social capital is not completely fungible but may be specific to certain activities.
>
> (Coleman 1988: S98)

As seen, Coleman postulates that the function of social capital is prescribed by social structure acknowledging the power of macroinstitutions. Thus the present study is generally in line with Coleman's conceptualization, but not entirely so because Coleman proposes social capital to be within the boundaries of a closed community, naturally blocking the possibility that this capital may be formed and utilized among dissimilar actors across group boundaries. Assuming this type of social capital within a closed community, Coleman voices great concern regarding the existence of generalized reciprocity as the backbone of exchange behaviors among rational actors. He was affected by Homans' exchange theory (1950) in conceptualizing social capital; however, he perceived that exchange behaviors are not confined to dyadic relations between actors but are able to generate externalities and public goods and bads (Coleman 1987). Thus social norms are important in producing "governmental and formal institutions to sanction" unconstrained actions by some selfish parties (1987: 153). In this context, generalized reciprocity is institutionalized as a sanction among people in a community after a long period of exchange and interaction. Coleman's conception of social capital therefore explains the specialized norm of reciprocity and trust among actors in some specific social settings; for example, Jewish merchants in New York engaging in exchanges of diamonds without formal insurance because of the preexisting norm of trust based on family, religious, and community ties, or student activists at Korean colleges in the 1980s recruiting new members from their own high schools, hometowns, or churches to form and maintain entrusted networks to avoid detection by the military regime then in power.

Bourdieu is similar to Coleman in focusing on the closure of social relations. Further, he thinks of it as resources that exist as potential and could actually be activated when in need among people of *institutionalized* relationships:

> Social capital is the aggregate of the actual or potential resources which are linked to possession of a durable network of more or less institutionalized relationships of mutual acquaintance and recognition – or in other words, to membership in a group – which provides each of its members with the backing of the collectivity-owned capital, a "credential" which entitles them to credit, in the various senses of the word.
>
> (Bourdieu 1986: 248)

Bourdieu's social capital is thus an exclusionary mechanism by which a ruling class constructs solid social relations within the class boundary and exchanges credits among its members alone, but rejects outsiders of lower classes. He developed this concept of social capital in order to discuss the conversion of economic capital into other types of capital, namely cultural and social capital. The reason he focused on such a conversion process was to argue that a ruling class has alternative ways to transfer its collective resources to the next generations when direct transmission of economic capital is prevented. In other words, for Bourdieu social capital functions as a channel of intergenerational transmission of class interests. As a result, lower classes are alienated from the process of production and reproduction of social capital and deprived of its benefits.

Thus for Bourdieu and Coleman social capital is a "collective asset" that can only be maintained and reinforced through investment in closed social relations within invisible but clearly existing class boundaries (Lin 2001: 23). For these two scholars, network closure is an indispensable assumption without which social capital cannot be generated and maintained (see Portes 1998 for how the social capital concept originated from these two theorists and, in particular, how Coleman was affected by Glen Loury in relating social capital to human capital).

Proposing that social resources, meaning resources accessed by social networks, positively affect outcomes of instrumental actions taken in the labor market, Lin (1999, 2001, 2006) broke open the closed boundaries (communities, classes, or social strata) containing social relations. His social capital concept is built on the social structure of occupational hierarchy and thus includes unequal distribution of economic and social resources. It affirms that a reproduction mechanism of social statuses across generations exists by acknowledging the advantage/disadvantage of better/worse social origins, called "the strength-of-position proposition" (Lin 2001: 64) – in brief, when one occupies a position in the occupational hierarchy, its hierarchical location tends to be significantly associated with others taken by one's adult children. However, Lin's unique contribution lies in that he did not set insurmountable boundaries for access and activation of social capital among classes and other kinds of social groupings. Also, he suggests that actors are not just passive subjects of structural forces by articulating the social-capital proposition: "Access to and use of better social capital leads to more successful action" (Lin 2001: 60). It should also be noted that the benefits of access and activation of social capital do not exclude members of lower classes.

With greater degrees of freedom in an open structure than in a closed one, Lin's actors also enjoy the advantage of being bridges themselves or being closer to bridges for instrumental actions. The remarkable thing about this perspective is that comparative studies across modernized societies become possible because the traits of the labor market structure from which social networks develop are similar. In this regard, note that labor markets under transition from state socialism to capitalism share consistent patterns of advanced capitalist labor markets in terms of labor force participation rates, unemployment rates, and even job placement services (Jenkins 2001). Therefore it is plausible to include China, a state socialist country, in a comparative study with other capitalist nations.

Below I present an in-depth review of two of the three key concepts of the current study: accessed social capital, activated social capital, and institutional constraints on social capital. The first two indicate that the status attainment process in labor markets can be associated with social capital, *ceteris paribus*, in the sense that (1) the total amount of social resources one retains, even without being activated, affects the status attainment outcome; and (2) a part of the social resources intentionally chosen and activated by job searchers increases the chance of upward mobility. However, it is hard to expect that accessed and activated social capital carry universally the same effects in different societies, considering that social capital effects may be buffered by local institutions. Thus the third concept, institutional constraints, delimits the effects of the two kinds of social capital so that we can expect variation in the efficacy of social capital across societies. The following chapter focuses solely on the review of institutional constraints.

Accessed social capital

According to Lin (2001), the status attainment process is composed of two steps. First, network resources, education, and initial positions of parents are predictors in explaining the variation of the attained status of individuals. Contact statuses, whatever tie strengths exist between actors and their contacts, are then expected to affect the attained status of job searchers. The network resources retained by an ego are called accessed social capital, whereas utilized network resources in the job search process are called activated social capital. To be sure, all network resources around an ego composed of his/her social ties are accessed social capital that is usually measured by position or name generators, whereby a representative map of the network and its potentiality to be utilized is captured; activated social capital is a part of the entire network resources for purposive actions taken by an ego (e.g., getting a job or recruiting new members of a civic association). Past social network research generally reached the conclusion that both accessed and activated social capital produce better instrumental and expressive outcomes. With regard to accessed social capital, the relevant review of the literature is as follows.

Campbell, Marsden, and Hurlbert (1986) examined the association between accessed network resources and socioeconomic statuses based on the 1965–1966 Detroit Area Study, and found that the resource composition of networks was significantly associated with attained statuses such as occupational prestige or family income. Apart from the general association between accessed social capital and socioeconomic status, accessed social capital was also revealed to exert positive effects on the reentry of the unemployed into the labor market. Using data on 242 middle-aged Dutch men, Sprengers, Tazelaar, and Flap (1988) found that those with better accessed social capital were more likely to be reemployed after a certain period of unemployment.

Further, accessed social capital was found to affect income levels. Boxman, De Graaf, and Flap (1991) found that both human capital (education) and accessed social capital, measured by work contacts in other organizations and memberships in clubs and professional associations, had direct and positive effects on income. This empirical finding on the relationship between accessed social capital and income is also supported by a study employing mathematical simulation: Arrow and Borzekowski (2004) found that 13–15 percent of the unexplained variation in wages is captured by accessed social capital (number of ties) after the effect of human capital is taken into account. The effect of accessed social capital applies to an isolated portion of foreign workers in the labor market. For instance, using data from the Mexican Migration Project, Aguilera and Massey (2003) found that accessed social capital of Mexican immigrants helped them find new jobs in the United States and get higher wages, especially when they were on un-documented trips. However, the story is not that simple, particularly in regard to coethnic ties of migrant workers. A qualitative study based on in-depth interviews with Polish migrants in London shows the complicated associ-ation between adaptation and social capital (Ryan et al. 2008). According to this study, the Polish migrants were more likely to be helped by accessing coethnic ties to fulfill basic requirements such as getting jobs and housing. However, too much dependence on coethnic ties exacerbated competition and exploitation in the migrant community, making diverse ties with local residents necessary for striking a balance in accessed social capital. The effect of accessing diverse ties applies not only to economic gains but also to quality of life, according to Erickson (1996). Erickson suggests that accessed social capital is a powerful source for generating cultural capital in the everyday life situations of working careers. Based on data from the private security industry in Toronto, she then found that the greater the network diversity, measured by the number of distinct classes included in a network, the more varied a worker's cultural resources. Note that this finding is markedly different from what was theorized by Bourdieu, who argued that economic, cultural, and social assets are exclusively possessed and transferred within high class.

In the present study I delimit the research scope in labor markets of the three chosen countries in which I examine whether accessed social capital is related to the socioeconomic status of respondents. In particular, accessed social capital is measured by the identical module of position generators employed in the questionnaires, which are explained in detail in Chapters 4 and 5. Again, the concern is if accessed social capital is efficacious in affecting labor market outcomes apart from activated social capital, the other com-ponent of social resources.

Activated social capital

Activated social capital denotes the effect of social contacts utilized for instrumental and expressive gains, even though the concept of social capital has been applied more often to instrumental outcomes than to expressive ones (for a review piece, see Song, Son, and Lin 2010). In other words, it is a part of accessed social capital mobilized for an immediate purpose. Simply put, when one has not developed good social relations – accessed social capital – in everyday life, it is less likely that one can depend on social ties in times of need and crisis unless altruistic network alters or strangers offer some help to meet the need without expecting returns.

In general, researchers assume that the successful use of activated social capital depends largely on the location of the mobilized contacts in the occupational hierarchy, which is usually measured by contact status in terms of occupational prestige or SEI (socioeconomic index) scores (Ganzeboom and Treiman 1996; Hauser and Warren 1997; Treiman 1977). From data on a representative community sample in metropolitan Albany, New York, Lin, Ensel, and Vaughn (1981) found that the higher the contact status the better the attained status of ego, controlling for parental status (recall the strength-of-position proposition) and education (as a measure of human capital). Marsden and Hurlbert (1988) also verified that the occupational prestige and industrial sector of a contact's status had significant effects on attained prestige and sector of ego, based on the 1970 Detroit Area Study.

The effect of activated social capital has also been corroborated by empirical studies conducted outside the United States. De Graaf and Flap (1988) conducted a comparative study among West Germany, the Netherlands, and the United States on the use of social ties in the job search process. They found that a contact person with relatively high prestige led to a job with higher prestige, especially in the Netherlands, which signals a plausible existence of cross-country variation in the effect of activated social capital. Wegener (1991) also found that contact status significantly affected the job prestige of respondents from the life history data of respondents in the former West Germany, and Völker and Flap (1999) identified a similar effect of social contacts in the former East Germany. Bian and Ang (1997) compared the utilization of social ties for job changes between China and Singapore and found that contacts' status had a positive impact on job changers' attained job status in both societies. Thus it is notable that political-economic differences between capitalist (West Germany and Singapore) and state socialist (East Germany and China) countries cannot be regarded as a cause that dichotomizes the effect of activated social capital as significant or not, even though such systemic differences may create variation in its effect.

Further, the supply side of activated social capital has been identified. Fernandez, Castilla, and Moore (2000) showed that job candidates who got employee referrals were more successful in getting jobs as customer service representatives at a large Midwestern phone center. In terms of the demand side of the labor market, they also found that referrals and employee social capital were beneficial to the company since they allowed the company to hire qualified employees at a lower search cost. An earlier study by Fernandez and Weinberg (1997) reached a similar conclusion, based on a retail bank and its employment process. Do organizations in a state socialist system also value the supply side of social capital? If so, it may signal that a state socialist country may have diverse and multifaceted features of social capital like those found in a capitalist country. According to Lin et al. (2009), Chinese organizations intentionally select and deploy workers with social capital to important edge positions where job holders will exchange with outside parties; this trend of selective deployment is more often seen in the private sector than in the state sector. However, relevant data on the supply side of activated social capital are difficult to obtain. For instance, when organizations utilize the social capital of their members to bring in human and material resources from outside, it becomes difficult to observe the activation process of social capital due to its routine institutionalization. This makes the determination of whether, how, and where social capital is activated even more complex.

The literature on activated social capital has also developed in segmented areas of migrant workers and race/ethnic enclaves. For instance, Aguilera and Massey (2003) found that having friends and relatives with migratory experience improves the efficiency and effectiveness of the job search, yielding higher wages for Mexican immigrant workers in the United States. Based on a specialized data set that sampled middle-aged non-Western migrant workers (i.e., Turkish, Moroccan, Antillean, and Surinamese migrants) in the Netherlands, Lancee (2010) reported that the bridging social capital of interethnic contacts resulted in a higher likelihood of employment and greater income for the migrant workers than bonding social capital composed of a dense network with family members. In particular, the effect of bridging social capital on income was found to be greater than that of language proficiency, generally regarded as one of the most essential skills for migrant workers. Regarding the use of social contacts by ethnic minorities, it is usually assumed that interracial relations with racial majority contacts conceptualized as weak or bridging ties matter significantly in the status attainment process (e.g., Briggs 1998, 2007; Burt 1992). In regard to coethnic contacts, Smith (2005) reported that whether poor blacks can activate black contacts of higher status hinges on helpers' careful consideration of the request, because those who are asked to help know that bad referrals would taint their own reputation at their workplaces. Portes also noted that too much dependence on coethnic ties can construct one of the critical causes of negative social capital: "cozy intergroup relations of the kind found in highly solidary communities can give rise to a gigantic free-riding problem, as less diligent members enforce on the more successful all kinds of demands backed by a shared normative structure . . . In the process, opportunities for entrepreneurial accumulation and success are dissipated" (1998: 16).

Although the effect of activated social capital has been generally supported in empirical studies, the effect of weak ties has not always been found to be effective in attaining better status. For example, based on a sample of employed adults in Chicago, Bridges and Villemez (1986) found that the effect of weakly tied and work-related informal contacts became insignificant once controls of human capital were included. Using German data of the life history of 604 adults, Wegener (1991) also showed that the effect of weak ties in the labor market was valid only for individuals with high-status prior jobs. A newly introduced concept of network diversity in place of weak ties seems promising in terms of its relative clarity as a guideline in categorizing relational entities by the dichotomy of homogeneity and heterogeneity, and its flexible applicability to different levels of analysis. However, the effect of network diversity has not been reported to be consistent across empirical studies. For instance, Eagle, Macy, and Claxton (2010) defined network diversity at the population level in the United Kingdom as social (i.e., number of contacts) and spatial (i.e., distance between caller and receiver) diversity in both mobile and landline phone calls in national communication networks. They then found that the composite measure of network diversity was significantly and positively related to the levels of community socioeconomic development measured by the UK Index of Multiple Deprivation, based on over 30,000 communities throughout the country. However, Goerzen and Beamish (2005) reported that alliance network diversity of multinational enterprises measured by the number of unique business partners and the number of unique industries of the partners was negatively associated with economic performance measured by returns on asset, sales, and capital (also see Table 1 in their study for a brief overview of mixed findings on the relationship between network diversity and performance of organizations).

As noted in the previous chapter, I introduce the structural layers of binding, bonding, and belonging in this study instead of strong/weak ties, given the mixed findings on the effect of weak ties and other relevant indicators in the literature, and in order to suggest a new way of categorizing social relations in future comparative studies designed at the individual level. Therefore, I test the effects of structural layers of social relations (see Chapter 5 for a detailed description) on labor market outcomes in the three societies, controlling for human capital and other confounders. I propose that the outer layer of belonging (participation in formal organizations) is generally better than binding (family-oriented ties) in predicting status attainment in the labor market and income because the former connects people to diverse social entities and ties outside the familiar boundaries of everyday life. Nonetheless, I propose that binding is a significant source of social resources in East Asian societies because social relations expand from family relations, according to the Confucian cultural legacy.

A major counterargument against the effect of activated social capital is worth noting: Mouw (2003) denies the effect of social contacts, showing that occupational homogeneity between ego and contact constructed spurious causal relations. Using the 1970 Detroit Area Study data used by Marsden and Hurlbert (1988), he argues that when the same occupational ties between a job searcher and contact, defined as having the same occupational codes, were excluded from the analysis, the effect of activated social capital became insignificant. However, I found that Mouw's argument is not supported because he failed to exclude the correct cases in which ego's "previous" job and contact's job were in the same occupational code. Instead, he deleted the cases where ego's "current/last" job and contact's job were in the same occupational code, which does not make sense considering that job seekers utilized their contacts when they were still in their previous jobs. When I replicated his model on the 1970 DAS data, deleting the correct cases, the effect of social contacts was significant. In the present study I employ the same method of deleting cases when respondents' previous jobs and their contacts' jobs fall in identical occupational codes (see Chapter 7; Table 7.5 on p. 111).

Conclusion

In this chapter I reviewed literature on accessed and activated social capital because they are the bipartite indicators of the social resources concept that will be used in a sequential manner in the chapters on empirical analyses. I stressed that accessed social capital is of a broader scope and subsumes activated social capital. It is expected that both will carry the explanatory power of an outcome; in other words, activated social capital directly affects the outcome while accessed social capital exerts its efficacy even after part of it is already taken up by activated social capital.

What makes accessed social capital remain significant when taking account of its activated portion? To understand this, we can draw from an example of perceived and received social support from the mental health and social support literature (Norris and Kaniasty 1996; Wethington and Kessler 1986). There, perceived support can be likened to accessed social capital in the sense that one has the information of who will be one's confidants when in crisis, and received social support is close to activated social capital because the specific help one asked for was indeed provided by the confidants. In general, the literature reports that stress or symptoms of mental illnesses are reduced not only by received support but also by perceived support – more consistently so in the case of perceived support (Ross and Mirowsky 1989).

Such findings in the social support literature are also applicable to outcomes related to socioeconomic gains; the nonutilized portion of social capital remains significant in affecting socioeconomic outcomes. The reasons may vary, as explained earlier, but I highlight an additional proposition here. It is plausible that an employer pays heed to the quantity and diversity of social capital that a job candidate would bring to the organization. In this case activated social capital by an actor – for instance, verbal or written references – may be regarded as a practical sample of the whole population of future utilizable social contacts (in other words, accessed social capital) that could be provided by a newly added member. In short, consideration of the supply side of jobs may help disentangle the mystery of the power of accessed social capital. But again, the existence of such an institutional calculation by organizations is hard to substantiate; some researchers thus call the power of unmeasured social capital the invisible hand of social capital, particularly when unsolicited job leads for nonsearchers are at issue (McDonald and Day 2010).

Thus far the two interlinked components of social capital have been discussed. The present study aims to employ them in the analytical model of the three societies in order to check for societal variations. What causes these variations? I assume that the institutional constraints in each society moderate the effect of social capital, and that the constraints are embedded in political economies and innate cultural legacies, among others. The following chapter introduces some plausible institutional constraints in the three case countries, particularly in the context of employment and the labor market.

[Handwritten annotations:]

Key Ques.

What is the relationship between institutional constraints → & individual choice?

↘ whether agency forms Structure or vice versa →

(to be studied): two representational → forms of institutional Constraint.
- political economy
- Culture

The power of insts. over human action

3 Institutional constraints

How do institutional constraints affect the form & function of Capitalism.
vm: Why put it as Constraint ⟵

We now turn to examining institutional constraints as the second of the
two main concepts of the present study along with social capital. How do
institutional constraints affect the forms and functions of social capital?
How do they vary in the three case countries? As briefly discussed in the first
chapter, an institution denotes a web of interrelated norms governing
social relationships (Nee and Ingram 1998). Then, more specifically, where do
institutional constraints come from? What is the relationship between
institutional constraints and individual choice (even before elevating to
the stage of social relations made by such choices)? These queries point to a
classic enigma in sociology and other social sciences, namely whether agency
forms structure or vice versa. I do not intend to delve into this philosophical
inquiry, considering that the focal point of this study is the international
comparison of social capital and its variations presumably generated by
disparities in institutional arrangements across nations. Nonetheless, it is
useful to check a few plausible ways of conceiving the relation between
institutional constraints and individual choice since doing so may help us
understand how institutional constraints and social capital are associated
with each other. It is also necessary to identify the two representative forms
of institutional constraints – political economy and culture. After a brief
review of these issues, I then proceed to introduce the literature regarding the
effect of institutional constraints on social capital, and show some specific
institutional conditions in each case country.

Key
PQ /
Asia
Def
Agency
VS
Structure

Institutional constraints and individual choice

Can institutions or institutional constraints come into being without humans
and their activities? This does not seem logically possible because humans and
their activities and relations must be the foundation of institutions; but once
institutions are formed they can then begin to constrain the activities and
relations of actors. In this study the delimiting power of institutions over
actors and their social relations is called institutional constraints. The next
query follows naturally: If human activities and relations constructed
institutions that in turn tend to impose their resultant constraints on actors,

Dy of
inst.
constraints

is it not plausible that actors can resist the institutional constraints or even try to reformulate institutions themselves when the severity of the constraints becomes unbearable?

According to both Marxist tradition and rational choice theory, it is possible to conceptualize institutions as creations rather than omnipotent and immutable external entities, but at the same time assume their pervasive influence on actors by way of, among others, established cultural norms, legal regulations, or political economic configurations (Grafstein 1988). To Marxists, institutions and institutional constraints are interpreted as none other than the bondage of capitalism created by capitalists and their class interests (Marx [1859] 1970). Thus it is logically possible that they may be replaced by communism and its accompanying institutions. Or significant changes may occur without a total replacement of the system. In this regard, Grafstein provides a practical example from Przeworski's analysis (1985) of how socialist developments can be contained within the capitalist political economy without experiencing revolution. The working class accepts the capitalist institution because capitalist political economy gives the working class as a whole a higher likelihood of realizing its material interests than the socialist system, especially when social and political disorder in the process of socialist revolution is taken into account. Simply put, both capitalists and workers agree to keep the capitalist social order in place. Grafstein (1988: 593) further argues that there can be interaction between the created institutions and their participants:

> Under the proposed interpretation, these institutions, however created, are not supernatural entities but exist *pari passu* with institutional participants. Yet in order to understand their constraining role, it is also important to appreciate that these institutions are distinct entities, ontologically on a par with each of the individuals who helps compose them . . . An institution, in this sense, can be understood as a connected group of such entities, be they classes, committees, or political roles. *Their interactions and thus their effect on participating individuals constitute the constraints of the institution* [emphasis added].

In other words, according to this rational choice perspective, an institution can exist when individuals agree to conform. Each individual can decide to conform when nonconformity could create greater losses due to formal punishment against it or socioeconomic disturbances than the benefits attached to conformity. In turn, such collective conformity generates regularity in social behaviors. Further, regularity in social behaviors stipulates what is naturally taken by the populace – in other words, constraining power over actors (Schotter 1981). It is therefore reasonable to assume that institutions are products of individual choices (Ordeshook 1986); nonetheless, institutions carry constraining power over actors as long as they are regarded as legitimately discrete entities.

Even when we accept that institutions are creations, it should also be asked whether every individual goes through the active process of rational calculation between conformity and nonconformity, as depicted by rational choice theory. In practice, not all individuals are critical of what is regarded as taken for granted. Conventions and routines as part of institutions and their constraints affect behavior in modern society as much as religious rituals in mystical premodern society (Douglas 1986). Geertz also regarded man as "an animal suspended in webs of significance he himself has spun" (1973: 5); he therefore argues that the analysis of the culture (that is, webs of significance) is an interpretive process, not an experimental science aiming to find law and principles of behavior. Further, the sociological theory of new institutionalism denies the view that choice governs institutions; choice can be preconfigured by the prevailing institution, which is close to the argument of bounded rationality – that is, a seemingly rational decision is limited and bounded by the incapability of decision makers not knowing all the relevant conditions, even when they themselves think that a decision is rationally made. In particular, Meyer and Rowan (1977) depict how modern organizations adopt structures and practices that symbolize rationality. They describe the rationalized practices found in organizations in terms of myth and ceremony. Organizations adopt practices that embody the myth of rationality in order to symbolize their commitment to efficiency. In other words, organizations seek rationality not purely because they are able to calculate its benefits, but because rationality is the dominant trend to follow. DiMaggio and Powell (1983) describe this nonrational copying of rationality as mimetic isomorphism, which happens particularly when organizations mimic the behavior of the leader in their field on the assumption that it behaves on the basis of the best strategy selected out of myriad alterative paths (e.g., Brouthers, O'Donnell, and Hadjimarcou 2005; Han 1994; Haveman 1993).

This divide between rational choice theory and new institutionalism on individual choice and institutional constraints is in line with the traditional characteristics of economics and sociology, as noted by Duesenberry: "I used to tell my students that the difference between economics and sociology is very simple. Economics is all about how people make choices. Sociology is all about how they don't have any choices to make" (1960: 233). Nonetheless, I take a moderate view between the two extremes. First, I agree that institutions are the products of humans and their activities and relations. Second, as institutions become deeply rooted in a society, they generate stronger constraints over actors to the point that people tend to succumb to them without asking if doing so is rational and legitimate. But third, some actors, if not all, are able to resist and renegotiate with institutions and their constraints in order to gain the best available outcomes, whichever way such outcomes may be defined; or, if the disagreement between institutions and actors gets too serious, then it is possible to see a drastic revolutionary change, as we did in the historical examples of the French Revolution in 1789, or the fall of the Berlin Wall in 1989 and the subsequent dissolution of the Soviet

Union in the early 1990s, or, more recently, in the Arab Spring in 2010 and 2011. Therefore I do not agree that actors are passive followers of institutions. Rather, actors make variations in the degree of their attachment or subscription to institutional norms and regulations. Thus the variation constructs a strong cause that complicates the social world and makes it hard to grasp with a simple dogmatic view. For instance, not all Chinese job searchers in the command economy accepted the principles of official job assignment; indeed, many of them exerted private efforts to get better jobs through the help of social contacts, sometimes using unlawful means such as bribery. On the other hand, suppose – although an unrealistic assumption – that without exception all Chinese workers and their families accepted the institutional official directive that disallowed the use of ties in the job assignment process; in this case the term *guanxi* would not be taken as one of the most important features of Chinese society, nor would it be meaningful to conduct this kind of comparative project when it is obvious that everything is already deterministically prearranged.

Institutional constraints in general

Institutional constraints generated from macro contrasts between capitalist and state socialist systems, and between Western and East Asian cultures may form qualitatively distinct types of social capital. For a feasible comparison among China, Taiwan, and the United States in the present study, the search for the causal relationship between social capital and institutional constraints will be confined to the labor markets in the three countries.

As mentioned, institutional constraints are the delimiting power of institutions over actors and their activities and social relations. The institutions of political economy and culture in particular may produce the most influential constraints. For instance, political regimes configure educational chances and employment patterns in certain ways; as a result, the overall tendency to make social networks in labor markets may differ among regimes. Likewise, strong cultural norms can divide people into segregative social relations between classes, races, and gender groups (e.g., caste in India, racial segregation in the United States and Europe, and general gender inequality in most countries). This conceptualization is critical because institutional constraints tend to form an overall framework of social capital for people, after which actors in the framework seek their own interests in the labor market with various types of access to and activation of social resources.

Political economy

There have been many studies that are directly or indirectly related to the theme of institutional constraints at the individual, organizational, or international level, but crossnational comparative research of social capital has much room for growth since it has not been actively conducted, partly but significantly due to the lack of a universal scale of social capital. To date, Eastern European countries and China have been the cases used to show the institutional constraints on social capital, in some cases with no comparative research design. To check the trend of comparative research on social capital, we need to start with a single-case national study in the United States.

Regarding the characteristics of social networks in the United States, Marsden (1987) utilized the 1985 General Social Survey (GSS), which was the first survey to gather personal network information from American people. Marsden found that American social networks are small, kin-centered, relatively dense, and homogeneous. In other words, a particularistic small network was characteristic of the personal relations of Americans. In tandem with the Marsden study, McPherson, Smith-Lovin, and Brashears (2006) utilized the 2004 General Social Survey to report that Americans' social network size had become significantly smaller in two decades with a decrease in the number of confidants.

Comparing the United States and China, Blau, Ruan, and Ardelt (1991) showed that a comparative study of interpersonal networks is feasible. With the 1985 GSS data used by Marsden and the 1986 survey data of 1,011 Tianjin city residents in China, they found that personal choices and relations in China, a socialist country at an early stage of industrialization and economic development, seemed to be remarkably similar to those in the United States, a capitalist country at an advanced stage of economic development. The reason articulated by these authors for this similarity is that particularism governs personal relations, regardless of cultural, political, or economic differences. However, their results may be strongly affected by the question they used in the surveys: "Who are the people with whom you discussed matters important to you?" This question from the name generators may have a strong connotation of strong ties for respondents, thus naturally invoking particularistic answers about kin or close ties around the respondents, regardless of institutional differences between countries.

With the replication of the 1986 Tianjin survey seven years later, Ruan et al. (1997) found that the number of ties of Tianjin people increased; a large portion of the increase pertained to friend ties and associates outside both family and workplaces. They inferred that the change in microsocial networks of Tianjin residents was caused by the macrosocial change of the partial introduction of the capitalist system selectively pursued by the communist government in one of the cities on the East coast.

In a similar vein, Völker and Flap (1995) conducted a retrospective survey on 489 residents in former East Germany to compare social networks before and after the fall of the Berlin Wall. Contrary to general expectations, they found that the size of East Germans' personal networks in 1993 and 1994 were smaller than those before the German unification. The density of networks decreased and the occupational diversity in social networks also declined; people's chances to obtain necessities through contacts became smaller than in the past. The authors explained that the reduction of social networks may have resulted from individual reactions to the ongoing unstable institutional changes. In other words, the uncertainty of the new system compelled them to remain with their old relations rather than add new ones. With the same data, Völker and Flap (1999) also found that East Germans utilized informal channels when they tried to find jobs under the Communist regime, but in order to reach contacts with high occupational prestige they needed to use strong ties, such as relatives or friends. This was the opposite of Granovetter's strength-of-weak-tie proposition based presumably on the labor market in the United States, but congruent with Bian's (1997) discovery of the value of strong ties in state socialist China. Adding consistency to these studies, Angelusz and Tardos (2001) found, based on 1987 and 1997 surveys in Hungary, that even after privatization the general network resources of Hungarians were affected by political involvement indirectly measured by self-reports of interest in political issues and the frequency of political discussions. Further, they argued that this may hint at the continuing power of the old political institution on social network composition. Kääriäinen and Lehtonen (2006) identified the relative deficiency of social capital in postsocialist countries in their multinational comparative study. When they compared bridging social capital measured by civic engagement among 21 countries categorized into five types of welfare regimes – Nordic, liberal, conservative, Mediterranean, and postsocialist – using the ISSP (International Social Survey Program) 2001 data, they found that the postsocialist regime (i.e., Czech Republic, East Germany, Hungary, Latvia, Poland, Russia, and Slovenia) had the least amount of bridging social capital. Further, they also found that the postsocialist and Mediterranean regimes had more bonding social capital based on ties of family and close friends than the other three types of regimes; the combined results thus indicate that individual social networks in the postsocialist regime are mainly composed of strong ties with intimate persons rather than weak ties known through activities in civic associations.

Culture

It is more difficult to find studies that compare nations of different cultural legacies and test the effect of culture on social capital. Comparative studies in this area mainly deal with the changes in political economy in certain parts of the world, such as Eastern Europe and China. Regarding the influence of culture, religion is the most frequent measure of cultural differences, while the rate of volunteering is sometimes used as a proxy measure of social capital (e.g., Candland 2001; Greely 1997). Note that voluntarism should not be equated with social capital, especially when individual social network composition and its utility are the main research interest. However, the literature is worth checking in terms of the effect of different religiosity as a distinct measure of culture on voluntarism, because it seems plausible that, at the very least, voluntarism provides more chances to widen one's social network –

or it is also possible that the wider the network the higher the rate of volunteering – even though the two are not directly related. In the relevant literature Protestantism has been assumed to be a better basis of social engagement, communal spirit, and participatory civil culture in the United States and other countries than other religions, particularly Catholicism (Bella et al. 1985; Ladd 1999; Tocqueville [1840] 2003; Wuthnow 1991, 1999). Based on a comparative study in regard to the effect of religion on voluntarism using the 1991 World Values Survey (WVS), Woolley (2003) reported that membership rates in voluntary organizations are generally higher in countries with a higher proportion of Protestant denominations. Using WVS data from 29 countries, Lam (2006) found that the higher the percentage of Protestants in the population, the higher its people's propensity to be members of voluntary associations, while the higher the percentage of Catholics in the population, the lower the likelihood that its people would be members of voluntary groups. Specifically, Lam states, "The estimated average membership rate for Protestant nations is 58.7 per cent, compared to the average of 26.9 per cent for Catholic nations, and 20.8 per cent for nations with other religious tradition" (2006: 186). Thus this study supports the traditional argument of the advantage of Protestantism over Catholicism. However, Curtis et al. (2001) found that mixed Christian countries (e.g., Canada, Netherlands, Northern Ireland, Germany, or the United States) where neither Protestantism nor Catholicism constitutes 70 percent or more of the religious composition have a significantly higher level of membership rates in voluntary associations than those in nations of other religions (e.g., Bulgaria, Estonia, Japan, South Korea, or Russia). In addition, there is no statistically significant difference in membership rates between predominantly Protestant and Catholic countries and nations of other religions. It is thus argued that "religious competition" arising from heterogeneous religious composition causes religious organizations to aggressively recruit new members; overall membership rates thus become higher than those in countries with a dominant religious tradition (Musick and Wilson 2008: 361). It is likely that the inconsistent findings between Curtis et al. (2001) and Lam (2006) may lie to a large extent in the differences in the ways that they measured religions (i.e., imposing a 70 percent cut-off point to distinguish a dominant religion vs. percentage of each religion). Yet Schofer and Fourcade-Gourinchas (2001) hint at another possibility – that religiosity in general is conducive to volunteering. Based on WVS data from 32 countries, they found that those who answered that they believe that religion is very important are more likely to become members of associations, regardless of religious and/or denominational differences.

Considering the results reported by the studies, it seems that cultural characteristics such as religiosity make a difference in volunteering rates among nations. It might also be presumed that culture creates variations in individual social network composition and its utilization, that is, accessed and activated social capital among countries. Further, to my knowledge the literature lacks efforts to identify if American and East Asian cultures are distinctively associated with individual social capital. I assume that the individualistic American culture is more conducive to the expansion of social networks outside the boundary of close ties with family than collectivistic and Confucian East Asian culture.

These empirical studies relating to political economy and culture and their effects on social capital remind us of two critical points for a comparative project of this kind. First, institutions within a society affect the size and composition of individuals' social networks. For example, the research findings in the Eastern European countries and China verify this plausible within-country shift in social capital before and after drastic changes in their political economic institution. Note that such changes at the macro level are not specifically measured in most of the studies but naturally assumed to be controlled by the fact that surveys at different time points, that is, before and after the incidents of macroscale change, were used. This is based on the presupposition that features in social networks are robust across time; if some significant changes in them are found, it is likely that a transformation in the social milieu such as an institutional change, though hard to be measured, may have triggered them, other things being equal. Second, the studies show that it is necessary to compare social capital of individuals across various societies. Few international comparative studies of social capital have been conducted, partly because it was rare to find the same measurement of social capital in different societies. Even in comparative studies that used the name generator method (Blau, Ruan, and Ardelt 1991; Völker and Flap 1995), its tendency to generate the names of mostly intimate alters limited its explanatory power to describe the general composition of social networks, which should also incorporate weakly associated ties. In addition, the lack of a consistent measurement scheme of social capital led some studies to use any available measures in secondary data sets that might be related to social networks or social capital (e.g., bridging social capital as the number of memberships in civic associations; bonding social capital as the number or frequency of family and friends contacts). With these points in mind, I now analyze some specific local institutional constraints in the case countries before presenting specific theories, hypotheses, and the description of actual data used in the comparative study.

Institutional constraints in case countries

Let us suppose that we picked three countries out of the over 190 nations recognized as members of the United Nations. Let us also presume an improbable thing: those three countries share a very similar culture, history, race-ethnic composition, other demographic features, and political economic system, whatever those may be. Of course, the things listed above do not cover all the conditions that can differ among nations, yet let us suppose that we succeeded in selecting three countries that are remarkably similar to one another in all the characteristics we can think of at the population level – even though such countries do not exist in practice. If the assumption of such similarities among the three nations is fulfilled, would it not be natural that we find that the three nations also share similar ways of forming (or dissolving) social relations? In the end, this specific similarity in the formation of social relations would lead us to the conclusion, related to the main theme of this study, that those three countries are not differentiated in terms of accessed and activated social capital. Differences may exist among them, but the variance of the differences, if any, should be in the negligibly smaller range because the environmental factors that can affect social relations were preconfigured to be analogous, compared to those created by another set of three nations that had critical disparities in the so-called environmental factors. It seems likely that even in the former set there could be significant differences in social capital if internal factors, such as genetic features, differed among the populations. However, such innately biological factors cannot possibly be controlled in general in social research. The key argument here is that should institutions across countries be more similar to one another, we may identify smaller differences in social capital composition and utilization.

Coming back from a radically hypothetical set of nations to the actual cases of the study, the differences among the three countries clearly stand out. Let us first consider the two Asian countries. China and Taiwan share cultural and historical legacies – including the humiliating late nineteenth and early twentieth centuries in which Western powers and Japan victimized China as their de facto colony – until 1949 when Chiang Kai-shek, the then president of the Republic of China and leader of the Kuomintang (KMT: Chinese Nationalist Party), moved the government from mainland China to Taiwan after the KMT was defeated by the Chinese Communist Party in the Chinese Civil War. The two societies thus share the same people (even though it includes about 2 percent Taiwanese aborigines), culture, and history before their division in the mid-twentieth century. Since then they have developed markedly different political economic institutions based on the two ideologies, namely communism affected by the Soviet revolution and the Soviet Union's practical assistance, and Chinese nationalism rooted in Sun Yat-sen's three principles of the people or San-min doctrine [三民主義] (Sun 1981). These two competing ideologies are the bases on which state socialist China and developmental capitalist Taiwan were established. They perceived each other as enemies and entered into constant competition politically, diplomatically, and economically. Thus it can be roughly presumed that the mainland Chinese and the Taiwanese peoples have been influenced by different political economic institutions, other things being equal. If significant differences were found in the compositions and/or utilization patterns of social capital between the two peoples, the effect of disparate political economic institutions could be singled out as the main cause triggering such differences.

The other case country, the United States, is related in varying degrees across time to the development of this antagonistic relation between China and Taiwan. The United States did not have confidence in Chiang Kai-shek's

KMT when the KMT had to retreat from Nanjing to Taiwan in 1949 and so maintained a noninvolvement policy, expecting that the invasion of the communist army would lead to the imminent fall of the KMT (Maguire 1998). However, the situation changed drastically when the Korean War abruptly began in June 1950. First, mainland China could not carry out a military invasion of Taiwan when it had to watch the course of the war's development in the Korean peninsula, where the United States and the Soviet Union were already heavily involved; indeed, it took only about three months after the outbreak of the war before China dispatched its army to the peninsula. Second, as a result of this first major war after World War II and its implications for the geopolitical entanglement in East Asia, the United States could no longer ignore the existence of the anticommunist KMT in Taiwan, only about 200 kilometers away from the southeastern coast of China; thus it decided to offer military and economic aid to Taiwan that was vital for the survival of the nation. The United States maintained its diplomatic position in recognizing the Republic of China (Taiwan) as the legitimate government of mainland China until the late 1970s; however, it altered its long-standing formal stance, eventually normalizing its relations with the communist regime in the People's Republic of China (PRC) in January 1979. The United States has since maintained a strategic ambiguity in dealing with China and Taiwan and the cross-strait relations between them, even though it degraded its de jure tie with the Republic of China to de facto diplomatic relations with the so-called "governing authorities on Taiwan," as stated in the Taiwan Relations Act passed by the congress in April 1979 (Charney and Prescott 2000: 462). Almost from the beginning of the cross-strait relations between China and Taiwan, the United States has played its role because it found its own geopolitical and economic interests at stake. Particularly in the Cold War period, the United States heavily influenced the installation of a capitalist mode of production and socioeconomic development in Taiwan. Thus the United States and Taiwan share a common institutional make-up of capitalist political economy, even though they are heterogeneous in other important institutional dimensions such as culture, history, and race-ethnicity.

Then what kind of institutional constraints, particularly related to labor markets in the modern period, exist in each of the case countries? Also, what are some important local contexts that we should keep in mind before observing the empirical results of the comparative analyses? We now turn to each case, in the order of China, Taiwan, and the United States.

China

Before the state socialist era began in 1949, China was mainly a feudalistic agrarian society with a colonial-style industrial sector that forged a small and fragmented urban labor market. Thus the old system affected the labor market institution in the socialist regime to some extent. For instance, workers' wages were paid in kind, not only in agriculture, but also in some industries due to high inflation and the spatial limits of local currencies (Li 1992). The in-kind payment system, the scale of which was called *"gong-ji-fen"* (工资分), was adopted and maintained by the Communist Party until 1956, when the national wage scale was introduced whereby wages were set solely in monetary values (Knight and Song 2005).

In this incipient period of constructing the economy and labor market under state socialism, China had to model itself after the Soviet Union mainly due to the international isolation imposed by the United States and the United Kingdom in the Cold War. In this regard, it is well known that Mao Zedong, the leader of the socialist China, decided to follow the Soviet model by saying "choose one side (一边倒)". However, conflict over hegemony in the communist bloc of the world caused the relationship between China and the Soviet Union to deteriorate, which resulted in the cessation of aid from the Soviet Union to China in 1957. Notwithstanding the break-up with the Soviet Union, a centrally-managed socialist economy was fully established in China. The legitimacy of this institutional arrangement was not challenged until the late 1970s when a new generation of political leaders headed by Deng Xiaoping started its reform.

Urban–rural division of labor

Like many other underdeveloped nation-states after World War II, China set industrialization as its imperative developmental strategy (Lin, Cai, and Li 2003). For a nation deeply rooted in one of the oldest agriculture traditions in the world, industrialization necessitated that the rural economy had to be sacrificed for industrial projects in urban areas that required huge investment of capital and labor. In order to sustain industrial workers, the government kept the prices of agricultural goods low. Low prices of agricultural goods suppressed not only the income of peasants but also the need to increase wages for urban workers; nonetheless, the widening gap between urban and rural incomes was inevitable. Consistent enforcement of low pricing of agricultural goods enabled the state to use the profits created out of the relatively higher prices of industrial goods for subsequent cycles of their reproduction (Knight and Song 2005).

Under the circumstances, it is obvious that residents in rural areas would want to migrate to cities and get urban jobs – note that such migration had actually happened when the civil war ended. If allowed, such migration based on individual rational choices might have caused the socialist control system to fail due to its direct impact, such as the lack of peasants in rural areas to produce crops for the whole population at low cost on the one hand, and the resultant excessive labor in urban areas on the other hand, not to mention other indirect impacts related to probable social, industrial, and political unrest. Therefore the state controlled the rural-to-urban migration and implemented strict management of urban job allocation. Specifically, the household registration system (*Hukou* [户口]) was put into effect for all citizens whereby people were not allowed to move from the places they legally belonged to in their lifetime; if they moved they were not given jobs, public services such as education and medicine, or food quota. *Hukou* prohibited migration from rural to urban areas or from small to large cities except for short-term visits to non-*Hukou* areas; these trips had to be approved by the government. Although its enforcement has weakened over time, the registration system still deprives migrant workers in urban areas and their families of some important life chances such as regular jobs, education of their children, and medical treatment. On top of this restriction on migration, the state established a job assignment system for urban residents, which will be elaborated in the following section. To put it simply, individuals could not choose their jobs; rather jobs were assigned by the state. Illegal migrants were naturally excluded from job assignments.

Job assignment to labor marketization

In terms of the organization of production heavily influenced by the agrarian tradition, the family was the main unit of production before the state socialist system that bound most people to members of their own families (Lee, Ruan, and Lai 2005). However, the economy was revamped from family-based to collective organization under the socialist regime: individual economic activities were integrated into a hierarchically controlled system that aimed to fulfill periodic national economy plans. That is, Soviet-style five-year national production plans ("五年计划") were implemented by the government. To mobilize and allocate laborers for specific goals of the plans, rural farmers were organized in the form of "people's communes" while urban workers were organized in work units called *danwei* (单位) (Bian 1994; Knight and Song 2005; Lee, Ruan, and Lai 2005). The work unit was not simply a production system but also a general social institution that conducted a wide range of sociopolitical and welfare functions. For instance, it distributed essential necessities and services to individual workers and their families, such as housing, medical services, pensions, and child care. At the same time, it also acted as a social control mechanism because it deterred workers from quitting their jobs and employers from firing workers (Shaw 1996). The affiliation with *danwei* was thus a lifetime deal that would determine most of the sociopolitical-economic life chances of a worker.

The mechanism of "getting a job" under the job assignment system did not depend on personal choice; in principle, the only rationale for it was how to match labor supply with the need of the national economy plans. Job assignment to work units was carried out through a government program from the mid-1950s to the early 1990s (Bian 1997). In principle, jobs were assigned without taking the wishes of either the employer or the employee into consideration. Reassignment to a different job was rare, as were transfers from one work unit to another. Under these conditions where entry into jobs and mobility between them were tightly restricted, the labor market, in the capitalist sense, did not actually exist in China. The following popular Chinese motto indicates the power of institutional constraint over individual choice: "I am a brick for the revolution, so place me wherever needed" (我是革命的 一块砖, 哪里需要哪里搬).

However, the strict job assignment system began to weaken after Deng Xiaoping adopted the Open Door policy in the late 1970s, by which foreign trade and economic investment were promoted. The foreign trade orders and investment provided a chance for the socialist government and local workers to observe how a "labor market" can function. Meanwhile, a series of labor reforms were initiated by the state, mainly aimed at improving the efficiency of the state sector in accordance with the foreign standards based on a capitalist market system. Specifically, the reforms brought irreversible changes to the job assignment system until the late 1980s. For instance, the state announced a plan in 1986, called "The Reform Plan of Job Assignment for College Graduates" (高等学校毕业生分配制度改革方案), whereby the old compulsory unidirectional job assignment system was replaced by bidirectional negotiation-based choices between college graduates and their future employers (Xinhua News Agency 2008). The reforms encountered an unexpected halt due to the Tiananmen Square protests in 1989; however, in the 1990s the quota system for job assignment in state enterprises was eventually put to an end, allowing enterprises to choose their own employees. In other words, the state gradually reduced its responsibility to plan and match the supply and demand of labor in order to increase the function of the labor market. To support this marketization of labor the state introduced the Labor Law in 1995, which basically acknowledges employers and workers as independent and autonomous players in the market.

However, even though the proportion of economic transactions in the marketplace increased, the state authority governing the economy remained intact, showing a mixture of market economy and state planning (Lieberthal and Lampton 1992; Walder 1995; Zhou 1995). Naughton defines the results of the economic reform from the late 1970s to early 1990s as a product of the dual-track policy of the state, whereby the main elements of the planned economy were kept while economic development was pursued in some newly introduced and confined sectors of the market economy (1995). The evolutionary and gradual labor marketization from job assignment to individual choice in the labor market was thus aligned with the dual-track policy, which perceived the existence of free labor away from strict state control as a sine qua non for economic development.

The embedded Confucian culture

The establishment of state socialism in mainland China in 1949 can be regarded in principle as the end of the feudalistic social order including, most notably, the Confucian culture. In fact, the Confucian culture was criticized since "the May Fourth Movement" in 1919 because nationalists suspected that Confucian values were out of date and thus caused the failure of the Qing dynasty. Mao and his followers also tried to modernize China by demolishing the Confucian culture. They stigmatized Confucianism because, according to their argument, it advocated the feudalistic social order justifying a close coordination among the emperor, the bureaucratic elite, and landlords. Anti-Confucianism reached its peak in the Cultural Revolution (1966–1976), in which Maoists tried to terminate anything traditional and Confucius was a major target to be destroyed in this mass movement. However, in reality Confucian values were so deeply ingrained in the Chinese culture and social relations that they functioned in concert with communist ideology (Ralston et al. 1999; Whyte and Parish 1984). Levenson captures this strong embeddedness of Confucianism with a long-term historical perspective: "If, in such a timeless, noumenal version of continuity, China were 'always China,' the place of Confucius in Communist China would be pre-ordained, and empirical inquiry gratuitous or fussily misleading" (1962: 2). Paradoxically, the Chinese government nowadays tries to revive the Confucian culture in China and promote Confucian institutes further afield globally.

Specifically in regard to gender equality, patriarchal male dominance based on Confucian culture did not disappear in socialist China. Wolf comments, "Contemporary China proves beyond a doubt that socialism and patriarchy can exist in stable harmony" (1985: 261). For instance, the constitution guarantees that equal work will be rewarded with equal pay. It then follows that both genders will receive the same remuneration for each workpoint; however, in general female workers are given fewer workpoints than males even when they perform the same tasks (Ruskola 1994). Things worsened for female workers after the Open Door policy was implemented because they were hired last but fired first, unprotected by the state (WuDunn 1993; Palmer 1995). Therefore I assume that the Confucian cultural legacy works as an institutional constraint against female workers and their job search activities through social contacts. The Confucian legacy and its plausible impact on labor market outcomes will be discussed in detail in the next chapter.

Taiwan

Before Taiwan was returned to the Republic of China at the end of World War II, Japan colonized the island from 1895 to 1945. The Japanese modernized Taiwan's infrastructure, building roads, railroads, and harbors, and setting up irrigation and sewage systems as part of the colonial exploitation policy according to which Taiwan had to produce agricultural and industrial products to support Japan and its wars in the Asian region, including mainland China. For instance, the *Chianan* canal irrigation system, completed in 1930, significantly increased the area for planting rice in the southwestern part of the island, from 5,000 to 150,000 hectares (Roy 2003). Due to these improvements Taiwan became a large producer of rice and sugar, although most of the crops were shipped to Japan. Nonetheless, the agricultural and industrial infrastructure set up by the Japanese was essential to the economic development of Taiwan after it was released from colonial rule (Ranis 1995).

While Japanese colonial rule in Taiwan was not as harsh as in other colonies such as Korea, the local Taiwanese were discriminated against in education and employment. The locals were increasingly exploited over time. Beginning in the late 1930s the colonial administration employed a policy of *Kominka* (皇民化: becoming subjects of the Japanese emperor) that aimed at the complete assimilation of the Taiwanese, replacing their local traditions with Japanese culture and enforcing the exclusive use of the Japanese language and the adoption of Japanese names, forcing them to abandon their original names (Roy 2003).

Thus when the KMT launched its government in Taiwan, one of the first momentous tasks it embarked on was to get rid of Japanese colonial legacies while also establishing social order by imposing martial law, insisting that the civil war against the communists in mainland China was not ended. In so doing the KMT applied one-party state rule, disallowing other parties and persecuting dissidents ruthlessly under martial law until 1987 – for instance, a remarkable incident called the 228 Massacre happened on February 28, 1947 in which the KMT led by mainland Chinese violently repressed the Taiwanese antigovernment movement. In the authoritarian period that was prolonged for almost four decades, the KMT and the government were indistinguishable, as was the case with the Chinese Communist Party and the Chinese central government; nor was there a clear distinction between government and party property and public property (Fell 2011). Therefore both Taiwan and China similarly went through authoritarian political rule by single parties, whether nationalistic or communist, until the late 1980s, after which Taiwan ushered in democratization – of course, the Taiwanese had more autonomy and freedom than the Chinese under the socialist regime even when Taiwan was under authoritarian regime. In addition, it is notable that North and South Korea are analogous to China and Taiwan in this respect because the two Koreas were divided with the ideological differences of communism and capitalism but shared the experience of stubborn authoritarian rule until 1987 – the same year that Taiwan's martial rule ended – when South Korea adopted the direct presidential election system that marked the end of military regimes. However, the most significant divergence between Taiwan and China occurred in the economic arena, as described in the following section.

Planned market economy

In contrast to its monopoly of power and authoritarian control over the political sphere, the KMT took a markedly different laissez-faire stance on economic activities. Even though the KMT-led government maintained its ownership of the majority of the sizeable and capital-intensive enterprises in key national heavy industries, it did not regulate most small businesses so that they could flourish in the internal and international markets (Lee 2004).

In the first place, most of Taiwan's large enterprises were formed in the 1950s. They were owned and managed mainly by entrepreneurs from the mainland who retreated to Taiwan with Chiang Kai-Shek's KMT regime. It was mainly due to their political loyalty to the KMT that they received governmental support for their businesses (Maguire 1999). These firms also tended to be Chinese family-run businesses accustomed to relying on family resources for financing; managerial positions were thus dominated by family members. The practice of nepotism in densely related family groups has been noted as one of the reasons that Chinese family businesses failed or did not grow further into conglomerates – to be fair, some exceptions such as Acer, Tatung, or Mitac exist. Basically, the companies shunned those outside their families even when they needed more investment to diversify their business areas or increase the size of business operations. The usual course of action for many large corporations was to divide the business among the children of the founders rather than expand the size of the firm by absorbing diverse businesses within a single large umbrella organization.

This tradition of Chinese family-run businesses with weaker government regulation coined a distinct feature of the Taiwanese economy in which small and medium-sized family enterprises (SMEs) became the main engine of development, whereas large conglomerates called *Chaebol* led the economic development in South Korea, another country belonging to the NICs (Newly Industrialized Countries) in East Asia (Amsden 1992; Evans 1995; Kim 1997; Lin, Fu, and Hsung 2001). Further, the Taiwanese institutional arrangement located SMEs in primary manufacturing and export sectors, while the Korean counterpart put them in marginal sectors mainly in charge of domestic consumption (Feenstra and Hamilton 2006). These differences in institutional arrangements then created particular interfirm relations in Taiwan and Korea that generated autonomous developmental momentum apart from the effects of state bureaucracy or macroeconomic factors (Hamilton et al. 2000). For instance, as indicated above, Taiwan does have some large conglomerates, but their role has been limited in specialized areas due to the preconfigured institutional arrangement. Amsden and Chu (2003) maintain that since the 1990s the role of large nationally owned conglomerates in Taiwan has been particularly remarkable in high-tech industries and modern service sectors, along with typically selective governmental intervention, while enjoying the so-called second-mover's (latecomer's) advantages. In other words, it is difficult to form a Japanese-style *Zaibatsu* or Korean-style *Chaebol* holding hierarchical control of diverse business entities in Taiwan even when the government wants it because a certain type of interfirm relations does not allow its development.

Thus while suggesting the common typology of several successful East Asian countries (i.e., Japan, Korea, Taiwan, Hong Kong, Singapore) as planned rational political economies in which the strong guidance of the states is identified, Henderson (2011) subcategorized the Taiwanese political economy as coordinated proprietorial capitalism. It is a blended type of capitalism that combines government planning and autonomous market agencies; specifically, a planned rational economy was applied in some state-owned sectors such as banking or aerospace, while other sectors were freely run by family-proprietorial companies.

Economic development and the labor market

The economic development of Taiwan developed in approximately three phases. First, from 1950 to 1962 Taiwan pursued an import substitution strategy aimed at nurturing primary industries that mainly responded to local demand, for instance, food processing and textiles (Maguire 1998). At the initial phase this plan helped facilitate the growth of Chinese family businesses as well. Once the domestic market for labor-intensive industries was exhausted in the early 1960s, the state policy shifted its focus to an increasingly export-oriented, labor-intensive industrialization (Ranis 1994). The next phase, between 1962 and 1980, was marked with a specific type of production called Original Equipment Manufacturing (OEM). In this type of production US multinational companies, for example, subcontracted manufacturing to Taiwanese firms; the products made in Taiwan were then sold under US brand names in the United States and elsewhere. In particular, the local electrical and electronic industries grew significantly in this OEM period. In the third phase, since 1980, a newly introduced type of production, Original Design Manufacturing (ODM), not only gave specific national identities to Taiwanese products in the global market but also enabled Taiwan to begin its production of more sophisticated consumer goods. In particular, high-technology industries have grown significantly in this period.

The exceptional performance of the Taiwanese economy was significantly due to the able and hardworking labor force (Fields 1992; Lee 2007). Across the three phases, Taiwanese workers were quick to migrate from the low-paying agricultural sector to the high-paying industrial sector, and from blue-collar jobs to professional and service jobs (Lee 2007). Meanwhile, the state prioritized the need to increase the number of skilled laborers in the areas of science and technology (Maguire 1998). As a result, an increasingly higher rate of tertiary educational attainment from the 1960s led to occupational upgrading among workers, allowing them to leave agricultural and blue-collar jobs behind (Fields and Kraus 2007). However, the association between educational level and occupational attainment weakened from the 1990s as a larger proportion of highly educated workers flooded the labor market; some with higher education thus had to take semi-skilled jobs.

The capital–labor relationship was not constantly peaceful. Especially when martial law was abolished in 1987, many protests and incidents of sabotage occurred, with demands for higher pay and better working conditions. Due to these heightened expectations, collective movements by workers, and the increasingly intense global competition, many industrial producers either moved their production overseas, such as to Southeast Asia and China, where they could employ cheaper labor, or imported foreign workers to Taiwan. The government initially limited the hiring of this foreign labor, but employers demanded that the quota be increased, threatening to move overseas. The government thus increased the inflow of foreign labor. As a side effect, this expansion, concurrently with the presence of overqualified local workers, contributed to the increased unemployment rate of local workers.

The performance of Taiwan's labor market began to deteriorate in the 1990s. The unemployment rate reached a record high of 5.9 percent in 2010 (source: http://www.indexmundi.com/g/g.aspx?c=tw&v=74). Other indicators of general economic performance, such as the economic growth rate, the rise in real wage rates, improvements in the occupational mix, and improvements in income distribution, have also gone through downturns (Lee 2007). Government officials have attempted to explain away the rapid deterioration in economic conditions and the high level of unemployment as due to the global recession, particularly in the aftermath of the Asian financial crisis in 1997. However, this argument is hardly convincing since it has been observed that most other Asian NICs maintained lower unemployment rates even though some of them were directly hit by the financial crisis: for instance, the unemployment rates were 2.1 percent in Singapore, 3.3 percent in South Korea, 3.5 percent in Malaysia in 2010, and 4.3 percent in China in 2009 (source: http://www.indexmundi.com/), all lower than in Taiwan. Failures of governmental policies have thus been blamed for the serious gap between labor supply and demand.

Nevertheless, governmental regulation of the labor market in Taiwan has been administered at the industry level, not at the individual level; simply put, employers created jobs and job searchers freely chose their jobs with their individual credentials, with no job assignment by the state. In practice, government employment services are the least popular method in recruiting blue-collar workers, while use of informal channels such as employee referrals is the dominant recruitment method; formal channels are used more than informal channels for white-collar jobs (Lee 1995). The state rather concentrated on designing the entire industrial structure and bringing in strategic industrial upgrading (Amsden and Chu 2003), removing itself from micromanagement of the labor market. For example, the high unemployment rates in the recent decade show that it is not the main task of the state to match job searchers with jobs. The free choice of Taiwanese job searchers contrasts with the job assignment policy of socialist China until the early 1990s.

Orthodox Confucian culture

When the KMT was defeated in the civil war, one of its first priorities was to ship as many exquisite traditional Chinese masterpieces and treasures as possible from mainland China to Taiwan, and later they were placed in the National Palace Museum. It is arguable that not only the physical artifacts of the Sung, Yuan, Ming, and Qing dynasties, but the orthodox Confucian culture was also moved to Taiwan, even more so in light of the fact that the mainland socialist government officially detached its people from the feudal legacy of Confucianism.

Specifically, the aforementioned three principles of the people proclaimed by Sun Yat-sen were also deeply based on the orthodox Confucian view of the relationship between the state and its people; one of the principles in particular advocates a paternalistic obligation of the state to take care of its citizens' livelihood. As a way of realizing this principle, Chiang Kai-shek, Sun's successor, created the New Life Movement in the 1930s, even before he came over to Taiwan, proposing that Confucian moral values could save a nation marred with corruption and opium addition. Thus the founding fathers of Taiwan shared the Confucian ideology, believing that it is the backbone of the Chinese social order.

Even in modern Taiwanese politics, Confucianism still functions as an indispensable element. Ling and Shih (1998) summarize that modern democratic politics in Taiwan holds three competing normative domains: the Western-style frame of liberal political institutions; a Taiwanese nativist or nationalist ethos; and a Confucian moral legitimacy commonly expected from political leaders. In regard to socioeconomic development, Confucian values such as frugality, discipline, and diligence were claimed to have contributed to the successful modernization and industrialization of Taiwan. It is thus argued that Taiwan is one of the representative cases of the East Asian nations that suggest that Confucian capitalism can exist independently from imported Western capitalism (Yao 2002).

In accordance with this historical lineage and implicit political inheritance of Confucian values and their practical impact on the work ethics of laborers in postcolonial socioeconomic development, Confucianism has pervasively affected Taiwanese people as a strong cultural institution. This influence also naturally involves strict hierarchy and male dominance in social relations, which in turn may affect social capital composition and utilization.

The United States

In this book the United States serves as a comparative reference to the two East Asian nations. The development of US labor is briefly overviewed in what follows. According to the multiauthored cooperative volumes led by John R. Commons on US labor history (Commons et al. 1918), the wage-earner class formed over three centuries in the United States, setting up a socioeconomic and political position independent from farmers, merchants, and employers. The organization of wage earners had its origin in the earlier efforts of artisans to protect their interests from merchant-capitalists. Organized labor based on trade unionism was active in various social movements for shorter working hours, public schools, prohibition of child labor, and abolition of imprisonment for debt in the 1820s and 1830s, all of which were related to basic rights of citizenship. National unions such as the

Knights of Labor and the American Federation of Labor were formed in the late nineteenth century, the latter of which eventually merged with the Congress of Industrial Organizations in 1955 to create the AFL-CIO, the largest federation of unions in the United States (Lichtenstein 2002).

An underregulated labor market

In regard to the formation of the labor market, supply and demand of labor were met mainly through informal means without state involvement; for instance, employer associations or labor unions ran ad hoc private offices to match unskilled manual labor vacancies with job seekers. However, the pressing need to control widespread unemployment facilitated the establishment of public employment offices beginning in the 1890s (Commons et al. 1918; Phan-Thuy 2001; Rees 1966). Public employment offices were nonprofit governmental organizations; one of their main functions was to protect job seekers from fraudulent activities committed by private employment agencies (Lee 2009). America's entrance into World War I in 1917 clarified the need to organize the labor market. Industries lost experienced workers to the army, and private and public employment services without national purview could not provide systematic solutions that could have rearranged the overall supply and demand of labor. It was only in 1933 when the Wagner-Peyser Act was enacted that the United States was able to establish a national employment service (Guzda 1983). However, its operation was far from systematic, as can be seen from what happened when World War II broke out: females were asked to fill the manual labor jobs that males vacated when they were drafted, but most of these female workers were asked to give the jobs back to males when they returned from war (Acemoglu, Autora, and Lyle 2004). According to the Bureau of Labor Statistics in the Department of Labor (source: http://www.bls.gov/news.release/pdf/empsit.pdf), the unemployment rate as of September 2011 at the national level was 9 percent – this means that 14 million persons were jobless. This also indicates that the US government does not have the capacity to regulate the labor market in an economic recession. Even apart from such extreme cases of wars or recessions, the federal government's efforts to regulate the US labor market have not been effective.

The lack of state regulation concurrently generates advantages and disadvantages. It may be good because actors – both job seekers and employers – are free to choose the best available options in the market; however, it could be bad when job seekers are discriminated against in the underregulated market due to ascribed statuses such as race, ethnicity, or gender.

Race and gender disparities

Racial and ethnic discrimination has a long history in the US labor market largely due to the slavery of African-Americans and its negative legacy for nonwhite workers. Gender discrimination against females has also been strong, relying on the old stereotypical perception that women were not intellectual or physically capable of doing factory or office work (Braude 1975). Although not as strong as in the past, race and gender disparities still exist in the labor market.

According to Tomaskovic-Devey (1993), there are two main theories that explain segregated employment structures. First, statistical discrimination theory proposes that employers discriminate against members of a particular group when their perception, based on either direct experiences or indirect information from other employers, dictates that those members are less productive or more expensive to train. Second, the explicit or implicit segregation of the labor market seeks the interests of the majority group by maintaining social closure. Simply put, segregation is used to maintain in-group interests, and not necessarily because out-groups are innately inferior or bad. Parkin provides an operational definition of social closure as: "the process by which social collectivities seek to maximize rewards by restricting access to resources and opportunities to a limited circle of eligibles" (1979: 44). Similarly, Tilly (1998) describes segregation as a result of the mechanism of "opportunity hoarding," by which a majority group reinforces its control over hoarded resources by its power to "include or exclude other members with respect to language, kinship, courtship, marriage, housing, sociability, religion, ceremonial life, credit and political patronage" (1998: 154–5).

Whatever the causes of discrimination and segregation, various social movements, including the civil rights movement, brought significant institutional changes to race and gender discrimination in the labor market through legislation and legal enforcement. The Civil Rights Act of 1964 is a representative achievement; it created the EEOC (Equal Employment Opportunity Commission) in 1965 to implement and enforce laws that prohibit discrimination based on race, color, religion, sex, national origin, disability, or age in hiring, promoting, firing, setting wages, testing, training, apprenticeship, and all other terms and conditions of employment. Specifically relating to gender discrimination, the Equal Pay Act of 1963 prohibited sex-based wage discrimination, while the Pregnancy Discrimination Act of 1978 illegalized discrimination against females because of pregnancy, childbirth, or a medical condition related to pregnancy or childbirth.

Even with this legislation, actual disparities in earnings and socioeconomic status among races and genders remain significant; they are still the main areas of US sociological research on social stratification (e.g., Huffman and Torres 2002; Smith 2000; Wilson 1987). Why do such actual disparities among racial majority and minorities and between genders persist? It is likely that the actual disparities are largely due to informally ingrained discrimination against racial minorities and females in terms of employment practices (Bertrand and Mullainathan 2004; Royster 2003). A structural reason that allows this informal discrimination may lie in the fact that the education and employment systems in the United States are relatively weak in their degrees of standardization when compared to other advanced economies.

The educational administration in the United States is highly decentralized, and this lack of standardization then affects hiring practices in the labor market. This is because employers are less able to rely on certificates in the hiring and remuneration process, as Allmendinger points out: "Poorly standardized educational structures deflate the value of certificates as passports for entry in the labor market" (1989: 64). Instead, employers have to develop their own strategies – including the use of social networks – and use their own selection procedures to find the best available employees. Reskin and McBrier (2000) also found that when the degree of formalization and standardization of personnel practices is higher, the impact of informal social networks on occupational outcomes is lower. Therefore, in the process of hiring, where informal criteria are frequently employed in invisible ways, racial minorities and females are more likely to be victimized, considering that legal enforcement of equal employment opportunity cannot catch all the nuanced informal discriminatory practices.

Conclusion

In this chapter we have examined how institutional constraints and individual choices are related. Institutional constraints delimit the choice set available to individuals. However, one cannot assume that individuals blindly follow whatever conditions are given by institutions. It is plausible that some individuals do not take institutional constraints into account, or simply ignore them in their choices of social relations and social actions. These inevitable noninstitutional or abnormal behaviors add a degree of complication to the social world. What matters is whether institutional constraints have the efficacy to create a solid pattern of individual choices in a society distinctly different from those of other societies that are free from such constraints. Among other forms of institutional constraints, I selected political economy and culture as the two comparative axes cutting across the three nations, China, Taiwan, and the United States.

The three countries have differential composition of institutional constraints. First, China has a socialist political economy and embedded Confucian culture. In particular, the socialist political economy enforced a strict job assignment system on its people at the national level for about four decades. Thus the concept of a labor *market* was new to the Chinese people when it was introduced in the early 1990s. Second, the Taiwanese developmental state planned the economy to realize a condensed version of socioeconomic development under the authoritarian regime. Nonetheless, its regulation of the economy was applied at the industrial level, following its priority of strategically allocating more resources to certain selected industries (e.g., information technology). Thus labor supply and demand were not as strictly regulated by the state as those in China. Still, its culture is supposed to be more dominated by Confucian doctrines and values than that in China, which led to the ideation of so-called Confucian capitalism among some scholars.

It is expected that the stronger the Confucian legacy the more severe the gender inequality in labor market outcomes. Lastly, the United States is free from a socialist political economy and idiosyncratic premodern cultural legacies. Nevertheless, its underregulated labor market and less-standardized educational system compared to other advanced Western countries enlarged the role of informal means and credentials, such as social networks in status attainment in the labor market. This informal nature of the labor market makes it difficult to provide fair opportunities to racial minorities and females that have been traditionally affected by discriminatory practices.

Based on the understanding of such institutional constraints, we now turn to forming some theoretical statements on the relationship between social capital and the status attainment process of individuals in the case countries (Blau and Duncan 1967; Sewell, Haller, and Portes 1969; Sewell and Hauser 1975). The next chapter defines each theoretical model of institutional arrangement of the three case countries and presents some specific hypotheses to test the causal sequence from accessed social capital to activated social capital to status attainment in labor markets.

Theoretical models and hypotheses

The present project principally aims to compare social capital among three societies: China, Taiwan, and the United States. The systematic differences in social networks in these three societies, presumably caused by institutional constraints, are analyzed in terms of accessed and activated social capital. In this chapter I provide specific theoretical statements on the relationship between social capital and institutional constraints, relying on the discussion of each in the previous two chapters. The position generators as a method for measuring accessed social capital are introduced, and then activated social capital is differentiated from accessed social capital and related to the labor market outcome. The hypotheses to be tested via empirical analyses are presented in the latter part of the chapter.

Models of institutions and institutional constraints

Why do institutional constraints – political economy and culture – affect people's social networks in the labor market? Over the last three decades social network research has performed a key role in reviving a strong tradition in sociology that captures the power of social structure in affecting people's daily lives (Beckert 2002; Block 1990; Granovetter and Swedberg 2001; Swedberg 2003). If one compares political, economic, or cultural institutions, specifically between capitalist and state socialist nation-states or between Western and Confucian East Asian countries, the institutional differences among nations must be given due consideration in regard to their power of organizing types of social relations. These affect people's life chances – directly with their own structural forces and indirectly with different patterns of social networks. Thus it makes little sense to argue that a free labor market and a state job allocation system result in undifferentiated types of social networks. In a similar vein, it is not feasible that the authoritarian social fabric of a Confucian country and the democratic social structure of a Western country generate indistinguishable effects on forming and using social ties in labor markets. It is thus reasonable to first focus on the effect of institutions on the formation of social relations before observing the effect of social relations on labor market outcomes. I present the models in the order of China, the

United States, and Taiwan because the latter has mixed features of the former two cases.

China: A socialist control model

How do political economic and cultural institutions form social networks in different societies? I argue that the degree of social controls by states affects the formation of people's social networks. At the macro level, China maintained a command economy in which the market was under the control of state planning. The representative examples of such socialist control initiatives are the Great Leap Forward and Cultural Revolution introduced by Mao Zedong from the late 1950s to the mid-1970s, and the Reform and Open Door Policy by Deng Xiaoping in the late 1970s (Chan 2001; Chen and Deng 1995; Goldman1994; Zang 2000; Zhang 1996). As discussed in the previous chapter, the command economy affected the everyday life of the Chinese people through the distributive systems of education, jobs, housing, food, and medicine. The life chances of Chinese people were considerably controlled by the state. I propose that in this situation people's social networks could not avoid the formational power of state bureaucracy. For instance, individuals did not choose their jobs or work colleagues; they were assigned by the state's job allocation system until the early 1990s (Bian 1994; Walder 1983; Zhou, Tuma, and Moen 1996). Therefore I call the ideal type of the Chinese political economic institution the "socialist control model."

China: A Confucian model

The cultural institution of China has been much affected by its Confucian tradition, although the cultural tradition was weakened to some extent by the introduction of communist ideology. Still, social hierarchies of age (seniority) and gender (male dominance) continue to prevail in China (Baker 1979; Shu and Bian 2003; Yu, Yu, and Mansfield 1990). To a large extent the constraint of the Confucian tradition on social networks is due to the fact that Confucian social relations are mainly based on hierarchical social order, for instance between monarch and subject or between father and son, as defined in the Confucian rule of "Three Bonds and Five Moral Rules" (Hamilton 1990). It thus reduces the freedom to form ties across the social boundaries of age groups and gender, among others (Li 2000a, 2000b; Zhou 2006). I thus call the Chinese cultural institution the "Confucian model."

The United States: A market-dominant model

The American people have not experienced this state enforcement of social controls, since the operation of American political power was based on the basic principles of democracy and free market. In regard to labor market entry and changing jobs, educational credentials and skills of individuals are matched with the needs of employers. In other words, the American labor market is quite free of state control except in monitoring illegal labor practices or injustice by employers. I call the ideal type of the American political economic institution the "market-dominant model" (Appleby 1984; Robbins 1994).

The United States: An individualistic model

Further, the American culture was built on the philosophy of individualism (Bobo 1991; Gans 1988; Tocqueville [1840] 2003). In principle, individual values are more important than collective ideology and interests, and people are free to choose their own course of action if it does not affect the basic sociolegal order. Maintaining and respecting privacy is thus an important rule in their lives and social relations. On the other hand, too much stress on individual values makes it hard to solve collective problems such as racial inequality. The legacy of racism dating back to the seventeenth century has not been cleared away, even after the strong civil rights movement in the 1950s and 1960s (Feagin 2000). Color-blind racism deeply rooted in individualism has been one of the reasons that the American society is less effective in achieving race equality because it refuses to acknowledge the existence of collective disadvantages due to physical skin color; rather, it is argued that an individual should be responsible for solving his/her own problems regardless of their structural sources (Bonilla-Silva 2006). Even though American individualism has experienced setbacks in solving collective problems, it nevertheless allows free choice in forming social ties and use of contacts. I thus call the cultural institution of the United States the "individualistic model."

Taiwan: A model mixing market dominance and Confucianism

Taiwan is a unique case that lies between the two opposite types of the United States and China. In terms of a political economic institution, it belongs to the market-dominant model. However, it swings toward the Confucian model when it comes to its cultural institution. To put it simply, it shares a political economic institution with the United States while holding a common cultural institution heritage with China. Its political economic institution was established mainly in opposition to the state socialism of mainland China, although it has unavoidably had the same cultural and historical background. Therefore the Taiwanese case consolidates two heterogeneous types: the market-dominant model in terms of political economy, and the Confucian model in regard to cultural institution. Of course, its political economy diverges somewhat from a purely market-dominant model in the sense that the Taiwanese developmental state created a planned rational economy in which the state takes the role of mastermind and regulator (Henderson 2011). Yet in a broad sense it is clear that planned rationality belongs to the market-dominant model. As Chang (2002, 2007, 2010) argues convincingly, based on relevant historical data, the Western advanced economies also passed through a developmental stage in which the states strongly regulated markets using the planned rationality that they now deny and ask developing countries to abandon, while pressing them to unconditionally open their markets. The Confucian nature of Taiwan's cultural institution is assumed to be somewhat stronger than that of China, considering that socialist China officially denied Confucianism since it was associated with the feudal monarchy. However, China later found it impossible to eliminate the deeply embedded Confucianism from its cultural foundation.

In terms of interaction between Confucianism and capitalist development, it has been argued that a Confucian revival functioned positively for the importation of and adjustment toward the market system by mobilizing Confucianism's traditional symbolic resources such as work ethic and social solidarity (Gold 1991; Tu 1991). Additionally, I note that the degree of this interaction varies even in countries with mixed models of Confucianism and market dominance, such as Taiwan, Korea, Japan, and Singapore, mainly due to the differential strengths of state intervention in the economy and society (Hamilton and Biggart 1991; Migdal 1988).

However, it should be noted that these models are all ideal types that cannot account for the complicated realities of political economies and cultures in each country. In effect, each society can contain diverse elements to varying degrees. Related to this agenda, another critical aspect is that I have no direct measures of these models in the three societies. Thus in examining the patterns of social networks in the three societies I am assuming that institutions and their constraints in each country affect social networks differently. In terms of the impacts of political economic models, I expect that patterns of social networks will be different between China on the one hand, and Taiwan and the United States on the other. Regarding the Confucian model, I propose that its effect on social networks is similar in China and Taiwan, which may create significant differences from the pattern of social networks in the United States. In regard to the interaction between Confucianism and market dominance in Taiwan, the pattern of social networks in Taiwan should indicate a mixture of that in China and the United States. Even though the reality is muddier than the ideal types, and within-society variations of the various models are unmeasured, I propose that significantly different patterns that emerge from the data can be considered conservative estimates of the potential effects of these various models among other plausible institutional causes.

To identify the relationship between the general structure of social networks – note that in this book this structural composition of social networks is equivalent to accessed social capital – and institutional constraints, it is necessary to determine how social networks in the three societies can be measured with a universal scale. As mentioned earlier, there are a few different ways of measuring accessed social capital; this book employs the position generator method. It is also necessary to clarify the difference between accessed and activated social capital since the position generator measures the former because it shows a static map of an individual's network within the structure of an occupational hierarchy. Accessed social capital thus differs from activated social capital, which consists of some portion of the accessed social capital that a job seeker utilizes for status attainment – finding or changing jobs – in the labor market. These concepts are explained in detail in the next two sections.

The position generator and accessed social capital

A comparison of accessed social capital in the three societies is made possible by the same scale of position generator questions in the surveys. As Van der Gaag (2005) mentioned, the position generator method is useful for a comparative study among different countries because it asks about the same positions to all the sampled respondents from various countries, whereby the sociostructural features of individual networks in each society is captured by utilizing the information of social ties' objective positions dispersed across a labor market. In other words, this method is appropriate for searching for various patterns of social networks in labor markets in different countries since it focuses on capturing information about an ego's network members that hold occupational titles (Lin 2001; Lin and Dumin 1986; Van der Gaag, Snijders, and Flap 2007). Specifically, according to a systematic comparison among the various methods of measuring social networks, the position generator better fits the studies in which instrumental actions, such as searching for a job, are the key outcomes rather than those where expressive actions, like perceived support when in need or sharing sentiments, are to be explained (Van der Gaag, Snijders, and Flap 2007). Part of the reason is that the information on an ego's network members that one gets from the position generator method excludes some social ties outside the labor market, such as homemakers, students, the retired, and the unemployed, who could offer as much expressive help as those inside the labor market. Therefore, in brief, the comparative sites of the study – labor markets in three different societies – are well matched with the position generator method.

The position generator method asks respondents whether they know occupants in certain jobs on a given job list. For the researcher, each job is associated with an occupational prestige or socioeconomic index score. The criterion of "knowing somebody" is defined as knowing someone by face and name. Thus the answers from the respondents can vary from knowing none of the occupants on the job list to knowing all of them. From this we can check how network members of an ego are embedded in the occupational hierarchy. There are three components in the position generator method that facilitate an understanding of the structural features of a social network: first, *upper reachability* shows the highest position in terms of prestige scores that a respondent knows from the job list in the occupational hierarchy; second, *range of prestige* offers information on how wide a respondent's upper and lower network limits are, in terms of prestige or socioeconomic (SEI) scores of occupations; third, *extensity* sums up the number of positions in the job list in which a respondent knows personal ties. Each of these three indices is utilized to compare the accessed social capital of individuals in the three societies. In predicting the indices of accessed social capital, structural layers of binding (ties with and through spouse), bonding (daily contacts), and belonging (memberships in voluntary associations) are employed to test if they are sources of accessed social capital. In order to systematically compare the amount of accessed social capital across the three countries, a single factor variable of accessed social capital that holds shared variation of the three indices is generated by confirmatory factor analysis. A latent mean comparison is then employed to determine which country has the greatest (or smallest) amount of accessed social capital.

Activated social capital and its outcome

Analyses of activated social capital in the three countries identify whether there are different patterns among the countries in the utilization of social contacts for instrumental purposes in the labor markets. One focal point of comparison with regard to activated social capital is first, whether higher contact status produces a beneficial effect for a job seeker, and if so to what degree. In other words, this second part of the analysis offers a chance to examine the relationship between contact status and its returns in three different labor markets to test the proposition of social resources on status attainment.

Second, role relations between an ego and contact(s) are compared across the three countries. The analysis of role relations shows the proportions of family vs. nonfamily ties in each of the three countries, possibly indicating the differential composition of activated social capital, if any. It is assumed that the Confucian culture exerts centripetal force that naturally favors family contacts, and at the same time makes it difficult for East Asians to go upstream in activating nonfamily contacts; this is more so in socialist China in which contacting helpers for job searches was prohibited.

Third, the examination of social group levels of inequality between gender groups in all three countries and racial groups in the United States is another crucial comparison. Gender and race are sociostructural elements because they are not only biological characteristics but also socially constructed borderlines among social groups that hold different amounts of economic resources, political power, and social resources. The principle of homophily governs social relations so predominantly that it categorizes race and gender into inner and outer groups (Homans 1950; Lazarsfeld and Merton 1954; McPherson and Smith-Lovin 1986, 1987). The social worlds of racial and gender groups tend to form and maintain an unequal distribution of resources whereby so-called racial majority/dominant gender and racial minorities/ nondominant gender become structuralized along with demarcation lines of class, status groups, and power (Bielby and Bielby 1994; Bonacich 1972; Goldin 1990; Marx 1994; Weber 1958). Following the relevant literature, I propose that activated social capital is another scarce resource, along with financial resources, property, or educational credentials, that is unequally distributed along gender and racial lines in society.

Fourth, the chain length of contacts renders another comparative point between capitalist (United States and Taiwan) and state socialist (China) nations, and between Western (United States) and Confucian (China and Taiwan) cultural entities. I propose that the average length of job search chains is shorter in capitalist and/or Western societies than in state-socialist and/or Confucian societies because in the former fewer institutional constraints offer greater degrees of freedom for actors to directly reach out to the best available contact situated in a wanted position in the occupational hierarchy, whereas more institutional constraints compel actors to activate more indirect, trustable contacts or culturally appropriate bridging ties that can lead job seekers to their final target contacts. Who are these bridging contacts and why are they needed? Trustable bridging contacts were necessary when private use of contacts for job searches was prohibited in socialist China; and culturally appropriate bridging contacts need to be evoked in a hierarchical Confucian society such as China or Taiwan. For instance, a young female job seeker may not be allowed to directly contact a male manager at a target company that she does not know; rather, she is expected to utilize a male relative who knows both the job seeker and the manager. By doing so she gives the impression that she is well versed in the Confucian hierarchical order of seniority and male dominance and is willing to comply with it.

Thus far I have presented key theoretical statements. It is now time to convert them into two sets of falsifiable hypotheses. The first set aims to test if accessed social capital has significant variation across the three countries, while the second set seeks to identify the effects of activated social capital and compare them among the three nations.

Hypotheses

In brief, the hypotheses focus on two main domains: differential composition of accessed social capital among the three societies; and various patterns of activated social capital. I propose that the differentials in accessed and activated social capital were formed by a varying degree of institutional constraints represented by the socialist control model and the Confucian model. Hypotheses 1-i are related to aspects of accessed social capital, while Hypotheses 2-i deal with activated social capital. All the hypotheses take various controls into account in order to tease out the partial effects of key variables.

Comparison of social capital composition

The Hypotheses 1-i series predicts consequences in accessed social capital in the three societies due to the institutional constraints of socialist control and Confucian models compared to market-dominant and individualistic models. Discussion then turns to the issues of the deficit in accessed social capital in racial minorities and females. Three indices of accessed social capital are used in actual comparison among the three countries: extensity, which is a count measure of number of network alters; upper reachability, which indicates the highest occupational prestige score attached to the jobs of network alters; and range of prestige scores, which denotes the gap between the highest and lowest prestige scores attached to the jobs of network alters.

Despite its recent embarkation into the market transition process, the state socialist system of China has exerted extensive constraints on its people in the form of governmental regulations over the distribution of education, jobs, and housing; the right to move from a residential region (household registration); religion; political participation; and speech (Deng and Treiman 1997; Houn 1958; Lin and Bian 1991; Bian 1997; Walder 1989). Capitalist societies do not explicitly practice these kinds of direct governmental intervention into the various life domains of their citizens. These constraints can prevent actors from reaching social contacts of high status. In regard to the job assignment system in China up until the early 1990s, one was usually placed in a work unit in a specific industry for one's lifetime and not allowed to transfer to another work unit, not to mention moving to a different region. This tended to lock workers in a small segment of occupational stratum in a region often insulated from higher strata in the same or other industries. In contrast, people in the United States and Taiwan have had a relatively greater chance of encountering and making contact with persons in the upper echelons of an occupational hierarchy since there are no governmental regulations affecting career mobility.

> *Hypothesis 1-1*:   People in China have less upper reachability in terms of highest prestige score attached to the jobs of network alters than their capitalist counterparts in the United States and Taiwan.

For similar reasons as above, the range of prestige scores of network members in China may not be as wide as those among Americans and Taiwanese at the aggregate level. The relatively narrower range of prestige of Chinese people may signal that the job assignment system and other various governmental regulations have hindered expansion of social network boundaries compared to cases in the United States and Taiwan.

> *Hypothesis 1-2*:   People in China have a smaller range of prestige in terms of accessed social capital than their capitalist counterparts in the United States and Taiwan.

Extensity (number of ties) can also reveal the depressed networks characteristic of Chinese people, since a count of number of ties indicates the density of a network and is intrinsically related to the other two indices, upper reachability and range of prestige scores.

> *Hypothesis 1-3*:   On average, people in China have a smaller number of ties in their accessed social capital compared to their capitalist counterparts in the United States and Taiwan.

Let us turn to the issue of gender inequality in accessed social capital. Disparity by gender group in access to valuable resources is an almost universal social phenomenon, but the double institutional constraints in China of socialist control and the legacy of male-dominant Confucian culture constitute additional drawbacks for Chinese females. Although not depressed by double constraints, Taiwanese females also suffer from the cultural legacy of Confucianism whereby females have traditionally been placed in an inferior social status. However, American females have not had these constraints from the peculiar political-economic and patriarchal cultural models, although they are not an exception to the universal baseline female inequality. Chinese females may therefore be the most disadvantaged with regard to accessing network resources, while American females are the least disadvantaged, with Taiwanese females in the middle of the two. Two relevant hypotheses follow in regard to general gender inequality and intersocietal variation of this inequality in China, Taiwan, and the United States.

> *Hypothesis 1-4*:   Females in the three societies experience disadvantages compared to males in formulating accessed social capital (upper reachability, range of prestige, and extensity).

> *Hypothesis 1-5*:   Chinese females are the most disadvantaged among the three female groups in obtaining accessed social capital due to the double constraints of state socialist and Confucian models. American females are the least disadvantaged among the females in the three societies since they suffer only a baseline gender inequality and no additional institutional constraints. Taiwanese females, affected by the Confucian cultural disadvantage in addition to baseline gender inequality, fall somewhere in between the most (China) and least (United States) disadvantaged female groups.

As indicated, gender inequality is a universal phenomenon that has been prevalent across almost every society. However, some societies, including the United States, have retained another kind of social group inequality. Racial inequality has been recognized as a serious social issue in the United States, given that it experienced slavery and, more recently, the civil rights movement. Practical inequality in its labor market and residential segregation against African-Americans and other nonwhite race/ethnic groups has persisted as well (Bonacich 1972; Hirshman and Wong 1984; Portes and Truelove 1987; Wilson 1987). I suggest that a comparison of accessed social capital by racial groups will reflect the overall racial inequality in the United States. This hypothesis will thus identify the intrasociety variation of accessed social capital by racial groups in the United States.

> *Hypothesis 1-6*:   When racial inequality in the United States is identified by the analysis of social capital composition, whites have greater accessed social capital (upper reachability, range of prestige, and extensity) than nonwhites.

Another important agenda regarding accessed social capital is the comparison of the structural sources of accessed social capital in the three societies. As discussed, the present research introduces three structural layers of social relations: binding (family-oriented ties); bonding (daily contacts); and belonging (participation in voluntary organizations). I assume that the belonging layer is the main source of accessed social capital. In addition, I suspect that binding is a significant source of accessed social capital in the two East Asian societies, given their Confucian focus on family cohesiveness.

> *Hypothesis 1-7*:   Among the three structural layers of social relations, the outermost layer of belonging is the main source of accessed social capital because memberships in voluntary associations increase the probability of contacting diverse social ties.

> *Hypothesis 1-8*:   Among the three structural layers of social relations, the innermost layer of binding is a significant source of accessed social capital in the two East Asian societies, but not in the United States.

Comparison of the status attainment process

Next, the Hypotheses 2-i series argues the positive effect of activated social capital across the three societies, regardless of their political-economic or cultural differences. I highlight the intricately different mechanisms of social contact activation among the three societies. In addition, gender and race inequalities in activated social capital are hypothesized in accordance with the parallel hypotheses of such inequalities in accessed social capital.

The effect of activated social capital is positive in predicting the attained status of respondents, regardless of institutional differences among the three countries. American people are free to use either formal or informal methods of job searches in order to maximize return from the process. Although the mobilization of social contacts for job searches was not legitimate in China, the effect of social capital is expected to penetrate these legal and institutional blockades.

> *Hypothesis 2-1*:   The higher the status of the contact person, the better the attained status of ego in China, Taiwan, and the United States.

However, it is expected that the impact of activated social capital will be differentiated across the three societies. I suspect that activated social capital (contact status) has the strongest impact on status attainment in the United States, whereas China has the weakest impact due to the dual institutional constraints on activation of social contacts for job search.

> *Hypothesis 2-2*:   The magnitude of the effect of activated social capital (contact status) is greatest in the United States and smallest in China, with that in Taiwan lying between these two societies.

Since the use of contacts for getting jobs in the labor market was legally prohibited in socialist China under the command economy period, Chinese people had to go through trusted persons rather than directly reaching out to those making decisions on desired positions (Bian 1997). In addition, the Confucian indoctrination of a hierarchical and patriarchal social order is likely to restrict the pool of contacts for job seekers to mainly the family domain. These institutional constraints increase the length of the chain of activated contacts in China.

> *Hypothesis 2-3*:   The chain of activated contacts for getting a job is longer for Chinese than for Taiwanese or Americans.

Composition of contacts usually involves most trustable parties, who fall mainly within family boundaries in China because use of low-trust contacts could have resulted in legal punishment when the state job allocation system was active. In contrast, Americans are more likely to link directly to helpers outside the family. Thus the differential composition of contacts in terms of family vs. nonfamily ties among the three peoples indicates the effect of the institutional constraints of the socialist-control and Confucian models.

> *Hypothesis 2-4*:   Chinese people tend to activate more family ties than nonfamily ties in the job search process, whereas Taiwanese and American people utilize more nonfamily ties than family ties.

What are the returns of this mobilization process of contacts by different gender groups? Generally, males in all three societies are better than females at utilizing their pool of social capital in order to achieve wanted returns from the labor market. Specifically, the gender gap in returns from the labor market is smallest in the United States (no additional constraints except for baseline gender inequality), but largest in state-socialist China (double constraints of socialist control and the Confucian model), with Taiwan in the middle of the spectrum (constraint of the Confucian model).

> *Hypothesis 2-5:* In all three societies males are more likely than females to achieve better status attainment through activated social capital. The gap between males and females in returns of activated social capital from the labor market is largest in China. The smallest gap between gender groups occurs in the United States.

Let us proceed to the issue of racial inequality in activated social capital in the United States. Because nonwhites are the disadvantaged racial group in terms of accessed social capital, their inequality in the labor market is evident when they have to rely on activated social capital drawn from their poorer accessed social capital in their job searches.

> *Hypothesis 2-6:* In the United States whites obtain greater returns in the labor market from their activated social capital than nonwhites.

Lastly, in terms of the direct effects of structural layers of social relations on status attainment, I propose that belonging (participation in formal organizations) has the strongest impact on status attainment across the target societies because it leads people to diverse social resources that cannot be acquired by educational or occupational credentials (Musick and Wilson 2008; Ruiter and De Graaf 2009). In addition, I also hypothesize that binding (family-oriented ties) exerts significant impact on status attainment in the two East Asian societies but not in the United States, due to the family-centered Confucian social order.

> *Hypothesis 2-7:* Among the three structural layers of social relations, the outermost layer of belonging has the greatest effect on status attainment in the three societies.

> *Hypothesis 2-8:* Among the three structural layers of social relations, the innermost layer of binding has a significant effect on status attainment in the two East Asian societies, but not in the United States.

I thus suspect that the bonding layer's effect will generally lie between the binding and belonging layers in the three societies.

Conclusion

As reviewed in Chapters 2 and 3, institutions and institutional constraints moderate the effect of social capital. Therefore I proposed ideal typical models of institutions and their constraints by each country. China has retained the socialist control model as its political economic institution and the Confucian model as its cultural institution. In Chapter 3 I pointed out that the Confucian legacy is inextricably embedded in Chinese society, even though the socialist regime and its Cultural Revolution tried to eliminate it. The United States is a representative reference case in which the market-dominant model is organically coupled with an individualistic culture. Not tilting toward either of these two extremes, Taiwan generates a model that mixes market dominance and the Confucian culture.

I also explained how accessed and activated social capital are specifically measured and deployed in a causal sequence of status attainment process in the labor market. The two sets of hypotheses were presented; the first set focused on the variation in social capital composition across the three countries due to their institutional constraints; and the second series of hypotheses aimed to test the actual status attainment process, focusing on the relationship between activated social capital and labor market outcomes. Racial and gender inequalities were also considered in both sets of hypotheses. In the following chapters the hypotheses are tested at both bivariate and multivariate levels of analyses. In the last chapter I revisit the hypotheses to determine if they were supported. Before proceeding to the multivariate analyses, the details of the data sets from the three countries, methods, and specific measures and their univariate and bivariate analyses are presented in the next chapter.

5 Data, methods, and measures

This study uses data sets from the same module of surveys administered in China, Taiwan, and the United States; the crossnational surveys were conducted between November 2004 and April 2005 in a synchronized fashion. The surveys were organized and funded by the Academia Sinica in Taiwan. The project, under the title "Social Capital: Its Production and Consequences," aimed to conduct a large-scale comparative study of social capital in the three societies.

Overview of data from the three societies

The sample size was in excess of 3,000 respondents in each country. The data sets from the United States and Taiwan were nationally representative, and the Chinese data set covered major regions and cities. Therefore demographic characteristics of the three data sets seem to be quite representative of each country, though the Chinese data did not cover rural areas. The age of respondents uniformly ranged between 21 and 64 in all three surveys, which targeted respondents currently or previously employed at the time of interview.

The key factor of the surveys is the almost identical position generator module for respondents from the three countries, in which a respondent answered whether he or she knows specific persons who hold 22 (the United States and Taiwan) to 24 (China) occupations. Actual occupational positions in the Chinese position generator module differed slightly from the American and Taiwanese modules in order to reflect the peculiarity in China's occupational structure. Specifically, the Chinese module included three jobs that were not listed in the modules of the United States and Taiwan: leader of work unit; higher manager of work unit; and public service personnel of government offices. The first two jobs are found in state or collective sectors in China that do not exist in American and Taiwanese industries. The third occupation (public service personnel) appeared in the list because it is widespread in Chinese society, and the job's influence could be an important ingredient of Chinese social capital. The occupation of congressman was omitted from the Chinese module but included in the US and Taiwanese modules, because the Chinese political system has not developed a Western-style legislative body. This slight variation in position generator modules between China and the other two societies aimed to take into account major differences in their occupational structures. It did not affect the systematic comparison among the three societies since the study employs only the major common portion of the modules. The position generator is based on the identical 21 jobs across the three samples to maintain comparability (see Table 5.1 and Appendix A).

It is first necessary to review how the surveys were conducted in each society so that the comparability of the data sets and the generalizability of the following statistical analyses can be identified.

The Chinese survey

The target sampling frame of the survey was adults ranging from 21 to 64 years of age, currently or previously employed, and registered and residing in urban cities in China. The sampling scheme employed was a multistage systematic probability sample in which households in all selected urban cities were sequenced to produce clusters of 19 consecutive households as the basic units of sampling. An eligible respondent in each household was then selected following the same standard of birth date closest to July 1. Beginning at the top of the list of all households by cities, clusters of households were sampled, producing 184 clusters from 167 cities.

Professional interviewers conducted personal interviews between November 2004 and March 2005. After up to three attempts with each designated respondent and further sampling from adjacent households if previous households failed to yield respondents, the response rate was about 40 percent, a total sample size of 3,514. The relatively low response rate was due to several factors. We held the sampled respondents rigidly and without replacement. Respondents who could not be contacted and interviewed after the initial attempt and follow-ups were counted as lost. We also found that more and more urban residents in China are less willing to be interviewed, and we made no effort to force their participation. The effects of the low response rates are difficult to estimate. It is difficult to find the appropriate census data from the sampled cities for currently or previously employed adults aged 21 to 64; however, strong correspondence in key parameters assures us that the sample provides credible estimates for the population under study. To further ensure against possible sample biases, the study incorporates critical control variables in all analyses.

The Taiwanese survey

The Taiwanese survey was conducted with a multistage systematic probability sample based on the island-wide national sampling scheme targeting adults aged 21 to 64, with current or previous working careers. The response rate was 48 percent, with 3,278 responses from eligible respondents in the selected households out of 6,829 face-to-face interview attempts by professional interviewers. The response rate seemed low, but it fell within a normal range of national surveys in Taiwan. The consistently low response rates in Taiwan were mainly due to the fact that over 85 percent of the population is living in urban areas, thereby producing several obstacles to the process of face-to-face interviews. For instance, interviewers routinely had difficulty gaining permission from security guards when attempting to enter high-rise buildings where selected households were located. Also, in not a few cases, sampled individuals and their families simply refused any attempts for interviews because they did not allow strangers into their households. A small proportion of refusals occurred during the interview, particularly when it took longer than the urban residents had expected.

A goodness-of-fit chi-square test was performed to assess the representativeness of the survey sample for the whole population in terms of "gender," "age," and "age (five categories) X gender." This confirmed that the sample is representative of the general Taiwanese population.

The US survey

The US survey utilized adults aged 21 to 64 who were currently or previously employed, selected from the whole population, as its sampling frame. The telephone survey method of Random Digit Dialing (RDD) was used for the national survey. Total attempts to reach the selected households numbered 6,915, from which 3,000 eligible persons whose birth dates were closest to July 1 responded to the interview requests, producing a response rate of 43.4 percent. The average length of the survey was 34.1 minutes. The response rate of this survey is not exceptionally low considering the declining trend of response rates in national telephone surveys since the 1990s (Keeter et al. 2006). Using two surveys that employed identical questionnaires, Keeter and his colleagues report that even though their response rates were 36 percent and 60.6 percent, no significant differences were found between the two surveys. They conclude that a low response rate does not deteriorate survey estimates (Keeter et al. 2000; Keeter et al. 2006).

One thing to note is that when the survey reached about two-thirds of the expected number of respondents, the research team found that racial minorities, especially Hispanics, were underrepresented in the sample. The team then decided to employ quota sampling for the rest of the sample, aiming to get a racial composition comparable to the 2000 US census. Thus the racial distribution in the final sample successfully reflects the actual structure of the US population. To capture potential statistical biases, if any, from the quota sampling, I use the dummy variable "quota" in the analyses. Specifically, when the variable "quota" equals 1, it means that such cases were from quota sampling.

Methods

One of the primary research interests of this study lies in the comparison of the three indices (upper reachability, range of prestige, and extensity) of accessed social capital from the position generators. Thus it is necessary to first understand how the three indices are constructed. The relevant statistical methods for comparison of social capital among the three societies are then presented.

As mentioned in the previous chapter, the three indices of accessed social capital measure different aspects of the social capital composition of each respondent. For instance, upper reachability tells us the highest job among a respondent's network members in terms of prestige scores within the given boundary of the structured occupation list of the position generators. Range of prestige shows the upper and lower limits of one's social network in light of occupational prestige scores. That is, if a respondent's range of prestige is greater than others, then the person's social network may consist of more varied occupational positions in the labor market. Through the extensity measure we can see how many network members a respondent has, since it simply counts the number of network members in a given job list of the position generators. Thus all three indices quantify certain essential aspects of one's social network.

The analysis is conducted by using simple descriptions of the indices as a starting point, then t-tests for differences in means are performed between social groups (e.g., gender and race) among the three societies. The t-test results are expected to show whether there are unequal distributions of social capital in social groups, and whether in fact there are intersocietal differences in social capital formation. The regression models considering the features of outcome measures were then utilized to identify associations between the indices and various explanatory variables in Chapter 6 (Dietz, Frey, and Kalof 1987; Johnston 1984; Wonnacott and Wonnacott 1981)

Structural equation modeling (SEM) is then used for comparing latent means of accessed social capital among the three countries in the latter part of Chapter 6. I also utilize it for a full-scale multigroup (that is, multinational) path analysis of the effects of structural layers of social relations, accessed and activated social capital on status attainment in Chapter 7 (Bollen 1989; Collins and Wulgalter 1992; Klein and Moosbrugger 2000; Muthén and Muthén 2010). Lastly, using SEM I conduct a series of tests of parameter invariance to identify statistically significant differences in the structural coefficients across the three societies in the latter part of Chapter 7 (Bollen 1989).

Measures and descriptive analyses

As already mentioned, the surveys in the three societies used almost identical questionnaires, although there were some trivial differences among them that reflect the idiosyncrasies of each society. However, this study employs only the identical measures in order to reasonably conduct an international comparative study. This section presents the variables of interest from the three data sets before proceeding to the empirical tests of the hypotheses. Note that in this chapter and those following the results are shown in the order of the United

States, Taiwan, and China. I put the United States first as a reference with the fewest institutional constraints, China last as the case with the most institutional constraints, and Taiwan in between the two countries as a moderate case.

Outcome and intermediate variables

The outcome and intermediate variables are selected to test the hypotheses presented in the previous chapter regarding the composition and comparison of accessed social capital and activated social capital across the three societies. At the first stage, the composition of accessed social capital is examined across the three focal societies. Further, using the latent mean structure model in structural equation modeling, I compare the overall volume of accessed social capital across the three societies. Second, activated social capital measures are introduced in the analyses, allowing accessed social capital to predict the actual usage of social contacts. Note that activated social capital denotes the utilized portion of accessed social capital in the process of status attainment. As the indices of activated social capital, I selected four measures – presence of contact, chain length, contact status, and routine job information. Among them, contact status is the main indicator of activated social capital because it is closely related to the quality of social resources. Third, measures in regard to occupational status and income become the outcome variables when the focus of the study turns to analyzing the effect of activated social capital on status attainment, controlling for all other covariates. At this latter stage accessed social capital changes its role to one of the explanatory variables for predicting occupational status and income of respondents. Comparisons of the status attainment processes in the three societies identify the structural similarities and dissimilarities at the societal level. This section focuses on the relevant variables that help test the aforementioned hypotheses.

Indices of accessed social capital

Accessed social capital in each society was measured by the same set of position generator indices (Lin, Fu, and Hsung 2001). As explained earlier, in the surveys the position generator asked if respondents knew occupants of specific jobs in the list of 21 occupations at the time of getting their current/last position (see Appendix B for actual position generator questions). First, the survey inquired into the respondents' social networks at the time of interview: "I am going to ask some general questions about jobs some people you know may now have. These people include your relatives, friends, and acquaintances (acquaintances are people who know each other by face and name). If there are several people you know who have that kind of job, please tell me the one that occurs to you first." The respondents were then asked, "Is there anyone you know who is a (job title)?" Although the questions followed a random order, the 21 occupations in the questions were associated with occupational prestige scores of Treiman's Standard Industrial Occupational Prestige Scale (SIOPS) (Ganzeboom and Treiman 1996; see Appendix A for the list of 21 occupations with their full job titles in the order they appeared in the survey). The survey then asked respondents the same set of position generators for the time when they got their current/last position. The social capital indices at the time of interview are used to compare accessed social capital among the three societies, while those at the time of respondents' taking current/last positions are employed as controls when examining the effect of accessed social capital on the occupational status of the respondents. Table 5.1 shows how many of the respondents in the three societies knew position holders in the 21 occupations. I report the percentages twice – when respondents took current/last job, and at the time of interview.

The descriptive information reflects some significant differences resulting from the differential levels of socioeconomic development and cultural features of the three societies. For instance, varied degrees of educational development are manifested in the percentages of people who answered that they knew professors; US respondents had the most contacts with professors, while Chinese respondents had the least among the three societies. This is quite understandable when we look at the data showing that 39 percent of the US sample had a BA or graduate degree, whereas only 19 percent of Chinese respondents had a BA or higher degree. It is also interesting that over half of the US respondents, double the percentages of the other two societies, knew lawyers, demonstrating the reality of the highly developed legal industry and its concomitant culture of rampant lawsuits in the United States. In contrast, the percentages of respondents who knew farmers show the opposite side of the occupational structure of the three societies. Over 70 percent of Chinese respondents answered that they knew farmers, while 41 percent of US respondents did. This speaks to the fact that China is in transition from an underdeveloped to a developing economy. Whether respondents knew taxi drivers reveals another cultural difference in the degree of economic development. Less than 10 percent of US respondents knew taxi drivers, while over 40 percent of Chinese respondents knew taxi drivers at the time of interview. This is not unexpected, given that the United States has the highest rate of car ownership in the world, whereas about 7 percent of households in China's key cities owned cars at the time of the survey (ACNielsen 2005). In addition, it should be noted that the percentages of knowing a lawyer, CEO, or teacher (ranked 2–4 in terms of prestige scores) were higher in China than in Taiwan, which may affect the distribution of upper reachability in the sample. The reason for the higher percentages of these jobs may be partly due to the rapid marketization and socioeconomic development in China.

As shown, the position generators effectively reflected socioeconomic and cultural differences in the three societies and showed its efficacy in capturing the variability in occupational structures across countries. Further, the indices of accessed social capital based on the position-generator items guarantee consideration of the hierarchical aspect of occupational structures by utilizing

Table 5.1 Percentage of respondents knowing specific jobholders in the three societies

Occupation (SIOPS prestige score)*	US		Taiwan		China	
	When taking current/last job (N=3,000)	*At the time of interview* (N=3,000)	*When taking current/last job* (N=3,278)	*At the time of interview* (N=3,270)	*When taking current/last job* (N=3,435)	*At the time of interview* (N=3,514)
1. Professor (78)	37.2	36.4	22.5	30.4	18.6	21.1
2. Lawyer (73)	51.1	54.3	14.4	21.7	22.2	25.6
3. CEO (70)	19.9	19.7	22.4	27.3	24.2	28.5
4. Teacher (60)	44.5	47.9	40.9	51.2	63.8	68.0
5. Production manager (60)	20.9	16.6	25.1	30.3	26.6	29.9
6. Personnel manager (60)	33.8	32.4	43.2	52.9	34.2	40.1
7. Writer (57)	19.7	21.2	5.3	6.6	7.1	6.1
8. Nurse (54)	59.8	68.8	36.4	45.2	44.7	49.1
9. Admin. assistant (53)	32.9	30.9	27.5	34.8	15.1	16.0
10. Programmer (51)	41.8	48.0	29.6	42.7	15.1	18.3
11. Bookkeeper (49)	32.6	30.7	47.7	55.9	56.0	61.1
12. Farmer (47)	41.1	41.7	57.3	62.5	70.0	72.3
13. Policeman (40)	45.4	49.5	33.8	45.6	39.4	46.4
14. Receptionist (38)	46.7	38.1	25.2	31.3	13.3	15.5
15. Operator (34)	29.9	25.0	49.4	56.6	37.1	41.7
16. Hairdresser (32)	56.6	59.0	44.2	55.9	25.3	30.3
17. Taxi driver (31)	9.4	8.6	27.9	36.4	33.4	43.8
18. Guard (30)	26.8	24.1	35.0	46.2	30.5	35.6
19. Janitor (25)	31.0	28.1	27.5	35.4	20.5	23.1
20. Babysitter (23)	29.5	26.6	23.7	32.5	13.2	15.7
21. Bellboy (22)	3.6	2.7	24.7	28.9	19.8	19.9

Note: *The occupational prestige scores of Treiman's Standard Industrial Occupational Prestige Scale (SIOPS) are in parentheses beside occupation titles (Ganzeboom and Treiman 1996).

the prestige scores attached to each occupation and also take into account the width of network ranges in the occupational structures. The specific social capital indices constructed on the position generators are introduced below. As noted, the indices were measured when respondents were starting current/ last position of employment as explanatory variables to be used in a multivariate context later.

EXTENSITY

The first indicator of accessed social capital is the number of jobs that a respondent knew from the list of 21 occupations. For instance, if a respondent knew nine jobs out of the list, then the extensity score is nine. Extensity can thus vary from 0 to 21. It is desirable to check the actual distribution of extensity in the three samples of the study. The mean and standard deviation of the measure are presented and subjected to a t-test to identify any significant differences among them at the univariate level.

As shown in Table 5.2, the mean extensity was the greatest in the United States and the smallest in China, with Taiwan's mean in the middle of the two. According to the t-test results, the differences among the three societies are statistically significant.

UPPER REACHABILITY

The remaining two indices are related to the prestige scores attached to each occupation in the list. Upper reachability denotes the highest prestige score among the jobs that a respondent knew, and thus captures how rich the social networks of the respondents are. For instance, if a respondent answered that he or she knew nine job occupants out of the position generator items, of which a CEO of a large company had the highest prestige score, then its prestige score (70) is assigned as the upper reachability score of the specific respondent.

At the univariate level, it turns out that the United States had higher upper reachability than the other two East Asian societies, according to the t-tests as

Table 5.2 Comparison of extensity

	US (mean (SD))	Taiwan (mean (SD))	China (mean (SD))
Extensity	7.14	6.64	6.30
(range 0–21)	(4.59)	(5.04)	(4.32)
N	3,000	3,278	3,435
t-test	US > Taiwan***		
		US > China***	
			Taiwan > China**

$* p < .05; ** p < .01; *** p < .001$ (two-tailed test).

Table 5.3 Comparison of upper reachability

	US (mean (SD))	Taiwan (mean (SD))	China (mean (SD))
Upper reachability (22–78 SIOPS score) N	69.03 (11.25) 2,830	62.18 (12.83) 3,084	64.09 (10.66) 3,390
t-test	US > Taiwan ***	Taiwan < China ***	US > China ***

$* p < .05; ** p < .01; *** p < .001$ (two-tailed test).

reported in Table 5.3. However, China had higher upper reachability than Taiwan. These results are opposite to the hypothesis that predicted the disadvantage of socialist society in allowing average citizens to mingle with higher positions in the occupational hierarchy. What is the reason for this? I reported above that Chinese people had greater percentages than their Taiwanese counterparts in knowing upper-echelon jobholders such as lawyers and CEOs (see Table 5.1). The reform, Open Door policy, and recent rapid marketization of the Chinese socialist government have made it possible to introduce and increase prestigious and market-oriented jobs like CEOs in its labor market; its people thus have better probability than in the past for making contact with such jobholders, including expatriate CEOs from the West (Fernandez and Underwood 2006; Wong 2005).

RANGE OF PRESTIGE SCORES

The third indicator of accessed social capital also utilizes the prestige scores assigned to the jobs. In particular, this indicator measures how wide the network alters of a respondent is in terms of having diverse occupations on the job list. Specifically, it is calculated by subtracting the lowest prestige score from the highest prestige score among the jobs known to a respondent. For example, let us suppose that a respondent knew 10 jobs out of the 21 position generators. Next, let us also assume that among the 10 alters of the respondent a CEO of a large company had the highest prestige score (70), whereas a driver had the lowest score (31). The range of prestige scores for the specific respondent is calculated by deducting the lowest score from the highest $(70 - 31 = 39)$.

According to t-test results in Table 5.4, the range of prestige was the greatest in the United States, followed by Taiwan and China. Since the index of range of prestige, along with the extensity index, captures the diversity of the social network, it seems at least at the univariate level that Americans enjoy the most diverse ties in their networks, whereas the Chinese have the least diverse ties in terms of occupational heterogeneity in their social networks.

Table 5.4 Comparison of range of prestige

	US (mean (SD))	Taiwan (mean (SD))	China (mean (SD))
Range of prestige	38.57	32.47	31.69
(0–56 SIOPS score)	(15.97)	(17.35)	(16.19)
N	2,830	3,084	3,390
t-test	US > Taiwan ***		
		US > China ***	
			Taiwan > China *

$* p < .05; ** p < .01; *** p < .001$ (two-tailed test).

THE INDICES AND GENDER INEQUALITY IN THREE SOCIETIES

It is worth checking social inequality patterns in the three societies through the accessed social capital indices. The proposition regarding gender inequality was that the two East Asian societies would exhibit more inequality than the United States. The plausible reason behind the proposition is related to Confucianism. Confucian ideology generates a strong norm of male dominance and legitimizes unfair treatment of women in East Asian social contexts, even though a reinterpretation of Confucianism has occurred that asserts the possibility of Confucian contributions favoring harmonious gender relationships (Li 2000a, 2000b). In particular, East Asian females have traditionally been confined within households following "the Confucian doctrine of the roles of men and women as that of the external (*wai*) and the internal (*nei*)" (Li 2000b: 188); this has deprived women of the chance to contact diverse job-holders in social spaces outside their homes. Since modernization has been pursued in the two East Asian societies, the degree of oppressive practices against females is expected to have decreased. Nonetheless, it is proposed that the overall comparison between the American and the two East Asian societies will reveal the societal level of gender inequality in the latter societies.

We now check gender inequality reflected in the indices of accessed social capital. According to t-test results in Table 5.5, there appears to be no female

Table 5.5 Gender inequality in the United States

Index	Male (mean (SD))	t-test	Female (mean (SD))
Extensity	6.90	<**	7.28
	(4.04)		(3.90)
Upper reachability	69.01	=	69.46
	(10.61)		(10.41)
Range of prestige	37.16	<***	39.68
	(15.17)		(14.27)

$* p < .05; ** p < .01; *** p < .001$ (two-tailed test).

Table 5.6 Gender inequality in Taiwan

Index	Male (mean (SD))	t-test	Female (mean (SD))
Extensity	8.77 (5.49)	>***	7.81 (5.33)
Upper reachability	65.33 (12.14)	>*	64.31 (12.62)
Range of prestige	37.58 (16.42)	>***	35.52 (17.43)

* $p < .05$; ** $p < .01$; *** $p < .001$ (two-tailed test).

disadvantage in the United States; instead, females had more extensity and a wider range of prestige than males. There was no significant gap in upper reachability between the two gender groups. Thus it seems that in the United States there is no gender inequality in accessed social capital in the traditional direction of female disadvantage.

The Taiwanese case shows a very different pattern of association between gender and accessed social capital indices in Table 5.6. In all three indices Taiwanese males had significantly greater means than females, which denotes a gender inequality that disadvantages females. On average, Taiwanese females had one less social tie than males; additionally, it appears that females were less likely to have network alters that occupied high-prestige jobs, which eventually reduced the average range of females' social network in the occupational hierarchy compared to that of males.

In Table 5.7, China shows further gender inequality in a more escalated manner; all three indices indicate that Chinese females had significantly smaller means than males. In other words, it is clear that in China males have richer and more diverse accessed social capital than females. Even though we are still at the basic descriptive level of statistical analysis, it seems clear that (1) China suffers from lack of accessed social capital compared to the United States and Taiwan; and, moreover (2) its degree of female disadvantage in accessing social capital is the highest among the three societies.

Table 5.7 Gender inequality in China

Index	Male (mean (SD))	t-test	Female (mean (SD))
Extensity	7.67 (4.75)	>***	6.51 (4.20)
Upper reachability	66.30 (10.47)	>***	63.89 (10.43)
Range of prestige	35.73 (15.19)	>***	32.28 (15.39)

* $p < .05$; ** $p < .01$; *** $p < .001$ (two-tailed test).

As we observed, the three indices of accessed social capital are effective in capturing the markedly different distribution of gender inequality between the American and the East Asian societies. Further, it is shown that gender inequality in accessed social capital is more prevalent in China than in Taiwan. It seems that this different degree of gender inequality between these two East Asian societies may be due to the disparity in economic development, which is mainly associated with their different political economic institutions. Related to this issue, it is known that the level of economic development has a positively significant impact on the relative status of women, controlling for patriarchal institutional arrangements (Forsythe, Korzeniewicz, and Durrant 2000). Nonetheless, it still remains to be tested if such gender inequality patterns among the target societies hold at the advanced multivariate analyses.

THE INDICES AND RACIAL INEQUALITY IN THE UNITED STATES

Let us now see if racial inequality in the United States is captured by the accessed social capital indices. At the first cut, I compare the indices between whites and nonwhites.

As shown in Table 5.8, whites were significantly superior to nonwhites in all the dimensions tapped by the three accessed social capital indices. From this we learn that whites have richer and more diverse accessed social capital than nonwhites. In turn, let us identify the significance of the gaps between whites and each racial minority group in the United States. Comparing whites and African-Americans, there was no seriously significant disadvantage for African-Americans except for upper reachability in Table 5.9. Although nonsignificant, African-Americans had slightly greater means in extensity and range of prestige than whites.

However, whites had unequivocally better accessed social capital than Latinos; all three indices report that whites had significantly greater means than Latinos in Table 5.10. Thus it is likely that the major reason for the overall gap between whites and nonwhites above is due to disparity in accessed social capital between whites and Latinos.

Table 5.8 Racial inequality between whites and nonwhites

Index	White (mean (SD))	t-test	Nonwhite (mean (SD))
Extensity	7.29 (3.85)	>***	6.66 (4.19)
Upper reachability	69.73 (10.0)	>***	68.07 (11.57)
Range of prestige	39.05 (14.16)	>**	37.26 (15.97)

$p < .05$; ** $p < .01$; *** $p < .001$ (two-tailed test).

Table 5.9 Race inequality between whites and African-Americans

Index	White (mean (SD))	t-test	African-American (mean (SD))
Extensity	7.29 (3.85)	=	7.36 (4.14)
Upper reachability	69.73 (10.0)	>*	68.48 (10.81)
Range of prestige	39.05 (14.16)	=	39.30 (14.29)

* $p < .05$; ** $p < .01$; *** $p < .001$ (two-tailed test).

Table 5.10 Race inequality between whites and Latinos

Index	White (mean (SD))	t-test	Latino (mean (SD))
Extensity	7.29 (3.85)	>***	6.19 (4.30)
Upper reachability	69.73 (10.0)	>***	67.51 (12.11)
Range of prestige	39.05 (14.16)	>***	36.02 (16.80)

* $p < .05$; ** $p < .01$; *** $p < .001$ (two-tailed test).

The remaining comparison addresses the last subset within minorities. As expected from the prior comparisons reported above, Latinos had worse access to social capital than African-Americans in extensity and range of prestige as shown in Table 5.11. This means that Latino social networks lack diversity compared to those of African-Americans.

These results point out that in the Unites States a within-minority inequality in accessed social capital has gone unnoticed but is a serious problem. Part of the reason could be that (1) Latinos have had a shorter immigration history

Table 5.11 Race inequality between African-Americans and Latinos

Index	African-American (mean (SD))	t-test	Latino (mean (SD))
Extensity	7.36 (4.14)	>***	6.19 (4.30)
Upper reachability	68.48 (10.81)	=	67.51 (12.11)
Range of prestige	39.30 (14.29)	>**	36.02 (16.80)

* $p < .05$; ** $p < .01$; *** $p < .001$ (two-tailed test).

than African-Americans; and, relying on the first cause to some extent (2) some Latinos are significantly lacking in the capacity for English-language communication, which is vital to having greater access to social relations in their host society.

Note that I did not break minorities further into, say, Asians or Native Americans because these groups did not occur with enough frequency for such statistical comparison.

FACTOR SCORE OF THE THREE INDICES

Van der Gaag and his colleagues (2007) argue that the three indices of accessed social capital can cause multicollinearity problems because they are positively correlated with one another – for instance, the more extensive a network, the wider its alters' range of prestige scores. Further, upper reachability and range of prestige tend to deviate from normality and thus be skewed in their distribution. In order to control multicollinearity, I conduct factor analysis of the indices from the three data sets (principal component method, varimax rotation, a criterion of an eigenvalue equal to or greater than 1, and scoring coefficients based on varimax rotated factors).

As shown in Table 5.12, a single factor solution is produced in each of the three data sets. The factor variable is employed in multivariate statistical analyses instead of putting all three indices in the regression equations. The single factor explained 81 to 85.7 percent of the total variance created by the three indices. In addition, the three social capital indices in the data sets have factor loadings of at least .86 on the single factor, which supports the efficacy of the factor variable in the analyses. It is notable that the range of the prestige

Table 5.12 Factor analysis of accessed social capital when starting current/last position

Variable	US (N=2,830)	Taiwan (N=3,084)	China (N=3,390)
Factor eigenvalue			
I	2.43	2.57	2.48
(% of explained variance)	(81.0%)	(85.7%)	(82.7%)
II	0.41	0.33	0.37
III	0.15	0.11	0.15
Factor loading on factor I[a]			
Extensity	0.86	0.89	0.89
Upper reachability	0.89	0.92	0.89
Range	0.95	0.96	0.95
Factor scoring on factor I[a]			
Extensity	0.35	0.35	0.36
Upper reachability	0.36	0.36	0.36
Range	0.39	0.38	0.38

Note: [a]Principal component, minimal eigenvalue of 1, and coefficients based on varimax rotation.

scores had slightly greater loadings on the factor than the other two indices in all three data sets; it is thus expected that diversity in social networks is well represented by the single factor variable.

Measures of activated social capital

Whether job seekers use social capital in their job search process partly depends on how much social capital they have in the first place, but there can be variation in activation of social capital even among people with the same amount of accessed social capital. In other words, some activate much or some of accessed social capital, others not at all. Thus it is necessary to distinguish activated social capital from accessed social capital when analyzing the job search process to identify if either of the two is related to job search outcomes.

There are several dimensions involved in the activation process of social capital. First, it should be clear whether job seekers used contacts in their job search. If they did, we can then be sure that they activated accessed social capital, the potential social resources embedded in their social network. Second, the number of contacts mobilized in the job search process must be checked. I suspect that a longer chain involving more contacts would be used more frequently in the two East Asian societies than in the United States because bridging ties between the job seeker and helpers are a byproduct of Confucian culture, which stresses the value of close ties within the family. It follows that job seekers would mobilize more closely related contacts to potential helpers even when they themselves knew the helpers. Further, it would be imperative to use a longer chain involving only trustable contacts when the use of contacts was prohibited under the job assignment system in China. These first two dimensions are related to the presence and quantity of activated social capital. Third, we must also take into account how resourceful the activated contacts are. This is called contact status, measured by the location of the contact in the occupational hierarchy. I propose that contact status is more strongly associated with job search outcomes than presence of contact and number of contacts used because quality of contact should have more impact on status attainment. Thus the third dimension captures the quality of activated social capital. Lastly, we need to consider whether job searchers are situated in structural positions to which routine job information flows without being requested. This last dimension tries to explain some variation in unsolicited activation of social capital.

In order to take quantity and quality of activated social capital and unsolicited routine job information into account, I introduce four measures in the analysis: presence of contact, length of contact chain, contact status, and routine job information. Among these measures, contact status is a focal variable of activated social capital because it captures the quality of activated social capital. Nonetheless, other indicators are also included as controls because they are expected to show crossnational variation.

Table 5.13 Use of contacts in the three societies

	US		Taiwan		China	
	Freq.	*%*	*Freq.*	*%*	*Freq.*	*%*
No contact	1,389	46.4	1,832	56.0	2,133	60.7
Contact(s) used	1,607	53.6	1,439	44.0	1,381	39.3
N	2,996	100.0	3,271	100.0	3,514	100.0

PRESENCE OF CONTACT

The survey asked respondents in all three countries, "During the process of getting your [current/last] job, how many people helped you? [This can include all kinds of help, e.g., telling you about a job opportunity, putting in a good word for you, etc.]" I then created a dichotomous variable where 0 means no contact used and 1 means contact(s) used in job search.

Social contact was most frequently activated in job searches in the United States, while it was least used in China, with Taiwan in the middle, as shown in Table 5.13. T-test results show that the differences in using contact(s) among the three societies were statistically significant. I assume that the least use of contacts in China is due mainly to institutional intervention by the communist government, which assigned jobs and made it illegal to utilize private ties in the job search process until the early 1990s; the experience of the institutional intervention over four decades might dissuade the job seeker from using contacts even after the labor marketization. Also, the comparatively less-standardized educational system and underregulated labor market in the United States are structural causes that make informal job search channels flourish, including the use of contacts by the job seeker.

LENGTH OF CONTACTS' CHAIN

The survey also probed for more information about helpers in the job search process. Specifically, the survey collected information about up to four helpers in regard to their gender, race, and occupation. I construct the length of helpers' chain variable that captures the quantity of activated contacts in the job search process.

As shown in Table 5.14, the length of chain in China was significantly longer than those in the other two societies. There is no significant difference found between the United States and Taiwan, the two capitalist societies. Note that not a single respondent used a fourth contact in the United States. Again, it remains to be examined in what circumstances the length of chain was extended and how it affected the status attainment process in the three target societies. The reference category (0) of the variable was given to no-tie users in a reconstructed variable of chain length employed in the actual analyses.

Table 5.14 Length of chain in the three societies

Length of chain	US		Taiwan		China	
	Freq.	*%*	*Freq.*	*%*	*Freq.*	*%*
1	882	76.9	1,054	80.8	703	63.8
2	258	22.5	218	16.7	295	26.8
3	7	0.6	30	2.3	67	6.9
4	–	–	2	0.2	37	3.5
Total	1,147	100.0	1,304	100.0	1,102	100.0
Mean (SD)	1.24 (0.44)		1.22 (0.48)		1.49 (0.76)	
t-test	US = Taiwan					
			US < China***			
					Taiwan < China***	

$p < .05$; ** $p < .01$; *** $p < .001$ (two-tailed test).

To examine the composition of contacts, the survey asked (1) if the respondent and their most important helpers were linked directly or indirectly; (2) what kind of relationship they shared with the most important helpers (e.g., family, coworkers, friends, or neighbors); and (3) how close they and their contacts were.

As shown in Table 5.15, Chinese people had the smallest percentage of direct contacts (81.5 percent) within the most important helpers in comparison with the other two peoples. Next, percentages of family ties among direct contacts of the most importance indicate that the majority of direct contacts were family ties for Chinese people (57.7 percent), close to three times that of the United States (21.1 percent). This thus tells us that the majority of Chinese people's most important direct ties are their family members, including extended families. In addition, note that for Chinese people 18 percent of family ties in the most important direct contacts were parents, whereas the

Table 5.15 Proportion of direct contacts and family ties in the three societies

	US		Taiwan		China	
	Freq.	*%*	*Freq.*	*%*	*Freq.*	*%*
Direct contacts	1,452	90.1	1,314	92.3	850	81.5
Indirect contacts	159	9.9	109	7.7	193	18.5
Percent of family ties among direct contacts (SD)	21.1 (0.41)		39.2 (0.49)		57.7 (0.49)	
t-test (proportion of family ties)	US < Taiwan***					
			US < China***			
					Taiwan < China***	

* $p < 0.05$; ** $p < 0.01$; *** $p < 0.001$ (two-tailed test).

Table 5.16 Closeness between job searcher and the first contact

	US	Taiwan	China
Mean closeness between respondent and the first contact (1: not close at all – 5: very close) (SD)	3.77 (1.24)	4.30 (0.89)	4.51 (0.73)
N	1,611	1,425	1,127
t-test	US < Taiwan***		
		US < China***	
			Taiwan < China***

* $p < 0.05$; ** $p < 0.01$; *** $p < 0.001$ (two-tailed test).

figures are 4.9 percent and 11.2 percent for Americans and Taiwanese respectively. As the t-tests report, the differences among the three societies were statistically significant. This difference between the United States and the two East Asian societies may be due to a large extent to the Confucian social order that centers on family relations.

The psychological closeness between the job seeker and his or her contact is another venue that needs to be checked. In the literature the closeness or intimacy index has often been used to measure the strength of ties (Bian 1997; Granovetter 1973; Wegener 1991). Although this variable is not employed in the multivariate analyses because measures of structural layers are employed instead, it is notable that the closeness index reveals differences among the three target societies. According to the results in Table 5.16, it appears that Chinese people had the closest relation between job searchers and their first contacts compared to the other two peoples; in turn, Taiwanese people had closer relations with contacts than Americans. The differences in closeness among the three societies were all significant.

CONTACT STATUS

The socioeconomic status of contacts should be taken into account independently of the presence of contacts and the length of contact chain because the quality of contacts is expected to be strongly associated with job search outcomes. The survey asked respondents about the occupational information of up to their fourth contact. Thus it is necessary to stratify the contacts following a consistent procedure. To begin, the occupations of the contacts were given occupational classification codes following the standard occupational classifications in each society. The contact jobs of US respondents were given the occupational codes of the 2000 census occupational classification system, while those of Chinese contacts were assigned the occupational codes of the 1995 Chinese Standard Classification of Occupations. For Taiwanese contacts, the four-digit occupational codes from the Standard Occupational Classification System of Taiwan were employed (Li et al. 1999). The contact status variable was then created with the standardized information based on the occupational codes. Specifically, using the occupational code information of all the contacts, I categorized contact status into four categories: low class, middle class, professional, and executive.

In the next step I chose the highest occupational class among up to four contacts of each respondent. For instance, if a respondent reported that his/her first contact's occupational class was low class, the second middle class, the third professional, and the fourth executive, then I chose the occupational class of the fourth contact as the contact status since it is the highest contact status in the job search process. Thus regardless of where the contact of highest status lay within the contact chain, I selected those specific contacts with the highest occupational class, because in the literature high contact status has been one of the most significant measures of activated social capital (Boxman, De Graaf, and Flap 1991; Campbell, Marsden, and Hurlbert 1986; Lin 2001).

As shown in Table 5.17, it is noteworthy that the mean contact status was highest in the United States and lowest in China, with Taiwan in between. These gaps among the three societies were statistically significant according to t-tests. Much of the crossnational gaps can be explained by the different degrees in economic and occupational development among the three societies; still, part of the reason may be that the Chinese and Taiwanese do indeed lack resourceful contacts, even after controlling for other factors including differentials in economic and occupational development. However, I do not have a specific way to check if this argument is verifiable. Nonetheless, unequal distributions in activated social capital among the target societies are identified as being in the expected direction.

Table 5.17 Occupational classes of contacts

Occupational class	US	Taiwan	China
1. Low class (%)	226	238	525
	(20.2)	(18.3)	(47.6)
2. Middle class (%)	220	614	116
	(19.6)	(47.1)	(10.5)
3. Professional (%)	310	110	101
	(27.7)	(8.4)	(9.2)
4. Executive (%)	365	341	360
	(32.6)	(26.2)	(32.7)
N	1,121	1,303	1,102
Mean (SD)	2.73	2.43	2.27
	(1.11)	(1.06)	(1.34)
t-test	US > Taiwan***		
		US > China***	
			Taiwan > China***

* $p < 0.05$; ** $p < 0.01$; *** $p < 0.001$ (two-tailed test).

ROUTINE JOB INFORMATION

As explained, routine job information or unsolicited job information can be invoked as another dimension of activated social capital in the sense that job seekers may follow up on such information to obtain new positions, even though it is less likely for them to report that they used contacts for their job search. Specifically, the survey questioned if someone mentioned job possibilities, openings, or opportunities to a respondent in casual conversations (e.g., face-to-face, telephone, or email) during the past year without being asked. I locate this measure under the umbrella of activated social capital because routine job information is derived from a job searcher's network members; the literature on unsolicited job information assumes that it adds more explanatory power to social capital that traditional social capital indices cannot capture (McDonald 2005; McDonald and Elder 2006).

Table 5.18 shows that routine job information was richest in the United States, where about 41 percent of respondents obtained such information in one way or another in the past 12 months. The Chinese lacked such information compared to the other two societies; only 22 percent of its respondents reported that they received it. The gaps of quantity in routine job information among the United States, Taiwan, and China were statistically significant.

Indices of status attainment outcome

As briefly mentioned above, the outcome indices of status attainment should show where the respondents ended up in the occupational hierarchy, presumably affected by the effects of accessed and activated social capital, *ceteris paribus*. I use two indices for the outcome: occupational class and annual income.

OCCUPATIONAL CLASS

The first of the two outcome variables from the job search process employed in this study is the respondent's current or last occupational status in the labor

Table 5.18 Routine job information in the three societies

	US		Taiwan		China	
	Freq.	*%*	*Freq.*	*%*	*Freq.*	*%*
0. no information	1,661	59.3	1,753	63.1	2,455	78.0
1. got information	1,142	40.7	1,025	36.9	694	22.0
N	2,803	100.0	2,778	100.0	3,471	100.0
t-test	US > Taiwan**					
			US > China***			
					Taiwan > China***	

$* p < .05; ** p < .01; *** p < .001$ (two-tailed test).

Table 5.19 Occupational classes in the United States, Taiwan, and China

Occupational class	US	Taiwan	China
1. Low class (%)	948	872	2,355
	(31.7)	(26.6)	(68.7)
2. Middle class (%)	712	1,900	321
	(23.8)	(58.1)	(9.4)
3. Professional (%)	979	287	524
	(32.7)	(8.8)	(15.3)
4. Executive (%)	352	213	226
	(11.8)	(6.5)	(6.6)
N	2,991	3,272	3,426
Mean (SD)	2.25	1.95	1.59
	(1.03)	(0.78)	(0.97)
t-test	US > Taiwan***		
		US > China***	
			Taiwan > China***

* $p < .05$; ** $p < .01$; *** $p < .001$ (two-tailed test).

market at the time of interview. To begin, the occupations of the respondents were given occupational classification codes following the standard occupational classifications in each society, as was done for contact status.

An outcome variable of occupational class was created using the occupational codes. Based on the occupational code information of each current/last job title of the respondents, I categorized the jobs into four categories: low class, middle class, professional, and executive. As shown in Table 5.19, the United States had the greatest proportion of professional and executive jobs in its occupational structure. In contrast, the majority (69 percent) of Chinese respondents occupied low-class jobs. It is also shown that the United States had the highest mean in the occupational classes, Taiwan was second, and China had the lowest mean score. The gaps in the means among the three countries are statistically significant.

In the multivariate analyses to be reported later, I use the three-category variable of occupational classes, collapsing the two high-end categories to examine the dynamics of status attainment in the three societies. I collapsed the third and fourth response categories for two reasons: (1) the ordinal logit model could not be employed on the four-category variable because the proportional odds assumption across response categories was violated; and (2) I thus turned to the multinomial logit model for which the fewer response categories, the better the interpretability of statistical outcomes.

ANNUAL INCOME

Annual income is the other outcome variable of status attainment in the three societies. The variable was constructed to be semicontinuous with at

Table 5.20 Annual incomes in the United States, Taiwan, and China

	US (mean (SD))	Taiwan (mean (SD))	China (mean (SD))	Range
Mean annual income	16.04 (4.50)	5.99 (2.71)	6.68 (4.29)	US, China: 1–27 Taiwan: 1–20
*Amount in US dollars	$25,200	$10,795	$1,474	–

Note: * Mean income amounts were calculated converting the specific point of the mean between its two adjacent response categories into dollar amounts. The mean annual incomes in New Taiwan Dollars and Chinese Renminbi were changed to US dollars using the 2004 currency exchange rates.

least 20 (Taiwan) to 27 (United States and China) categories in the three data sets.

The United States had the highest annual income level among the three countries, China the lowest, and Taiwan in between according to Table 5.20. It appears that annual income was underreported by American and Taiwanese respondents, given that the United States recorded $40,309 and Taiwan recorded $25,300 of the GDP per capita in 2004, respectively. The mean annual income of the Chinese respondents was closer to its GDP per capita of $1,490 in the same year (sources: the United States and China http://data. worldbank.org/indicator/NY.GDP.PCAP.CD?page=1; Taiwan http://www. indexmundi.com/g/g.aspx?c=tw&v=67).

Although the response categories were not constructed identically across the three surveys, this should not raise any fundamental obstacles to statistical analyses capturing the dynamics of social capital and other covariates in obtaining better financial returns in the trisocietal labor markets.

Explanatory variables

The main focus of the study is to compare the effects of social capital and other covariates in the job search process across the three labor markets in the selected target societies, using models as identical as possible as permitted by the data. It is thus imperative to employ the same or most similar array of explanatory variables from the three data sets. I thus develop four types of explanatory variables: demographic variables, structural layers of social network, origin status, and socioeconomic status. Explanatory variables should precede the time points when the interviews were conducted in order to set the temporal order between independent and outcome covariates. In some cases I report variables of interest at both time of interview and time of starting current/last position to check consistency across time. However, the actual multivariate analyses employ the retrospective explanatory covariates at the time of starting current/last position.

Demographic features

Age, gender, and race are key demographic features of the respondents. Note that age is a time-varying variable that can take nonconstant values by events of interest, while the other two are time-invariant variables. To keep temporal order in the statistical models, I chose age at the starting point of the current/last position of the respondents rather than age at the time of the interview. I also note that race is a US-specific variable that cannot be applied to the other two societies. I could have employed a Han vs. non-Han ethnic divide in China and Taiwan, but I did not take it into account in the multivariate models because a predominant proportion of Chinese (97.1 percent) and Taiwanese (99.1 percent) respondents claimed that they were of Han ethnicity, thus lacking variability as a covariate.

AGE

The range of the variable at the time of interview was fixed across the three data sets as 21 to 64 years old as one of the eligibility criteria to qualify as a respondent. Chinese respondents were two to three years younger than the other two peoples according to the mean ages. Mean ages at the starting point of current/last position were at least eight years less than those at the time of interview in the three societies. In particular, Chinese respondents were about six years younger than American workers, which suggests that Chinese workers had lower rates of turnover or fewer job changes. This may be partly

Table 5.21 Descriptive statistics of explanatory variables: demographic features

Demographic variables	US (mean (SD))	Taiwan (mean (SD))	China (mean (SD))	Range/ categories of variable
Age	41.48 (10.57)	41.02 (11.66)	38.37 (10.30)	21–64
Age when starting current/last position	33.38 (9.87)	31.70 (9.63)	26.96 (8.73)	–
Male	0.46 (0.50)	0.52 (0.50)	0.49 (0.50)	–
White	0.69 (0.46)	–	–	0: nonwhite 1: white
Black	0.12 (0.32)	–	–	0: nonblack 1: black
Latino	0.14 (0.34)	–	–	0: non-Latino 1: Latino
Other	0.05 (0.21)	–	–	0: W+B+L 1: other
N	3,000	3,278	3,514	–

due to the fact that once jobs had been assigned, Chinese workers were not allowed to change their jobs or work units until the early 1990s. To maintain temporal order in the status attainment models, age at the starting point of current/last position is used in the analyses as explained.

MALE

Males composed 46 to 52 percent of the samples in the three societies. As hypothesized, this variable is employed to identify if there were different patterns of gender inequality in the job search process, accessed and activated social capital, and status attainment outcome across the target societies.

RACE

White, black, Latino, and other races are used in the models of the US data set. Whites constituted 69 percent of the sample while blacks and Latinos were 12 and 14 percent respectively. In the multivariate models the reference category is whites.

Structural layers of social relations

The social network is composed of a variety of social relations that can be differentiated in terms of strength of ties, duration of dyadic relationships, role relational categories, or demographic homogeneity/heterogeneity. I employ the conceptualization of concentric structural organization in the social network, distinguishing its three layers of social relations from inside to outside (Lin, Ye, and Ensel 1999; Son, Lin, and George 2008).

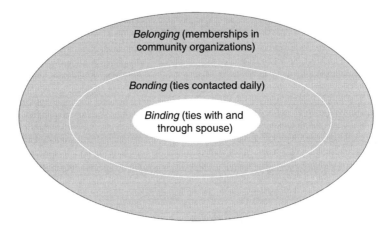

Figure 5.1 Structural layers of social networks

Specifically, the inner layer nearest to an ego is called *binding* (ties with and through spouse), while the middle layer is composed of *bonding* social ties that are contacted by an ego on a daily basis. Lastly, the outer layer in the social network is *belonging* (community participation), measured by the number of memberships in community organizations.

It should be noted that the *binding* and *belonging* variables were measured both when respondents were interviewed and when they started their current/ last position prompted by retrospective questions, while the *bonding* variable was measured only at the time of interview. Thus the multivariate analyses employ the retrospective measures of *binding* and *belonging* to set up a temporal order between explanatory and outcome variables, although I had to compromise by using the *bonding* measure at the time of interview.

I conjecture that these measures of social network structural layers are strongly associated with the accessed social capital indices because the former functions as the sources of the latter in the sense that accessed social capital captures part of the variance in the structural layers of social network.

BINDING (TIES WITH AND THROUGH SPOUSE)

This measure is composed of six categories ranging from 0 (not married), 1 (know almost none of spouse/partner's friends), to 5 (know almost all friends of spouse/partner). The measure is an indicator of wider family relations in the sense that marital union in East Asian societies is interpreted as being an expansion of family boundaries. Specifically, the measure takes persons with no marital relation as its base category in order to (1) include both married and unmarried respondents, and (2) set up differential degrees of familiarity to spousal ties. Put another way, the categories of 1 to 5 show the variations in network overlaps between respondents and their spouses/ partners while the category of 0 indicates that this network overlap is not possible due to the lack of a marital tie in the first place. Notice that according to Table 5.22 the spousal network was smaller at the time of current/last positions than at the time of interview in all three societies, implying the increased degree of assimilation in spousal ties across time. There was no systematic difference among the three countries according to the means and standard deviations in the spouse network item.

BONDING (DAILY CONTACT)

This measure is created by the question, "On average, about how many people do you make contact with in a typical day?" It had six response categories ranging from smallest to greatest possible number of contacts. According to the means of the variable, people contacted 12 to 14 persons on average in a typical day in the three societies. T-test results (not tabled) further indicate that the number of people contacted daily by Chinese respondents was significantly less than those by American and Taiwanese peoples.

Table 5.22 Descriptive statistics of explanatory variables: structural layers

Structural layers of social network	US (mean (SD))	Taiwan (mean (SD))	China (mean (SD))	Range/categories of variable
Binding 1: Spouse network at the time of interview	2.52 (2.14)	2.35 (1.87)	2.70 (1.59)	0: Not married 1: Almost none 2: A few 3: About half 4: Most 5: Almost all
Binding 2: Spouse network when starting current/last position	2.04 (2.15)	1.93 (1.93)	1.53 (1.79)	0: Not married 1: Almost none 2: A few 3: About half 4: Most 5: Almost all
Bonding: Daily contact (number of people contacted daily)	3.42 (1.50)	3.40 (1.37)	3.17 (1.18)	1: 0–4 2: 5–9 3: 10–19 4: 20–49 5: 50–99 6: More than 100
Belonging 1: Memberships in community organizations at the time of interview	2.01 (1.87)	0.63 (0.84)	0.16 (0.55)	US: 0–10 Taiwan: 0–5 China: 0–11
Belonging 2: Memberships in community organizations when starting current/last position	1.29 (1.53)	0.37 (0.66)	0.06 (0.33)	US: 0–10 Taiwan: 0–5 China: 0–11
N	3,000	3,278	3,514	–

BELONGING (MEMBERSHIP IN COMMUNITY ORGANIZATIONS)

This measure results from a series of questions that asked if respondents participated in specific types of community organizations (see Appendix C). Even though there were some disparities in the types and number of organizations in the three societies, differences in the mean numbers of memberships among them look significant. Nonetheless, in order to check if such seeming differences in the mean numbers of memberships were due to the nonidentical sets of community organizations listed in the surveys, I reduced the number of organizations to only three identical ones (i.e., religious, leisure or sports, and other) among the three societies at both the time of interview and the starting point of the current/last position. The unequal distribution in the means stayed similar to the original one: the United States had means of .77 at the time of interview and .54 when starting the current/last position; Taiwan .30 and .15 respectively; and China .03 and .01 respectively.

What can we deduce from these mean differences? First, the mean number of memberships was greatest in the United States, while that of China was smallest, with the Taiwanese mean in the middle. This pattern holds regardless of the two time points available in the data (i.e., belonging 1 and 2). Second, more specifically, Americans had significantly greater numbers of memberships in community organizations than the two East Asian countries according to t-test results at the .000 level (not tabled). Notice that the mean numbers of memberships were less than 1 in both Taiwan and China. Third, it should not be overlooked that there was also a statistically significant gap between Taiwan and China in terms of number of memberships in community organizations in terms of the t-test.

The results thus demonstrate that the institutional and cultural differences between American and East Asian societies were clearly reflected in the outer layer of the social network. That is, the effect of the participatory civic culture in the United States seems to create a significantly greater mean number of memberships in community organizations than those of the two East Asian societies, which supports the view that the United States is "a nation of voluntary associations that engage citizens in problem-solving and governance" (Boris 1999: 2). Further, the socialist deterrence against freedom of association may have resulted in the smallest mean of number of memberships in community organizations, even significantly less than that of Taiwan, although the latter also experienced long-term authoritarian rule until the late 1980s. Thus the peoples in the two East Asian countries were contextually constrained to form less of a belonging structural layer in their social networks due to the lack of democratic and civic tradition. A structural explanation of the deficiency in the belonging structural layer can be found in the literature on volunteering:

> Many years of experience of totalitarian regimes undermines generalized trust, which in turn discourages volunteering. Not knowing whom to trust, people retreat into the private sphere, into the realm of their family [similar to the *binding* layer] and closest friends [similar to the *bonding* layer] or into innocuous groups promoting government-tolerated cultural and recreational activities. The effect of these experiences lingers long after the totalitarian regime has collapsed.
>
> (Musick and Wilson 2008: 345–6)

Socioeconomic status

The covariates of origin and previous socioeconomic status are included in the analyses in order to first, control their effects in the job search models, and second, identify the institutional constraints reflected in different degrees of the effects of socioeconomic status in the three societies.

Regarding origin status, I select three terms: father's education, mother's education, and occupational class of father's job when a respondent was 16 years old. As shown in Table 5.23, the average parental educational level of US respondents was higher than that of their Taiwanese and Chinese counterparts. The occupational status of father's job in China was the lowest compared with the other two countries.

With regard to the socioeconomic status of respondents, I also chose educational and occupational achievements. Both categorical and continuous versions of education measurements confirmed that US respondents were

Table 5.23 Descriptive statistics of explanatory variables: socioeconomic status

	US (mean (SD))	Taiwan (mean (SD))	China (mean (SD))	Range/categories of variable
Origin status				
Father's education	4.95 (1.90)	3.34 (1.50)	3.71 (1.51)	1–8
Mother's education	4.97 (1.61)	2.55 (1.40)	2.88 (1.53)	1–8
Occupational class of father's job	1.76 (1.02)	1.91 (0.76)	1.49 (0.95)	1: low 2: middle 3: professional 4: executive
Socioeconomic status				
Education (Categorical)	6.05 (1.28)	5.11 (1.52)	5.29 (1.22)	1–8
Years of education	14.84 (3.24)	12.25 (3.71)	12.05 (3.08)	US: 0–35 Taiwan: 0–34 China: 0–25
Occupational class of first job	0.83 (1.11)	0.83 (1.08)	0.17 (0.58)	0: no first job 1: low 2: middle 3: professional 4: executive
Occupational class of previous job	1.53 (1.29)	1.42 (1.03)	0.58 (0.97)	0: no prev. job 1: low 2: middle 3: professional 4: executive
Quota sampling	0.44 (0.50)	–	–	0: nonquota 1: quota
N	3,000	3,278	3,514	–

more highly educated than their Taiwanese and Chinese counterparts. Note that education, with eight response categories, was employed in the multivariate analyses. Occupational class of first and previous jobs consistently showed that Chinese respondents had the lowest means. I note that both variables included the "0" category for those who had not had first or previous jobs. I found that 89 percent and 63 percent of Chinese respondents did not have first and previous jobs respectively, whereas about 50 percent and 30 percent of American and Taiwanese respondents had first and previous jobs, respectively, before their current/last job. This shows that most Chinese respondents tend to stay at the same job without progressing through multiple careers.

Lastly, it should be noted that the US survey employed a quota sampling to overcome underrepresentation of racial minorities in the sample. As shown at the bottom of Table 5.23, 44 percent of the sample was drawn by the quota sampling, for which a dichotomous variable of "quota" was included in the multivariate analyses to control for effects derived from the quota sampling.

Conclusion

Having explicated the surveys, methods, and variables of interest and their descriptive features, the next two chapters deal with the composition and activation of social capital and their impact on status attainment among the three societies. Specifically, Chapter 6 examines the composition of accessed social capital in the three societies. In particular, I determine how the structural layers of the social network are associated with accessed social capital, controlling for other covariates. A latent mean comparison technique in structural equation modeling is used to identify if there are significant differences in accessed social capital among the three societies.

Chapter 7 then analyzes how accessed social capital is associated with activated social capital, and how accessed and activated social capital affects status attainment outcomes in the labor markets employing regression models and SEM multigroup path analysis.

6 Accessed social capital among the three societies

This chapter presents the results of multivariate analyses on the composition of accessed social capital in China, Taiwan, and the United States. Since comparison of the accessed social capital indices at the descriptive level was addressed in the previous chapter, the main concern here is to identify how the accessed social capital indices are associated with structural layers of the social network, controlling for other covariates. Using the accessed social capital factor introduced in the previous chapter, it then shows how the latent variable of accessed social capital is related to structural layers of the social network across the three societies. Lastly, a latent mean comparison using the structural equation modeling tests if the amounts of accessed social capital significantly differ by the countries.

Figure 6.1 depicts this chapter's conceptual model. Its main interest is if and how strongly structural layers of social relations are associated with accessed social capital. This model is expanded in the next chapter in which the remaining steps of the mediatory path from social capital to status attainment are tested.

Indices of accessed social capital and structural layers

It is worth knowing how the structural layers of social networks are related to each of the three indices of accessed social capital. Such analyses offer specific information regarding if and how the structural layers generate the richness and diversity of accessed social capital. In this section I thus take the indices

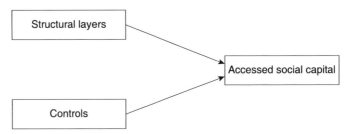

Figure 6.1 Structural layers of social relations and accessed social capital

of accessed social capital – extensity, upper reachability, and range of prestige – as the outcome variables predicted by the binding, bonding, and belonging measures of structural layers, the explanatory variables of interest.

Extensity and structural layers

The extensity index captures diversity in the social network because it shows the number of positions accessible through a person's network. In other words, the greater the extensity, the more diversity resides in a person's network. Given that it is a count variable, it is not proper to employ the OLS (Ordinary Least Squares) model. To get a clear idea of selecting a desirable multivariate regression model, I checked the distributional shapes of extensity when starting current/last position across the three target societies.

As shown in Figure 6.2, the extensity skewed to the left in all three societies. This denotes that it is difficult to know most or all of the occupational holders among the 21 position generator items. Note that all the means fell between 6 and 8 (refer to Table 5.2). I thus checked if the Poisson model distribution is suitable for the count variable, but its model fit was not good because of overdispersion in the distribution. A negative binomial model is more suitable than the Poisson model when a high probability of low counts exists so that variance of a dependent variable is significantly larger than its mean (Long and Freese 2006). The estimation of a negative binomial model is as follows:

$$\text{In } \lambda_i = (\beta_0 + \beta_1 x_i + \ldots + \beta_n x_{in}) + \varepsilon_i, \text{ where } \exp(\varepsilon) \sim \Gamma$$

λ is the rate at which a rare event occurs and the first part of the equation $\beta_0 + \beta_1 x_i + \ldots + \beta_n x_{in}$ represents the log rate of the rare event. The term ε_i is used for unobserved heterogeneity, which follows a gamma distribution. The two assumptions regarding its expected mean and variance are:

$$E(u_i \mid x_i) = \lambda_i$$
$$V(u_i \mid x_i) = \lambda_i(1 + \lambda_i \alpha)$$

In particular, α is the dispersion parameter and when $\alpha = 0$ a negative binomial model becomes Poisson. However, if α is significantly greater than 0, the negative binomial model captures the observed proportion of zero and low counts significantly better than Poisson.

I present the results of the negative binomial model on extensity with robust estimates of the standard errors by the three societies in Table 6.1. Controlling for demographic and socioeconomic covariates, bonding and belonging structural layers were significant sources of extensity in all three societies. In particular, belonging had the strongest impact on extensity among the three structural layers in all three societies in terms of odds ratios. This is quite understandable because the outer layer of relational structure provides more chances to be linked to many positions in the occupational structure.

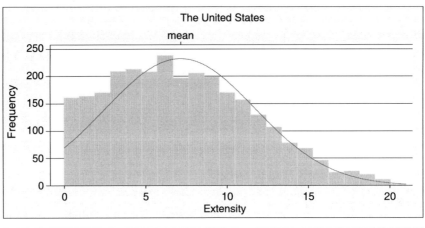

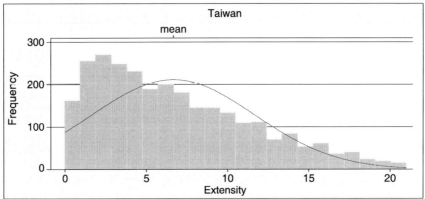

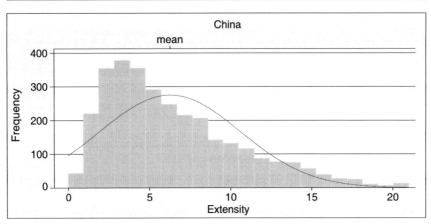

Figure 6.2 Distribution of extensity in the three societies

Table 6.1 Negative binomial regression of extensity

	US	Taiwan	China
Structural layers			
Binding	0.010	0.029***	0.007
Bonding	0.023**	0.102***	0.059***
Belonging	0.091***	0.139***	0.097**
Controls			
Age	0.014	0.037***	0.035***
Age^2	–0.000	–0.0003**	–0.0005**
Male	–0.016	–0.020	0.107***
Black	0.151***	–	–
Latino	–0.058	–	–
Other	–0.094	–	–
Education	0.052***	0.133***	0.079***
Previous job	0.034**	0.089***	0.052***
First job	0.030**	0.043***	0.050**
Father's job	–0.022	0.002	0.012
Father's education	0.015	0.015	0.002
Mother's education	0.022*	0.023	0.032**
Quota	–0.005	–	–
Log likelihood	–7,981.36	–8,375.78	–8,014.61
Wald chi-squared	539.03	915.06	337.77
α (dispersion parameter)	0.26***	0.31***	0.25***
N	2,823	3,013	2,970

* $p < 0.05$; ** $p < 0.01$; *** $p < 0.001$ (two-tailed test).

Nonetheless, it is notable that belonging mattered significantly in China and Taiwan where, as we have already seen, the mean number of memberships in community organizations was less than one (see Table 5.22). Note that binding was significantly associated with extensity only in Taiwan. This indicates that spousal (or family) ties were an important structural layer in one of the two East Asian societies that inherited the Confucian social order.

It is interesting to see that age had no effect on extensity in the United States – note that this inefficacy of age also applies to the other two indices of accessed social capital reported below – while it significantly impacted extensity in the two East Asian societies. The higher the age of a Taiwanese or Chinese person the more extensity the person obtains, even though according to the age-squared term the effect of age is drastically reduced in the later stages of life, perhaps after retirement. Being male was not significant in the United States and Taiwan; however, it was significant in China for having a more extensive network. In terms of relevant measures of socioeconomic background, education and prior occupational status (i.e., previous and first jobs) were significantly related to extensity in the three societies. Mother's education had a significant effect on extensity in the United States and China but not in Taiwan.

Race-related covariates were included only for the American sample, with whites as the reference category. African-Americans had significantly more extensity than whites. Extensity of Latinos and other racial groups did not show a significant gap compared to that of whites. This advantage of African-Americans in terms of extensity is not surprising considering that the bivariate analysis in the previous chapter (see Table 5.9) already showed that African-Americans had more social ties than whites, even though the gap was not statistically significant. To control the effect of quota sampling in the US survey the relevant variable was included, but it was not significant. The dispersion parameter of α was significant in all three countries, which indicates that the selection of negative binomial regression over the Poisson model was proper in capturing zero or low counts of extensity.

Upper reachability and structural layers

The upper reachability index gauges how rich a social network is because it hits the highest possible prestige score within a respondent's network alters measured by the position generators. Mainly due to the fact that the prestige scores were bounded by the lowest and highest prestige scores of the 21 position-generator items, the distribution should be censored at both ends. Specifically, the lowest score should not go below the prestige score of 22 (hotel bellboy) while the highest score cannot exceed the prestige score of 78 (professor) (refer to Table 5.1). Considering that the index was based on the position of the highest prestige score in a respondent's social network, its overall distribution is skewed to the right, as shown in Figure 6.3.

I selected the Tobit regression model to fit the data because the outcome measure has nonnormal distribution with censoring at both ends. The mathematical formula for this specific type of Tobit model is stated below.

$$y_i = y_i^* \text{ if } y_{Low}^* < y_i^* < y_{Upper}^*$$
$$y_i = 0 \text{ if } y_i^* \leq y_{Low} \text{ or } y_i^* \geq y_{Upper}$$
$$y_i^* = \beta x_i + u_i, u_i \sim N(0, \sigma^2)$$

In other words, it treats the observable variable of y_i as a latent variable when the latent variable y_i^* is between the lower and upper limits of the prestige scores. This model also assumes that the latent variable has a linear relationship with the vector of explanatory variables with normally distributed error terms (Takeshi 1973).

As shown in Table 6.2, the belonging layer was consistently significant in positive association with upper reachability in the three societies. Bonding was significant in Taiwan and China but not in the United States. However, binding had no significance in any of the three societies.

Age and age-squared terms were significant only in China; this indicates that Chinese people tend to obtain network alters of higher socioeconomic status as they age, but this benefit of seniority declines after a certain age.

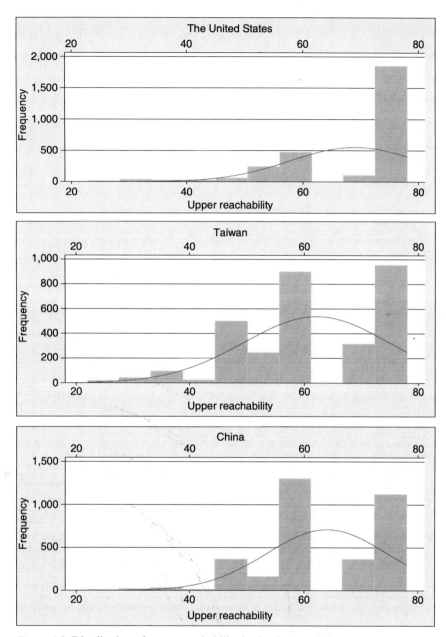

Figure 6.3 Distribution of upper reachability in the three societies

Table 6.2 Tobit regression of upper reachability

	US	Taiwan	China
Structural layers			
Binding	–0.03	0.16	–0.15
Bonding	0.18	1.03***	0.76***
Belonging	2.38***	2.18***	2.75***
Controls			
Age	0.08	0.30	0.55**
Age^2	0.00	–0.00	–0.01**
Male	0.77	–0.52	1.95***
Black	1.65	–	–
Latino	3.46**	–	–
Other	–0.58	–	–
Education	3.81***	5.14***	2.88***
Previous job	–0.06	0.68*	1.28***
First job	0.99**	0.81*	1.03*
Father's job	1.00**	0.32	0.03
Father's education	0.19	0.35	0.25
Mother's education	0.36	0.68**	0.66***
Quota	0.86	–	–
Log likelihood	–7,352.13	–9,187.58	–9,723.39
/sigma	14.80***	13.11***	11.58***
N	2,672	2,865	2,932

* $p < 0.05$; ** $p < 0.01$; *** $p < 0.001$ (two-tailed test).

Being male was also significantly related to upper reachability only in
China. Thus it follows that elderly Chinese males are more likely to access
social ties of higher socioeconomic status, indicating the efficacy of the
Confucian social order that favors seniority and male dominance. Education
and first job allowed the respondents to achieve significantly better upper
reachability in all three societies; note that in terms of standardized β
coefficients (not tabled) education was the strongest predictor of upper
reachability among the covariates in the United States and Taiwan, while it
was the second-strongest predictor in China after age. This shows that human
capital measured by education is strongly related to the richness of accessed
social capital. Previous job mattered in China and Taiwan but not in the
United States. Father's job increased upper reachability only in the United
States. Mother's education was significantly related to upper reachability in
Taiwan and China.

    Among the US-specific measures of race, Latinos had better connections to
highly positioned network alters than did whites. However, we have already
seen that Latinos were the most deprived social group with the smallest
mean score of upper reachability among all racial groups (see Tables 5.10 and
5.11). Thus the regression results may be indicative of the fact that the seeming

deficit of Latinos in upper reachability was due to a large extent to their disadvantages in socioeconomic status and origin status that were controlled in the model. The quota variable was not significant, which shows that there was no impact of the quota sampling in the US survey.

Range of prestige and structural layers

The range of prestige scores index aims to capture the degree of variety in a person's network by subtracting the lowest prestige score from the highest score attached to the positions known to the person in the position-generator items. For instance, if a respondent answered that she knew only one jobholder in the position-generator items, her range of prestige scores would be 0 regardless of which position she knew. In contrast, if another respondent knew, among other network alters, a policeman (prestige score: 40), a position with the lowest prestige score in his network, and a lawyer (prestige score: 73), a position with the highest score, his range of prestige scores would be 33 (refer to Table 5.1), showing the extent to which his network has the potential to be diverse.

Thus the range of prestige index also involves censoring at the lowest and highest ends of the prestige scores embedded in the 21 positions. Let us look at the actual distributions of the variable across the three societies. Figure 6.4 identifies that two walls were formed at the lowest and highest ends of the range of prestige scores. This means that a significant proportion of respondents answered that they knew only one jobholder (range: 0) or they knew both the highest- and lowest-prestige jobs (range: 56) (i.e., professor (78) and hotel bellboy (22)).

There was no distinctive common type of distribution among the target societies. However, it is notable that the range of prestige scores increased in an almost linear pattern in the US sample except for the relatively high distribution at the lowest bound, which means that American people tend to have more diverse jobholders in their social networks than the two East Asian peoples. This advantage of range of prestige scores for Americans was also reflected in the highest mean and lowest standard deviation of the measure among the three countries (refer to Table 5.4).

To account for the censoring effects at the lowest and highest ends of the distribution, I chose to employ the Tobit regression. The specific mathematical formulae were presented above in the subsection on upper reachability.

Table 6.3 shows that the binding layer was not effective in enlarging the range of prestige in any of the three societies. In retrospect the only case where binding became significant was when it predicted extensity in Taiwan (see Table 6.1); however, bonding and belonging were significant in doing so. In terms of standardized β coefficients (not tabled), the effect of belonging was about three times greater than that of bonding in the United States, while in the East Asian countries bonding's effect was a little greater than belonging, even though the unstandardized coefficients in the table

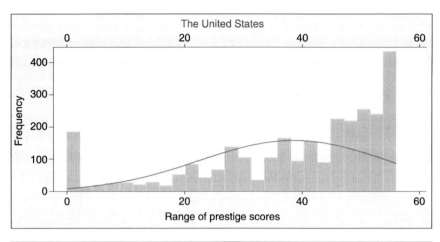

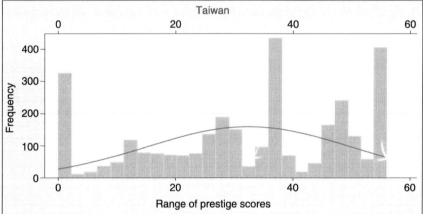

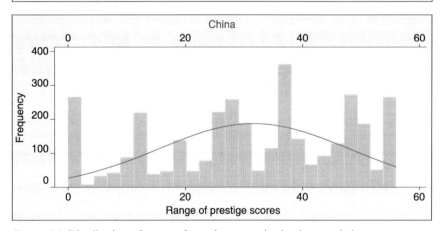

Figure 6.4 Distribution of range of prestige scores in the three societies

Table 6.3 Tobit regression of range of prestige scores

	US	Taiwan	China
Structural layers			
Binding	0.23	0.35	−0.10
Bonding	0.58**	1.91***	1.22***
Belonging	2.06***	3.13***	3.28**
Controls			
Age	0.17	0.54*	1.05***
Age²	−0.00	−0.00	−0.01***
Male	−1.72**	−0.23	2.94***
Black	3.49**	–	–
Latino	−0.59	–	–
Other	−3.95*	–	–
Education	2.06***	4.31***	1.87***
Previous job	0.19	1.78***	1.13**
First job	0.82**	1.07**	1.69**
Father's job	−0.00	−0.46	0.09
Father's education	0.12	0.52	−0.29
Mother's education	0.18	0.55	1.19***
Quota	0.79	–	–
Log likelihood	−10,529.26	−10,699.35	−11,285.46
/sigma	16.07***	7.53***	17.47***
N	2,672	2,865	2,932

$p < 0.05$; ** $p < 0.01$; *** $p < 0.001$ (two-tailed test).

seem to imply that belonging had a stronger impact. This indicates that the main structural source for increasing diversity in accessed social capital in the United States is community participation.

Age or age-squared terms were significant in China and Taiwan; however, age was not related to range of prestige in the United States. I thus conclude that age had no association with accessed social capital in the United States, since it was inefficacious in predicting the three indices of accessed social capital. Further, being male was highly significant in China for achieving a wider range of prestige scores in social ties, while being male was negatively related to range of prestige scores in the United States. Thus age and gender measures demonstrate that the cultural divide between the United States and the two East Asian countries is associated with diversity in accessed social capital.

Higher education and better occupational status in first and previous jobs significantly widened the range of prestige in China and Taiwan; but previous job did not matter in the United States. Among the measures of status origin, only mother's education mattered for having a wider range of prestige in China. The US-specific terms of race showed that African-Americans had a significantly wider range of prestige than whites, while other nonwhites had a significantly narrower range of prestige than whites. Again, the quota term was not significant.

Accessed social capital and structural layers

As explained in the previous chapter, the accessed social capital factor captures most of the variations in the three indices of accessed social capital (see Table 5.12). It thus provides an economic way of presentation regarding the relationship between accessed social capital and structural layers by consolidating the three indices of accessed social capital into a factor variable. The accessed social capital factor was already standardized in the process of exploratory factor analysis and has close to a normal distribution. I thus employed robust OLS regression model for the outcome measure as reported in Table 6.4.

The belonging and bonding layers had a significant impact on accessed social capital, while the binding layer was significant only in Taiwan; this reflects the fact that binding increased extensity in Taiwan. According to the standardized coefficients, it is clear that in the United States belonging (community participation) is indeed the primary source of accessed social

Table 6.4 Robust standardized OLS regression of accessed social capital

	US	Taiwan	China
Structural layers			
Binding	0.02	0.05**	−0.00
Bonding	0.04*	0.13***	0.09***
Belonging	0.23***	0.12***	0.06***
Controls			
Age	0.15	0.32**	0.48***
Age^2	−0.05	−0.19	−0.41***
Male	−0.02	−0.01	0.09***
Black	0.06**	–	–
Latino	0.01	–	–
Other	−0.03	–	–
Education	0.17***	0.36***	0.18***
Previous job	0.02	0.08***	0.08***
First job	0.06**	0.07***	0.06**
Father's job	0.01	−0.01	0.01
Father's education	0.03	0.03	0.00
Mother's education	0.02	0.05*	0.09***
Quota	0.02	–	–
Intercept	−1.80***	−2.75***	−2.27***
R-squared	0.17	0.29	0.12
N	2,672	2,865	2,932

* $p < 0.05$; ** $p < 0.01$; *** $p < 0.001$ (two-tailed test).

capital, whereas in the two East Asian societies bonding (daily social ties) seems to be a stronger source of accessed social capital than the other two structural layers of social relations. In terms of overall effect of structural layers, I conclude that they were the sources of accessed social capital even when other covariates were controlled. Further, the two outer layers worked better in producing accessed social capital in the occupational hierarchy than the inner layer (binding). Note in particular that in the United States belonging was the strongest predictor of accessed social capital; its effect was greater than education, a representative indicator of human capital.

Age or age-squared terms showed the significant impact of seniority on accessed social capital in China and Taiwan. Specifically, age had an inverse U-shaped influence in China, as indicated by the significant age and age-squared terms, while age was also significantly related to accessed social capital in Taiwan, although its effect seemed to be weaker than that in China; note that the effect of age was the strongest in predicting accessed social capital in China according to the standardized coefficients. In contrast, it was confirmed that age was not related to the accessed social capital of Americans since age and age-squared terms were never significant in the United States in previous regression models where three independent indices of accessed social capital were employed as the outcome measures. Being male was significant in obtaining more accessed social capital only in China. Thus the multivariate analysis confirmed that Chinese females suffer from gender inequality in accessed social capital.

Socioeconomic status measured by education and first and previous jobs generally had a strong impact on accessed social capital across the three societies. Among the three terms, education had the greatest magnitude in the three societies; education was the strongest predictor of accessed social capital in Taiwan. However, status of origin had a weak influence on accessed social capital. Only mother's education was significantly associated with accessed social capital in Taiwan and China. I suspect that this is due to the fact that mothers are strongly involved in building good networks for their children in East Asian societies, while fathers are usually less involved in their children's social upbringing and educational process.

In terms of US-specific measures of race, African-Americans had significantly more accessed social capital than whites; we observed above that African-Americans had more extensity and wider range of prestige scores than whites. Thus the next chapter tests whether African-Americans can realize this advantage of accessed social capital in terms of utilizing contacts of high status and obtaining better jobs and income.

Latent mean comparison of accessed social capital

The multivariate analyses of accessed social capital using the indices of structural layers of social relations showed that outer layers are better sources of accessed social capital. Further, demographic variables such as age and gender reflected differential formations of accessed social capital among the three societies presumably affected by cultural institutions. However, these multivariate regression models lacked the capacity to directly compare amounts of accessed social capital across the societies. It may thus be helpful to identify whether there is crossnational inequality of accessed social capital in China, Taiwan, and the United States by using latent mean comparison of the structural equation modeling.

As shown in Figure 6.5, in the context of confirmatory factor analysis, the latent variable of accessed social capital is composed of three observed indicators: extensity, upper reachability, and range of prestige. For a systematic comparison of the latent means of accessed social capital across the three societies, the three data sets were pooled together to be subject to empirical tests of latent mean differences.

The confirmatory factor analysis generated similar standardized factor loadings on the three indicators of accessed social capital across the three societies, as shown in Table 6.5. The factor loadings indicated that the three indicators worked as good observed sources of the latent measure of accessed social capital. Note that the factor loading of range of prestige was set at 1.00 as a reference indicator in all three groups of comparison.

At the next step, the means of latent accessed social capital were calculated based on the factor loadings of the three indicators. Again, the latent mean of the first group (the United States) was artificially set at 0.00 to serve as a reference point for the other two groups. The latent mean of accessed social capital in the United States was highest, followed by Taiwan and China. However, it is not certain if the seeming differences in the values of the latent means of accessed social capital are statistically significant. Thus I proceeded to the test of latent mean invariance to identify the latent group mean differences.

Specifically, the original confirmatory factor analysis model worked as a baseline to be compared to the subsequent models on which constraints of invariance on the latent means of accessed social capital were applied. The first

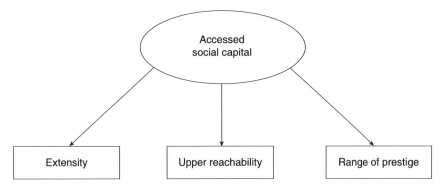

Figure 6.5 Confirmatory factor analysis of accessed social capital

Table 6.5 Latent mean comparison of accessed social capital

	US	Taiwan	China
Standardized factor loading			
Extensity	0.75	0.78	0.79
Upper reachability	0.80	0.87	0.80
Range of prestige	1.00	1.00	1.00
Latent mean of accessed social capital	0.00	–0.40	–0.47
Test of latent mean invariance			
US=Taiwan=China			
χ^2 (df=2)		393.16	
p-value		0.000***	
US=Taiwan			
χ^2 (df=1)		245.09	
p-value		0.000***	
US=China			
χ^2 (df=1)		347.73	
p-value		0.000***	
Taiwan=China			
χ^2 (df=1)		3.44	
p-value		0.064	
Model fit index			
CFI		0.98	
TLI		0.97	
SRMR		0.04	
N	2,830	3,084	3,390

* $p < 0.05$; ** $p < 0.01$; *** $p < 0.001$ (two-tailed test).

model in the test of latent mean invariance forced the latent means of accessed social capital to be the same across the three societies. The chi-squared value (i.e., 393.16) with the two degrees of freedom generated by the invariance assumption was great enough to get a highly significant *p*-value, which indicated that the subsequent model is worse than the baseline model. In other words, the assumption of total invariance in the latent means of accessed social capital across the three societies was rejected. Namely, there should be some significant differences among the three latent means of accessed social capital produced in three countries. The analytic task is thus to identify where the significant gap in accessed social capital can be attributed to.

The next model thus assumed that the United States and Taiwan have the same latent mean of accessed social capital, which was also rejected, as the chi-squared test result indicates. It was then clear that the United States has a significantly higher latent mean of accessed social capital than Taiwan. The third model proposed that the latent means of accessed social capital are not differentiated between the United States and China. However, the chi-squared test again confirmed that the latent mean of accessed social capital in the United States is far greater than that in China. In turn, the last model assumed that the latent mean of accessed social capital in Taiwan is equal to that in China. This latent mean invariance assumption produced a considerably lower chi-squared value than those from the previous steps; and the test result demonstrated that there is no significant gap in accessed social capital between Taiwan and China.

Therefore it was confirmed that the United States has significantly greater accessed social capital compared to the two East Asian societies. However, the volumes of accessed social capital in Taiwan and China are not differentiated from each other. This result may indicate that the differential between the American and East Asian cultures matters more in determining the volume of accessed social capital than the political economic differential between capitalist and socialist states.

Conclusion

This chapter showed that the outer structural layers of social relations (i.e., belonging and bonding) are better sources of accessed social capital across the three target societies. In particular, belonging is most significantly associated with accessed social capital in the United States, verifying the effect of voluntarism in widening social relations in the labor market that in turn can be related to socioeconomic returns (Musick and Wilson 2008; Ruiter and De Graaf 2009). However, the social relational layer of bonding (i.e., size of daily social ties) is more important than belonging in China and Taiwan. This may be due to the relative weakness of the volunteering culture in the two East Asian countries.

Regarding the binding layer, it is significant in increasing accessed social capital only in Taiwan. This indicates that spousal ties, presumably an indicator of family ties, are a significant source of accessed social capital in Taiwan. Considering that in Taiwan the binding layer was significant particularly in increasing extensity of the social network (Table 6.1), it appears that relations based on family ties are efficacious in expanding social networks in the occupational domain, thus implying the persistent legacy of the Confucian value of family orientation. To be fair, though, note that its effect on accessed social capital is less than half of the effect of the bonding and belonging layers in Taiwan (Table 6.4)

The presence of age stratification in accessed social capital was identified in China and Taiwan because seniority generates an advantage in obtaining more accessed social capital in the two East Asian societies. Further, the multivariate analysis presents the fact that Chinese males had more accessed social capital than their counterparts, other things being equal. This is remarkable because American and Taiwanese males had no such advantage over females. Given the strong combination of age stratification and male dominance in accessed social capital, the Confucian social order seems to be embedded in the fabric of Chinese social networks. Specifically, strong cultural principles favoring elderly males preconfigure the patterns of social relations causing disadvantage to young females in China. Compared to China under the double constraints of age and gender, the composition of Taiwanese accessed social capital is affected by age stratification but not by male dominance. American accessed social capital is found to be free from both; note that American males have a narrower range of prestige scores than American females (Table 6.3), even though this female advantage is not reflected in the overall factor measure of accessed social capital (Table 6.4).

In regard to the particular effect of race on US social networks, interestingly African-Americans retain more accessed social capital than whites (Table 6.4). Detailed analyses on each indicator of accessed social capital demonstrate that African-Americans have more extensity and a wider range of prestige scores than whites (Tables 6.1 and 6.3). In addition, Latinos' social networks are found to be richer in upper reachability than whites' networks (Table 6.2). It is now the task of the next chapter to test if and to what extent these minority advantages in accessed social capital affect status attainment and income in the labor market.

The multivariate analysis also verified that the volumes of accessed social capital are significantly dependent on socioeconomic status, such as education and prior job statuses, in all three societies. This means that human capital is significantly related to how resourceful and diverse the social capital that one can access is, notwithstanding crossnational differences. Further, the first or previous job status is related to more accessed social capital, indicating the advantage of better occupational origin in yielding returns to social resources.

In accordance with the standardized β coefficients in Table 6.4, we can identify what kind of factors most affected the volumes of accessed social capital by each country. In the United States the belonging layer of social relations (i.e., community participation) and education are most significantly related to accessed social capital, signaling the efficacy of a participatory civic culture and human capital in forming better social capital. However, education and age matter most significantly in Taiwan, showing the power of human capital and age stratification. In China age, education, and being male are the factors affecting how much accessed social capital one obtains; therefore the effect of the Confucian social order indicated by age and gender is prevalent, while education also significantly impacts accessed social capital. Three findings are remarkable. First, without exception, human capital is strongly associated with the volume of accessed social capital in all three target societies – note that not only education but prior occupational status (that could be an indicator of job experience, widely known as another plausible measure of human capital) was also significant in predicting accessed social capital in the three countries (Mosey and Wright 2007). This shows the existence of a solid linkage between human and social capital regardless of the institutional differences in political economy and culture. Second, the presence and absence of Confucian culture and its degree of strength are reflected in the measures of age and gender that were among the most significant predictors of accessed social capital in China (age and gender) and Taiwan (age). Lastly, the SEM (structural equation modeling) latent mean comparison of accessed social capital among the three countries using the parameter invariance test verified that Americans have more accessed social capital than Taiwan and China. However, the seeming gap in accessed social capital between Taiwan and China was not proved to be statistically significant. Therefore, Americans are richest in accessed social capital followed by the Taiwanese and Chinese.

What we have observed in this chapter is the first part of a causal mechanism explaining the relationship between social capital and status attainment, specifically composed of accessed social capital, activated social capital, and labor market outcomes. In particular, I aimed to test the sources of accessed social capital in the three countries using the concepts of the binding, bonding, and belonging structural layers of social relations, and also checked how demographic and socioeconomic features are related to accessed social capital in each society. The next empirical chapter analyzes (1) if and how accessed social capital is related to activated social capital, and in turn (2) whether accessed and activated social capital are related to labor market outcomes in the three countries.

7 Social capital and status attainment

Having identified the structural sources of accessed social capital in the three societies in Chapter 6, I turn to the next stage of multivariate analyses in which (1) the relation between accessed and activated social capital is checked, and (2) the impact of activated and accessed social capital on status attainment is tested, as depicted in Figure 7.1.

At the first step, the measures of activated social capital are regressed on accessed social capital and other controls. The measures of status attainment (i.e., occupational class and annual income) then become the final outcome variables of multivariate regressions in which activated and accessed social capital works as the explanatory variables along with other controls. It is thus a partial mediation model in which accessed social capital transfers its partial effect to status attainment via activated social capital and also directly affects status attainment. Note again that in this chapter all the explanatory variables except bonding (a structural layer of daily social ties) and education were measured when the respondents started their current/last job in order to keep temporal order against outcome variables. In the latter part of this chapter the entire conceptual model in the figure is subjected to a SEM (structural equation modeling) multigroup comparison analysis of the three societies employing only the compatible set of variables. Based on the SEM results, a set of tests of parameter invariance is then

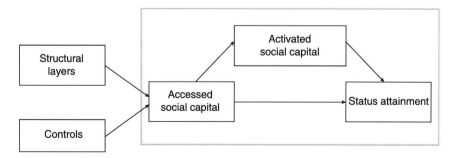

Figure 7.1 Accessed and activated social capital and status attainment

conducted to identify significant crossnational differences reflected in the structural coefficients.

Accessed and activated social capital

There are four measures of activated social capital that capture some critical features of contacts and their capacity utilized in the job search process; presence of contact, length of contact chain, contact status, and routine job information (see Chapter 5 for a description of these measures). I note that among the four measures, contact status performs the role of the main indicator of activated social capital in multivariate analyses on status attainment reported in the next section because it captures the resource dimension of activated social capital. In this section I test if accessed social capital is related to each of the four measures of activated social capital in the first place.

Accessed social capital and presence of contact

When considering the relation between accessed social capital and its practical activation, it is plausible for the amount of accessed social capital to be positively associated with the presence of contact – that is, the more social resources one accesses the more likely one will utilize the resources for instrumental action. Further, the analysis checks whether any disparities exist in the association among the three societies.

As shown in Table 7.1, accessed social capital was significantly associated with presence of contact in Taiwan and China, but not in the United States. The three structural layers of social relations were generally in weak association with presence of contact; however, the belonging layer in China had a positive and significant relationship with presence of contact, even though its bonding layer was negatively related to presence of contact. Socioeconomic status (education, previous and first jobs) was not strongly associated with presence of contact, although education was negatively associated with presence of contact in Taiwan and China, while previous job had a positive and significant impact in the United States and China. Origin status (father's job and parents' education) did not exert a significant effect on presence of contact in general, except for the positive association between father's education and presence of contact in China. One finding specific to the United States regarding race variables is that Latinos were more likely to involve contacts in job search process than whites. This may imply that a significant portion of Latino migrant workers found their jobs informally through their compatriots (Aguilera and Massey 2003).

Thus we learned that the volume of accessed social capital does not directly facilitate the use of contacts in the United States whereas it does in the two East Asian societies. Also, the analysis informs that the effect of general socioeconomic status is not consistently related to presence of contact in the three countries, although father's education was related to presence of

Table 7.1 Logit regression of presence of contact

	US	Taiwan	China
Accessed social capital	–0.00	0.11*	0.16***
Structural layers			
Binding	–0.02	0.02	–0.01
Bonding	0.02	–0.03	–0.08*
Belonging	0.05	–0.00	0.23*
Controls			
Age	0.03	0.00	0.02
Age^2	–0.00	–0.00	–0.00
Male	–0.03	–0.02	–0.11
Black	–0.08	–	–
Latino	0.54***	–	–
Other	0.08	–	–
Education	0.04	–0.09*	–0.06
Previous job	0.08*	0.06	0.14**
First job	–0.00	0.06	–0.07
Father's job	0.04	0.09	–0.01
Father's education	0.02	0.01	0.12***
Mother's education	–0.01	0.02	0.00
Quota	0.05	–	–
Intercept	–0.86	0.16	–0.76
Wald chi-squared	37.70**	26.30*	70.33***
N	2,669	2,861	2,932

* $p < 0.05$; ** $p < 0.01$; *** $p < 0.001$ (two-tailed test).

contact in China. In terms of demographic measures, gender does not affect the chance of having a contact in the job search process in any of the three countries.

Accessed social capital and chain length

The next measure of activated social capital is the chain length of contacts relied on in respondents' search for current/last job. Given that the measure is a count variable from 0 to 4, I first tried a Poisson regression model that resulted in a bad model fit; I thus employed a negative binomial regression (for a specific discussion of the mathematical formula of the model, see p. 87).

Remarkably, accessed social capital was not related to chain length in the United States while it was significantly associated with the length of the job search chain in the two East Asian societies, as shown in Table 7.2; note that its effect was highly significant in China. I inferred that rich and diverse accessed social capital induces the Chinese and Taiwanese to involve more contacts in their job search processes. In contrast, in the United States accessed social capital does not lengthen the job search chain of contacts. Considering the two multivariate analyses so far, it follows that accessed social capital is

Table 7.2 Negative binomial regression of chain length

	US	Taiwan	China
Accessed social capital	–0.01	0.06*	0.11***
Structural layers			
Binding	–0.00	0.00	–0.02
Bonding	0.01	–0.02	–0.04
Belonging	0.04**	–0.01	0.12
Controls			
Age	0.02	0.00	0.03
Age^2	–0.00	–0.00	–0.00
Male	–0.01	0.01	–0.10
Black	–0.02	–	–
Latino	0.27***	–	–
Other	0.09	–	–
Education	0.02	–0.03	–0.02
Previous job	0.05**	0.05*	0.11***
First job	–0.01	0.02	–0.04
Father's job	0.01	0.05	0.02
Father's education	0.01	0.01	0.08**
Mother's education	–0.01	0.02	–0.00
Quota	0.24***	–	–
Log-likelihood	–3,588.62	–3,857.99	–3,756.41
Chi-squared	102.10***	30.60**	83.65***
N	2,672	2,865	2,932

* $p < 0.05$; ** $p < 0.01$; *** $p < 0.001$ (two-tailed test).

related to neither presence of contact nor the length of contact chain in the United States, whereas it is associated with both presence of contact and chain length in China and Taiwan. In sum, accessed social capital is more strongly related to quantity dimensions (i.e., presence of contact and chain length of contacts) of activated social capital in China and Taiwan than in the United States.

Structural layers were not strongly associated with the length of the job search chain in Taiwan and China; however, the belonging layer was related to chain length in the United States. This may indicate that the belonging layer (community participation) in the United States offers additional chances for job seekers to activate contacts outside their normal and intimate boundaries of life. The demographic variables of age and gender report a weak relationship with chain length in the three countries. Among the socioeconomic variables, only previous job status was significantly associated with chain length in the three societies; it appears that people mobilized more contacts for their current/last jobs when they had higher occupational status in their previous jobs. It is notable that in China, father's education increased the length of job search chains as it was a significant predictor of presence of contact. Thus it appears that family background indicated by father's education provides contacts for Chinese job seekers.

The US-specific measures of race and quota showed an interesting pattern. Latinos had significantly longer job search chains than whites. The quota variable was significant, confirming that Latinos had disproportionately longer chains than other race-ethnic groups; recall that quota sampling was employed to increase Latinos in the sample. Thus it appears that Latinos are more likely to (1) use contacts than whites, given the results reported in the previous section, and (2) mobilize multiple helpers in locating their current job. It is plausible that Latinos depend on their connections in the job search process to make up for their lack in human capital and socioeconomic status in the host society.

Accessed social capital and contact status

As noted, contact status is the main indicator of activated social capital since it is closely related to the quality of contacts. For a simpler presentation of the results, I first combine the upper two categories ("executive" and "professional") in the original measure (refer to Table 5.17) to create "high" occupational class – note that I use the original measure of occupational class when it is employed as one of the predictors of labor market outcomes in the later stage. I then report the contrast between high vs. low occupational classes of contacts from a multinomial logit regression.

$$\ln\left\{\frac{\Pr(High|X_i)}{\Pr(Low|X_i)}\right\} = B_{i,High|Low}X_i$$

The formula indicates that the model is based on the log odds of belonging to a high-class occupation compared to that of belonging to a low-class occupation, other things being equal. I report logit coefficients of the explanatory variables in Table 7.3.

Accessed social capital was positively and significantly associated with contact status in the United States and Taiwan, but not in China (however, note that the results are different in the SEM multigroup analysis later; see Table 7.11 on p. 124). This is an interesting finding considering that in China we have observed that accessed social capital is significantly related to presence of contact and chain length of contacts, so-called quantity dimensions of activated social capital. However, it loses its explanatory power for contact status. In contrast, accessed social capital is not related to presence of contact and chain length in the United States; however, it is significantly associated with contact status, the quality dimension of activated social capital. In Taiwan accessed social capital is consistently related to the three indicators of activated social capital analyzed so far.

Structural layers lost their power in explaining the variation of contact status in the United States and Taiwan; however, the bonding layer was negatively related to contact status in China. Thus it seems that adding more daily contacts in China lowers the chance of obtaining help from high-class

Table 7.3 Multinomial logit regression of contact status

High vs. low class	US	Taiwan	China
Accessed social capital	0.21*	0.25*	0.03
Structural layers			
Binding	–0.03	0.02	0.02
Bonding	–0.01	0.00	–0.19**
Belonging	–0.01	0.01	0.40
Controls			
Age	0.05	0.09	–0.03
Age^2	–0.00	–0.00	0.00
Male	–0.32	–0.12	–0.03
Black	–0.17	–	–
Latino	–0.51*	–	–
Other	–0.31	–	–
Education	0.54***	0.47***	0.47***
Previous job	0.41***	0.18	0.06
First job	–0.06	0.06	–0.06
Father's job	0.22*	0.31**	0.54***
Father's education	–0.08	–0.02	–0.00
Mother's education	0.08	0.10	–0.00
Quota	–0.24	–	–
Intercept	–2.98**	–4.53***	–2.47**
Wald chi-squared	360.78***	220.08***	270.98***
N	2,669	2,861	2,932

* $p < 0.05$; ** $p < 0.01$; *** $p < 0.001$ (two-tailed test).

contacts. Thus it seems that the bonding structural layer cannot be the source of high status contact in China (refer to Table 7.11 in which a similar association between bonding and contact status in China is reported at the SEM context).

Demographic variables of age and gender revealed no significant relation to contact status. However, the socioeconomic measure of education and the origin status measure of father's job had significant associations with contact status. In addition, previous job status significantly improved contact status in the United States. Thus socioeconomic status (including origin status) seems more strongly related to contact status than to presence of contact and chain length.

The US-specific measures of race reported another interesting aspect: Latinos were less likely to have good contacts in the high occupational class than whites. Thus I conclude that Latinos rely more on the quantity of contacts (i.e., presence of contact and chain length) than on the quality of contacts, which may explain their lower job status in the US labor market. Also note that African-Americans were no better in getting better contacts than whites, even though they had greater accessed social capital (see Table 6.4).

Accessed social capital and routine job information

As explained earlier, routine job information probes how likely it is for job searchers to receive job-related messages from their contacts in casual ways. It thus has the potential to explain more variation in activated social capital by capturing unreported use of contacts in the job search process. Considering that the variable was dichotomous (0 = no routine job information; 1 = received routine job information), I employ the binomial logit regression model in Table 7.4.

A striking finding is that accessed social capital was positively and significantly associated with routine job information in all three societies – the more accessed social capital one has, the more routine job information that flows in. Among the structural layers, belonging was related to having routine job information in a consistently positive and significant way in all three target societies, which indicates a beneficial return to having more memberships in a variety of organizations. However, binding, the innermost layer, was negatively related to generating routine job information, and its negative association was significant in Taiwan. Bonding was positively and significantly related to routine job information in China.

Regarding the demographic variables, males in the three societies were more likely to report that they received routine job information than females. Age

Table 7.4 Logit regression of routine job information

	US	Taiwan	China
Accessed social capital	0.35***	0.31***	0.34***
Structural layers			
Binding	–0.03	–0.06*	–0.02
Bonding	0.05	0.02	0.15***
Belonging	0.12***	0.14*	0.35**
Controls			
Age	–0.04	–0.02	0.12**
Age^2	0.00	–0.00	–0.002**
Male	0.36***	0.30***	0.21*
Black	0.25	–	–
Latino	0.43**	–	–
Other	0.22	–	–
Education	0.02	0.06	0.01
Previous job	0.14***	0.06	0.12*
First job	0.12**	0.18***	0.26***
Father's job	–0.01	0.03	–0.13*
Father's education	0.03	0.05	0.10*
Mother's education	0.05	0.06	0.03
Quota	–0.10	–	–
Intercept	–0.58	–1.07*	–4.18***
Wald chi-squared	195.33***	209.96***	188.35***
N	2,672	2,864	2,918

* $p < 0.05$; ** $p < 0.01$; *** $p < 0.001$ (two-tailed test).

mattered only in China; seniority was positively associated with acquiring routine job information up to a certain point in life, after which a curvilinear drop of the likelihood began. Thus young females seem to be excluded from routine job information in China.

Among the socioeconomic status measures, first and previous occupational classes also mattered for receiving routine job information, except for the inefficacy of previous job in Taiwan. Nonetheless, education did not affect the presence of routine job information in the three countries. This seems to indicate that routine job information is closely related to the labor market experience of job seekers. In China, father's education mattered positively for receiving routine job information, while the effect of father's job status was negative. I suspect that if a Chinese father holds a good job status he may directly link an important contact to his adult children rather than passing on varied job information to them. The US-specific measures of race show that Latinos had a greater chance of receiving routine job information than whites. This hints at Latinos' dependence on informal channels for locating jobs; in sum, Latinos are more likely to activate contacts, further rely on a lengthier contact chain, and get more routine job information from network alters, but are less likely to utilize high-class contacts than whites.

Social capital and status attainment

I now turn to the last step of the multivariate regression analyses in which two final outcome variables of status attainment (i.e., occupational class and annual income of respondents) are regressed on accessed and activated social capital and other control measures. In this section the four measures of activated social capital and the single factor variable of accessed social capital are therefore the explanatory variables of main interest. Contact status goes to the forefront in the list of explanatory variables in the tables because, as explained, it is the most important indicator of activated social capital.

As stated earlier (see Chapter 2), I deleted cases from the sample where respondents' previous jobs and any of their contacts' jobs in the job search chain fell in the same occupational codes in order to control for occupational homogeneity (Mouw 2003, 2006). Another plausible option was also available – employing an interaction term to control for homophily between job searchers' previous jobs and the jobs of their contacts. Nonetheless, I chose to delete the so-called "homogeneous" cases to react to the causality argument more strictly, even though this resulted in losing some portion of the observations. I report the percentages of reduction in the sample compared to the number of respondents who reported that they used contacts.

As reported in Table 7.5, 4 to 11 percent of contact users were dropped from the samples. The percentage of reduction due to the same occupational codes for previous jobs of respondents and contacts' jobs is greatest in Taiwan among the three samples. There may be reasons for these crossnational

Table 7.5 Percentage of reduction in the three samples

	US	Taiwan	China
Contact use reported by respondents	1,607	1,439	1,381
Deleted due to occupational homogeneity	72	162	82
Percentage of reduction in the sample	4.5%	11.3%	5.9%

differences in occupational homogeneity, but it is not the main concern of this study. At any rate, this reduction in the sample sizes is reflected in the following multivariate regression analyses and SEM models.

In addition to the occupational homogeneity, another issue should be checked that is specifically related to the Chinese sample. As pointed out several times in this book (in particular, Chapter 3), the command economy in China employed a mandatory job assignment system from the mid-1950s to the early 1990s. It is therefore critical to check if the general pattern of association of accessed and activated social capital and status attainment outcomes stays similar between the two sets of results from the two subsamples, the first of which is composed of those respondents who got their jobs in the compulsory job assignment era, and the second of which after the era. This sensitivity check is performed at the end of the multivariate regression analyses.

Social capital and occupational class

As was done for contact status, the multinomial logit model was chosen for the occupational class of respondents. For simplicity of presentation, I combined the upper two occupational categories – executive and professional – and contrasted it against low-class jobs.

First, it is noticeable in Table 7.6 that contact status was consistently significant in leading job seekers to better occupational class, regardless of which of the three countries they lived in. Note that contact status remained efficacious after the occupationally homogeneous cases were excluded from the samples and a set of covariates, including indicators of human capital, demographic features, and socioeconomic status, was controlled, although the effect of contact status had been even stronger before the sample reduction. The other measures of activated social capital were not as consistently associated with occupational class of respondents as contact status. Presence of contact was not significant in the United States and Taiwan; it was significantly negative in China. I suspect that this insignificance of presence of contact is mainly due to the fact that the quality of contacts (contact status) was controlled. Chain length was significantly negative in the United States and Taiwan, but not in China. This finding indicates that using a longer chain of contacts was associated with worse occupational class in the United States and Taiwan. Routine job information did not have a significant association with occupational class in any of the three societies.

Table 7.6 Multinomial logit regression of occupational class

High vs. low class	US	Taiwan	China
Activated social capital			
Contact status	0.57***	0.91***	0.36***
Presence of contact	0.34	–0.27	–0.63*
Chain length	–0.75**	–1.00***	–0.15
Routine job information	–0.00	–0.30	–0.00
Accessed social capital	–0.03	0.27**	0.06
Structural layers			
Binding	0.02	0.12**	0.06
Bonding	0.03	0.01	–0.10*
Belonging	0.08	0.19	–0.27
Controls			
Age	0.02	0.04	–0.07
Age^2	–0.00	–0.00	0.001*
Male	–0.87***	0.50**	–0.23*
Black	–0.46*	–	–
Latino	–0.36	–	–
Other	–0.14	–	–
Education	0.91***	1.45***	0.85***
Previous job	0.45***	0.24*	0.27***
First job	0.11	0.70***	0.11
Father's job	0.17**	0.31**	0.13*
Father's education	–0.05	0.16*	–0.04
Mother's education	–0.04	–0.23**	–0.05
Quota	–0.05	–	–
Intercept	–5.23***	–10.69***	–4.63***
Wald chi-squared	621.13***	812.73***	552.82***
N	2,599	2,706	2,802

* $p < 0.05$; ** $p < 0.01$; *** $p < 0.001$ (two-tailed test).

The effect of accessed social capital on occupational class remained significant only in Taiwan. It is likely that the accessed social capital effect in the other two societies was fully mediated by activated social capital measures (particularly contact status). Nonetheless, this result should not be taken as conclusive because we have yet to check the other outcome measure.

The measures of structural layers were also generally in a weak relationship with occupational class because their effects are assumed to have been absorbed in accessed social capital, in accordance with the partial mediation model of this study. Specifically, in the United States none of the structural layers was significant. However, binding was significantly and positively related to producing more high-class jobs in Taiwan. This denotes that spousal (or family) ties matter significantly for Taiwanese job seekers for acquiring better jobs. It thus seems that the binding layer carries particular weight in Taiwan not only in accessing social capital (Table 6.4) but in obtaining status attainment outcome. As reviewed in Chapter 3, this unique effect of the binding layer seems to be related to the local milieu in which small- and medium-sized *family* enterprises (SMEs) make up the major portion of the Taiwanese economy and its labor market. In China the bonding layer was negatively related to occupational class. Thus multivariate analyses on the Chinese sample inform that the bonding layer of daily ties decreases both contact status (Table 7.3) and occupational class of job seekers. However, we should hold off on any conclusions until we see how bonding is related to income in the next step.

In terms of demographic measures, age was not significant in obtaining better occupations except for the significant curvilinear effect in China signaling the advantage of older workers. Gender showed mixed patterns of association with occupational class by country. In particular, males had lower occupational class than females in the United States and China. These results may not properly reflect the gender inequality in the two societies. It seems likely that the measure of occupational class with a limited number of categories cannot be sensitive enough to catch the inequality. A supplementary analysis (not tabled) employing socioeconomic (SEI) scores of current/last job of respondents in the US data showed that there was no significant association between gender and SEI scores, but the Chinese data set did not provide such a variable. Thus it is reasonable to identify the relationship between gender and income in the next step. Still, it is noticeable that significant gender inequality was found in Taiwan in regard to occupational class.

Variables of socioeconomic status generally reported strong association with occupational class. Education, an indicator of human capital, was consistently related to occupational class in all three societies. Previous job was also consistently associated with occupational class. First job mattered only in Taiwan. Father's job was also consistently related to occupational class of respondents in the three societies, showing a higher chance of intergenerational transmission of socioeconomic status. Educational level of parents did not matter in the United States or China; however, father's education was in a positive relation with occupational class of respondents in Taiwan, while mother's education was negatively associated with occupational class.

Among the US-specific measures, minority groups reported disadvantages in getting high occupational class jobs compared to whites; in particular, the disadvantage of African-Americans was statistically significant. Thus African-Americans' advantage in accessed social capital (Table 6.4) is not related to occupational class, one of the final outcome measures.

Social capital and annual income

The annual income variable had 20 to 27 response categories in the three data sets (refer to Table 5.20). The distribution was slightly skewed to the right in the United States, whereas it was skewed to the left in the two East Asian societies. Logging the variable was thus not a good solution to bring it closer to normal distribution because it would make the US distribution highly skewed. I therefore compared the two sets of results using unlogged vs. logged income variables. There was no noticeable deviation between the two sets of results. I decided to use the unlogged income variable in the OLS (Ordinary Least Squares) regression, employing Huber-White robust standard errors.

As shown in Table 7.7, contact status was significantly associated with annual income of respondents in the United States and Taiwan, but not in China; this result stayed the same when I used the logged income variable. It is thus clear that contact status did not produce significantly better income for Chinese job searchers. The other two measures, presence of contact and chain length, were not significant in the United States and China; note that presence of contact was significant and negative in Taiwan when controlling contact status. Routine job information was significantly associated with more income only in the United States.

Accessed social capital was consistently significant in association with earning more income across the three societies. This is remarkable because accessed social capital did not lose its significance even after a set of measures of activated social capital, more proximate explanatory variables to annual

Table 7.7 Robust OLS regression of annual income

	US	Taiwan	China
Activated social capital			
Contact status	0.33*	0.22**	−0.11
Presence of contact	−0.77	−0.50*	−0.06
Chain length	−0.14	−0.03	0.06
Routine job information	0.54**	−0.13	0.29
Accessed social capital	0.41***	0.25***	0.31***
Structural layers			
Binding	−0.04	0.12***	0.01
Bonding	0.15*	0.21***	0.52***
Belonging	0.09	0.32**	0.10
Controls			
Age	0.20**	0.17***	0.19**
Age^2	−0.003**	−0.002***	−0.003**
Male	2.25***	1.34***	1.58***
Black	−0.56*	−	−
Latino	−0.25	−	−
Other	−0.30	−	−
Education	1.00***	0.55***	0.75***
Previous job	0.19*	0.09	0.10
First job	−0.02	0.12*	0.32
Father's job	0.10	−0.01	−0.10
Father's education	0.02	0.02	0.20**
Mother's education	−0.04	−0.06	0.01
Quota	0.28	−	−
Intercept	4.84***	−1.77**	−3.38***
R-squared	0.23	0.33	0.18
N	2,004	2,682	2,818

* $p < 0.05$; ** $p < 0.01$; *** $p < 0.001$ (two-tailed test).

income, was taken into account. Also note that China had a significant and positive impact of accessed social capital, even though none of the activated social capital indicators was significantly related to annual income.

In regard to the structural layers of social relations, all three layers were significant and positive in Taiwan for acquiring more income. In particular, the binding layer kept its significance only in Taiwan as it did above for occupational class; thus the effect of the binding layer on status attainment seems to be unique to Taiwan. The bonding layer was significant in all three societies. Note that the bonding layer was negatively related to occupational class, but it helped increase income for Chinese workers; therefore the bonding layer is not unilaterally positive or negative in its relation to the two socioeconomic outcomes in China. In terms of demographic variables, age and being male were significant in bringing more income in all three societies. Thus it seems that the advantage of experienced male workers in acquiring more income is confirmed regardless of crossnational differences. It was found above that American and Chinese females belonged to better occupational class than males; however, this female advantage did not translate into more income.

Among the socioeconomic status measures, education was the only variable that maintained its significant effect across the three societies. Also note that it was consistently significant in its effect on occupational class as well. Previous job status was associated with more income in the United States, while first-job status increased income in Taiwan. Father's education was related to more income in China. In terms of US-specific measures of race, minorities earned less income than whites, and the gap between African-Americans and whites was significant. Thus I conclude that the African-American advantage in accessed social capital did not lead them to better contacts, occupational class, and income. We now turn to check whether the job assignment system in China caused any different pattern of association between social capital and status attainment.

China: The job assignment system and social capital

China offers a unique case among the three sampled countries in that it experienced two drastically different labor policies before and after the 1990s: from the mid-1950s to the early 1990s it maintained the state job assignment system, after which a capitalist-style labor market was introduced. It is therefore necessary to test if what we have observed thus far – in particular, the effect of social capital on occupational class and income in China – is an artifact due to the introduction of the labor market beginning in the 1990s. In other words, if individual agency was under the control of institutional constraints set up by the state policy of unidirectional job assignment from above, the effect of social capital should not exist in the period of mandatory job assignment.

The most accurate way to test the effect of job assignment should be to run the analyses on respondents who got their first jobs in the period of state job assignment. The survey did not ask when a respondent began his/her first or previous job, but it did query when a respondent started his/her current/ last job. Thus I kept only those respondents who got their current/last job beginning in 1955 (a minor portion of the sample began working when they were teenagers) to 1990 in the first subsample. Likewise, I left only those who got their current/last jobs from the year of 1991 in the second sub-sample. Note that this is a conservative criterion in dividing the sub-samples, because if respondents began their *current/last* jobs before 1991 they definitely started their *first* jobs roughly before the introduction of labor mar-ketization. I selected 1990 as the endpoint of the period given that there was no official closing of the job assignment system; it is widely accepted that it gradually came to an end in the late 1980s or the early 1990s. I compared regression outcomes of occupational class and annual income between the two subsamples.

The most important variables to compare between the subsamples in Table 7.8 are activated and accessed social capital. According to the regression results of occupational class, contact status, a representative indicator of activated social capital, was significant in both samples. In addition, it is remarkable that accessed social capital was significantly related to high occupational class in the subsample of the job assignment era but not in the other sample. It is thus confirmed that both accessed and activated social capital helped job seekers get better jobs in the mandatory job assignment period. In terms of annual income, contact status was significantly related to it in neither subsample. However, accessed social capital was significantly related to earning more income in both subsamples, although its effect seems weaker in the latter subsample. I therefore conclude that the effect of social capital on status attainment in China is not an artifact partially applicable to those workers who entered the labor market after the job assignment era. Rather, social capital had been efficacious in leading job seekers to better jobs even in the job assignment era and continued to be so after the labor marketization. Jobs were indeed assigned in the former era; but it was an open secret that those who were well connected were assigned better positions, as is confirmed by the statistical analysis. This is not to deny that the socialist institution constrained Chinese workers in utilizing personal contacts for jobs, but apparently not all of them were limited.

In terms of structural layers, belonging was related to low occupational class in the job assignment era. Note that group membership was centrally managed by the socialist government back then, so that people were assigned to social groups involuntarily. Thus being exposed to this compulsory membership is more likely to have affected people of lower socioeconomic status. Bonding did not have significant effect on occupational class; however, it increased income in both subsamples. In regard to demographic covariates, age was associated with high occupational class and more income in the job assignment era, whereas age carried significant effect on neither outcome measure in the labor marketization period. Being male was related to low occupational class under the job

Table 7.8 China: Sensitivity analysis on subsamples before and after compulsory job assignment

	Occupational class		Annual income	
	Subsample 1 (1955–1990)	Subsample 2 (1991–2005)	Subsample 1 (1955–1990)	Subsample 2 (1991–2005)
Activated social capital				
Contact status	0.37**	0.37***	–0.13	–0.03
Presence of contact	–0.19	–0.64	–0.02	–0.15
Chain length	–0.27	–0.14	0.02	0.11
Routine job information	0.45	–0.13	0.25	0.34
Accessed social capital	0.19*	–0.05	0.34**	0.27*
Structural layers				
Binding	0.12	–0.01	0.01	0.01
Bonding	–0.02	–0.11	0.38***	0.67***
Belonging	–1.07*	–0.10	0.02	0.78
Controls				
Age	–0.14	–0.06	0.27**	0.05
Age^2	0.003*	0.00	–0.004***	–0.00
Male	–0.48**	–0.11	1.76***	1.36***
Black	–	–	–	–
Latino	–	–	–	–
Other	–	–	–	–
Education	0.97***	0.81***	0.64***	0.89***
Previous job	0.24	0.39***	0.15	0.02
First job	0.06	0.16	0.22	0.78*
Father's job	0.01	0.18**	–0.16	0.00
Father's education	–0.02	–0.06	0.20*	0.21*
Mother's education	0.03	–0.03	0.01	0.09
Intercept	–4.58***	–4.57***	–3.33*	–3.06*
Wald chi-squared	265.78***	333.51***	–	–
R-squared	–	–	0.14	0.26
N	1,068	1,692	1,704	1,072

Notes: Those who belong to the subsample 1 obtained their current/last jobs from the year of 1955 to 1990 while those who belong to the subsample 2, from the year of 1991 to 2005. Multinomial logit model was applied to occupational class; robust OLS model was applied to annual income. $p < 0.05$; ** $p < 0.01$; *** $p < 0.001$ (two-tailed test).

assignment system, but not significantly related to occupational class in the labor marketization era. It was significantly and positively related to income in both subsamples. Among measures of socioeconomic features, education had the most consistent effect on the two outcomes in both subsamples. This indicates that the effect of human capital was important even in the job assignment era that included the Cultural Revolution by which the socialist government tried to nullify the effect of education.

Resuming the crossnational analysis (using the whole sample of the Chinese data), it is necessary to combine the two outcome measures – occupation class and annual income – at the next stage of SEM models for a simplified and consolidated presentation. I also constructed an identical model across the target societies, omitting the US-specific measures because it allows systematic comparison of the status attainment process across the three societies, which is the main purpose of employing SEM analysis.

SEM multigroup path analysis on status attainment

Having covered the status attainment process with a specific focus on the effects of accessed and activated social capital, I turn to the last step of the multivariate analyses in which by merging the samples a single structural equation model is employed using the common covariates across the three societies. The US-specific measures of race and quota were omitted at this step. The final outcome variables of occupational class and annual income were combined into a latent endogenous variable, "status attainment." Occupationally homogeneous cases remain excluded from the samples. I then ran a universal SEM multigroup path model on the three samples from the target societies. The results are reported first, followed by a series of the tests of parameter invariance that help identify whether the status attainment mechanism varies among the three societies.

Multigroup path analysis

Figure 7.2 summarizes the mediation process from the structural layers of social relations, social capital, and status attainment. Note that in order to construct a simple and universal model contact status is used as a representative indicator of activated social capital, excluding presence of contact, chain length, and routine job information at this particular stage. It is also notable that the path analysis results were fully saturated with the same set of control covariates of demographic and socioeconomic measures imposed every step of the way to the endogenous variable of status attainment; thus the standardized structural coefficients reported in the figure are conservative.

Regarding the relationship between structural layers and accessed social capital, the outermost layer of belonging was the main source of accessed social capital in the United States, while the binding layer was not significant. Taiwan was the only society where all three layers, including the binding layer, mattered significantly in increasing accessed social capital. China showed similarity to Taiwan in that bonding was the most significant layer followed by belonging, but the effect of binding was not significant. However, it is premature to conclude that the effects of the structural layers are significantly different among the three countries; this conclusion must be made after specific tests are conducted.

At the next step, accessed social capital changed its role as an exogenous variable to predict activated social capital and status attainment. The structural

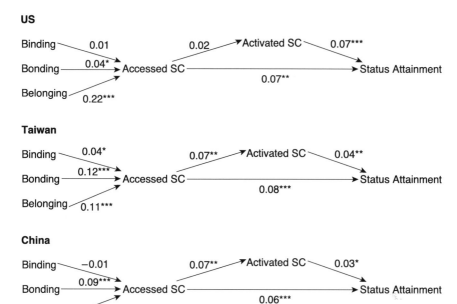

Figure 7.2 SEM multigroup path analysis

Notes: Standardized structural coefficients are reported; model fit indices CFI (Comparative Fit Index) = 1.00, TLI (Tucker-Lewis Index) = 1.00, RMSEA (Root Mean Square Error of Approximation) = 0.00; * $p < 0.05$; ** $p < 0.01$; *** $p < 0.001$ (two-tailed test).

relations between accessed and activated social capital are discussed first. It was shown that accessed social capital had a significant and positive relation to contact status, a representative indicator of activated social capital, in Taiwan and China, but not in the United States. In other words, it appears that the resourcefulness and diversity of one's social relations affects whether one can utilize a contact of higher status for a purposive action of job search in China and Taiwan; however, this link between accessed social capital and contact status was not found in the United States. This result seems to be different from that of the multinomial logit model (Table 7.3) where accessed social capital was significantly related to contact status in the United States and Taiwan; however, the difference may lie in the fact that the present model posits the relationship between accessed social capital and contact status as a part of the mediatory process from structural layers to status attainment outcome employing a common set of covariates among the three countries. To some extent, the reason for the inefficacy of accessed social capital on contact status in the United States may be that American people use varied ways of activating social contacts, such as routine job information in the labor market (McDonald and Elder 2006). It is also likely that American job seekers are able to reach out to unfamiliar contacts regardless of how much accessed social capital they have accumulated, which is not possible in the East Asian context where strong social relations have to be formed before any part of them can be activated. Nonetheless, it is too early to conclude that the relationship between accessed and activated social capital differs between the United States and the two East Asian countries; the test of parameter invariance must first be conducted.

The effect of accessed social capital was significant and positive on status attainment in all three societies. This tells us that even when the effect of activated social capital is controlled, accessed social capital has a direct impact on the status attainment outcome. Another important thing is to see if activated social capital is a significant predictor of status attainment. It was a significant predictor of status attainment in all three target countries; nonetheless, the effect seems stronger in the United States than in China or Taiwan. Thus it is now a concern to see if the seeming gaps in the structural coefficients in the path model across the three countries are statistically significant.

Test of parameter invariance

A question remains from the SEM multigroup analysis: whether exogenous variables (e.g., structural layers) had significantly different relations with endogenous measures (e.g., accessed social capital) across the target societies. I conducted a series of tests of parameter invariance in this section to identify if the apparent differences in structural coefficients across countries are statistically significant. To do so, the test assumes the invariance (or sameness) of structural coefficients across the three countries (Kline 2005; Muthén and Muthén 2010). If the assumption is refuted by the test, the seeming gap is confirmed to be real. Specifically, the test of parameter invariance follows three steps. First, an SEM model works as a baseline with a chi-squared model fit. Second, an assumption of parameter invariance on a specific structural coefficient is imposed across countries on an alternative SEM model. Third, the chi-squared model fit differences between the baseline and alternative models are used for a chi-squared difference test to determine if model fit stays the same or is worsened by the assumption of invariance. If the model fit sees no significant deterioration then the assumption of parameter invariance is confirmed, but if it shows a significant drop in model fit the parameter invariance assumption is denied, meaning that there is significant difference in the parameter among the societies.

To conduct the tests, I broke the SEM multigroup path model into three parts: (1) structural layers on accessed social capital; (2) accessed social capital on activated social capital; and (3) activated social capital on status attainment. Structural coefficients could thus differ from what was reported in Figure 7.2; nonetheless, the general pattern of association stays similar. In addition, I put all four indicators of activated social capital back at this final stage of empirical testing.

Structural layers on accessed social capital

The test of parameter invariance was performed on each exogenous variable in the SEM multigroup analysis. For instance, Table 7.9 shows how the test is conducted to see if the exogenous variable of bonding had the same impact on accessed social capital in the three countries. The second row in the table shows the structural coefficients of the bonding layer on accessed social capital in the three societies. The first test is called total invariance assumption because it assumes that the structural coefficients of bonding are the same across the three societies. The chi-squared value with two degrees of freedom due to the total invariance assumption generated a significant *p*-value, which indicates that the assumption is rejected. In other words, the structural coefficients cannot be the same across the societies.

Next, another assumption of parameter partial invariance between the United States and Taiwan was imposed in the second model. The model fit gap between the baseline and alternative models was statistically significant, which indicates that the effect of the bonding layer cannot be assumed to be the same between the two countries; that is, in Taiwan the bonding layer had a significantly greater effect on accessed social capital than in the United States, as informed by the magnitudes of the structural coefficients (i.e., Taiwan 0.12 vs. US 0.04). In turn, the next test of parameter partial invariance between the United States and China also confirms that the structural coefficients of the bonding layer cannot be assumed to be the same between these

Table 7.9 Test of parameter invariance on accessed social capital (presenting test procedure)

Outcome: Accessed social capital	US	Taiwan	China
Structural layer	0.04*	0.12***	0.09***
Bonding			
Total invariance (US=TW=CH)			
χ^2 (df=2)		13.091	
p-value		0.001**	
Partial invariance (US=TW)			
χ^2 (df=1)		12.571	
p-value		0.000***	
Partial invariance (US=CH)			
χ^2 (df=1)		5.854	
p-value		0.016*	
Partial invariance (TW=CH)			
χ^2 (df=1)		1.390	
p-value		0.238	
Crossnational comparison		Taiwan>US	
		China>US	

Notes: Standardized structural coefficients are reported; the MLMV (maximum likelihood parameter estimates with standard errors and a mean- and variance-adjusted chi-square test statistic) estimator is employed; * $p < 0.05$; ** $p < 0.01$; *** $p < 0.001$ (two-tailed test).

two countries. However, the last test of parameter partial invariance verifies that the assumption was supported between Taiwan and China, indicating that the effect of the bonding layer on accessed social capital did not differ between the two East Asian countries. Considering the three test results, the last row of the table reports that in Taiwan and China the bonding layer had a significantly greater impact on accessed social capital than in the United States.

Table 7.10 presents the full results of the tests of parameter invariance among the three countries having accessed social capital as the endogenous variable. It shows that in terms of the other two structural layers, significant gaps were not found among the three countries. For example, the structural coefficients of belonging seem to have disparities among the countries (e.g., US 0.22 vs. China 0.06); nonetheless, the gaps were not statistically significant. Next, the demographic measures of age and being male showed crossnational differences. It was true in the three countries that the older the worker the

Table 7.10 Test of parameter invariance on accessed social capital (full results)

Outcome: Accessed social capital	US	Taiwan	China	Test of parameter invariance
Structural layers				
Binding	0.01	0.05*	0.02	US=Taiwan=China
Bonding	0.04*	0.12***	0.09***	Taiwan>US China>US
Belonging	0.22***	0.12***	0.06**	US=Taiwan=China
Age	0.09***	0.14***	0.07**	Taiwan>US
Male	−0.03	−0.03	0.08***	China>US China>Taiwan
Education	0.18***	0.38***	0.19***	Taiwan>US Taiwan>China
Previous job	0.02	0.08***	0.09***	Taiwan>US China>US
First job	0.07***	0.07***	0.05*	US=Taiwan=China
Father's job	−0.00	−0.00	0.01	US=Taiwan=China
Father's education	0.03	0.03	−0.01	US=Taiwan=China
Mother's education	0.01	0.06*	0.10***	China>US
R-squared	0.17	0.29	0.12	–
Model fit index				
CFI		1.00		–
TLI		1.00		–
RMSEA		0.00		–
N	2,415	2,579	2,698	–

Notes: Standardized structural coefficients are reported; the MLMV (maximum likelihood parameter estimates with standard errors and a mean- and variance-adjusted chi-square test statistic) estimator is employed. The structural coefficients are different from those reported in the path model (Figure 7.2) because the present model deals with a specific part of the path analysis; age-squared term is omitted because it seriously deteriorates the model fit; * $p < 0.05$; ** $p < 0.01$; *** $p < 0.001$ (two-tailed test).

more accessed social capital he/she obtained. However, the effect of age was much stronger in Taiwan than in the United States, but its effect was not differentiated between the two East Asian countries (note that according to the structural coefficients there seems to be a greater gap between Taiwan and China than that between Taiwan and the United States; but the test confirms that the difference between Taiwan and the United States is significant). Being male was significantly and positively related to accessed social capital only in China, and its effect was significantly stronger than in the United States or Taiwan. Thus the tests detected the particular advantages of the elderly or males in the two East Asian countries.

In terms of socioeconomic measures, Taiwan had a stronger effect of education on accessed social capital than the United States or China, even though education was significantly associated with accessed social capital in all three countries. Previous job brought significantly greater accessed social capital for Chinese and Taiwanese workers than American workers. It thus appears that human capital is more strongly related to accessed social capital in Taiwan and China than in the United States. Interestingly, mother's education produced significantly more accessed social capital in China than in the United States.

Accessed social capital on activated social capital

At this second step of the tests of parameter invariance, the focus shifts to the relations between activated social capital and accessed social capital and other controls. I employed all four indicators of activated social capital as the endogenous variables.

CONTACT STATUS

The first indicator is contact status. Table 7.11 shows only a single difference found by a series of tests, that is, the effect of accessed social capital on contact status is significantly greater in China than in the United States. In other words, Chinese job seekers who had more accessed social capital activated a contact of higher status, while accessed social capital was not related to contact status in the United States. Note that the effect of accessed social capital on contact status was also significant in Taiwan, but not significantly greater than that in the United States. Recall that these results are not in line with those from the multinomial logit regression of contact status (Table 7.3). The difference between regression and SEM outcomes lies in the fact that the regression model ran on each sample independently, while the SEM multigroup model treated each country as a part of greater collectivity. I give priority to the SEM results because systematic comparison among the three societies is the main purpose of this study.

Other covariates did not differ in their effects on contact status among the three countries. For instance, the effect of father's job on contact status was

Table 7.11 Test of parameter invariance on activated social capital (contact status)

Outcome: Activated social capital (contact status)	US	Taiwan	China	Test of parameter invariance
Accessed social capital	0.02	0.07*	0.10***	China>US
Structural layers				
Binding	−0.04	0.01	−0.03	US=Taiwan=China
Bonding	0.02	−0.02	−0.05*	US=Taiwan=China
Belonging	0.07*	−0.01	0.03	US=Taiwan=China
Age	0.25	0.16	0.16	US=Taiwan=China
Age^2	−0.31	−0.21	−0.07	US=Taiwan=China
Male	0.01	0.01	−0.04	US=Taiwan=China
Education	0.03	−0.02	0.01	US=Taiwan=China
Previous job	0.07**	0.00	0.04	US=Taiwan=China
First job	−0.00	0.03	−0.02	US=Taiwan=China
Father's job	0.03	0.07**	0.09***	US=Taiwan=China
Father's education	0.01	0.03	0.08*	US=Taiwan=China
Mother's education	−0.06	0.03	0.02	US=Taiwan=China
R-squared	0.02	0.02	0.05	–
Model fit index				
CFI		1.00		–
TLI		1.00		–
RMSEA		0.00		–
N	2,412	2,576	2,698	–

Notes: Standardized structural coefficients are reported; the WLSMV (weighted least square parameter estimates using a diagonal weight matrix with standard errors and mean- and variance-adjusted chi-square test statistic) estimator is employed. The structural coefficients are different from those reported in the path model (Figure 7.2) because the present model deals with a specific part of the path analysis; * $p < 0.05$; ** $p < 0.01$; *** $p < 0.001$ (two-tailed test).

significant in China; nonetheless, the effect was not significantly greater than in the other two countries according to the tests of parameter invariance.

PRESENCE OF CONTACT

Similar to the previous result on contact status, Table 7.12 shows that accessed social capital is related to presence of contact in China and its effect is significantly greater than that in the United States. It thus demonstrates that in China those with more accessed social capital are more likely to activate contacts and try to reach contacts of higher status. This was also the case in Taiwan; as a result, the two countries were not differentiated by the test. However, the amount of accessed social capital was not related to whether job seekers activated contacts and intended to reach better contacts of higher status in the United States.

Education shows an interesting pattern in that it was positively related to presence of contact, but its effect was not significant in the United States, while it was negatively related to presence of contact in Taiwan and China. The test results indicate that the negative relationship between education and

Table 7.12 Test of parameter invariance on activated social capital (presence of contact)

Outcome: Activated social capital (presence of contact)	US	Taiwan	China	Test of parameter invariance
Accessed social capital	0.01	0.07*	0.10***	China>US
Structural layers				
Binding	–0.04	0.02	–0.02	US=Taiwan=China
Bonding	–0.01	–0.02	–0.06*	US=Taiwan=China
Belonging	0.05	0.00	0.05*	US=Taiwan=China
Age	0.10	0.03	0.18	US=Taiwan=China
Age²	–0.14	–0.12	–0.12	US=Taiwan=China
Male	–0.02	–0.02	–0.03	US=Taiwan=China
Education	0.03	–0.11**	–0.05	US>Taiwan
				US>China
Previous job	0.05	–0.01	0.04	US=Taiwan=China
First job	–0.01	0.03	–0.03	US=Taiwan=China
Father's job	0.02	0.06*	0.01	US=Taiwan=China
Father's education	0.01	0.02	0.12***	China>US
				China>Taiwan
Mother's education	–0.03	0.02	0.01	US=Taiwan=China
R-squared	0.01	0.02	0.04	–
Model fit index				
CFI		1.00		–
TLI		1.00		–
RMSEA		0.00		–
N	2,412	2,576	2,698	–

Notes: Standardized structural coefficients are reported; the WLSMV (weighted least square parameter estimates using a diagonal weight matrix with standard errors and mean- and variance-adjusted chi-square test statistic) estimator is employed; * $p < 0.05$; ** $p < 0.01$; *** $p < 0.001$ (two-tailed test).

presence of contact in Taiwan and China differed significantly from the positive relationship between them in the United States. Specifically, those who were less educated in Taiwan and China were more likely to rely on contacts in their job search. The effect of father's education shows the other side of the story. Chinese job seekers who had fathers with a higher level of education were more likely to have job search contacts than American and Taiwanese job seekers. Thus lack of human capital was compensated by the utilization of contacts in Taiwan and China; moreover, in China it was less-educated job seekers with fathers of higher level of education that activated contacts, probably with help from their fathers.

CHAIN LENGTH

The third measure of activated social capital, chain length, adds consistency to what we have observed so far. Table 7.13 indicates that accessed social

Table 7.13 Test of parameter invariance on activated social capital (chain length)

Outcome: Activated social capital (chain length)	US	Taiwan	China	Test of parameter invariance
Accessed social capital	0.02	0.07*	0.09**	China>US
Structural layers				
Binding	–0.02	0.00	–0.03	US=Taiwan=China
Bonding	0.00	–0.02	–0.07**	US>China
Belonging	0.07**	–0.02	0.03	US=Taiwan=China
Age	0.15	0.05	0.21	US=Taiwan=China
Age²	–0.20	–0.14	–0.15	US=Taiwan=China
Male	0.01	–0.01	–0.04	US=Taiwan=China
Education	0.02	–0.07*	–0.03	US=Taiwan=China
Previous job	0.04	0.02	0.04	US=Taiwan=China
First job	–0.01	0.00	–0.03	US=Taiwan=China
Father's job	0.01	0.05*	0.02	US=Taiwan=China
Father's education	0.01	0.02	0.11***	China>US
Mother's education	–0.05	0.03	0.00	US=Taiwan=China
R-squared	0.01	0.02	0.03	–
Model fit index				
CFI		1.00		–
TLI		1.00		–
RMSEA		0.00		–
N	2,415	2,579	2,698	–

Notes: Standardized structural coefficients are reported; the WLSMV (weighted least square parameter estimates using a diagonal weight matrix with standard errors and mean- and variance-adjusted chi-square test statistic) estimator is employed; * $p < 0.05$; ** $p < 0.01$; *** $p < 0.001$ (two-tailed test).

capital was significantly related to chain length of contacts activated in the job search process in China and Taiwan. It was more so in China; the gap between China and the United States, where accessed social capital was not related to chain length, was statistically significant as reported by the tests of parameter invariance. Thus I conclude that accessed social capital significantly affects contact status, presence of contact, and how many contacts are involved in a job search in China, but it does not matter in the United States; the gaps between the two countries are statistically significant – in other words, the gaps found between the two countries are real.

In regard to structural layers, the effect of bonding was significantly negative on chain length in China. Further, its negative association with chain length was confirmed by the tests of parameter invariance to be statistically significant in comparison to its neutral relation with chain length in the United States. What does this mean? Chinese job seekers who lacked the bonding layer or, in other words, had less daily contact with people were more likely to use a longer chain of contacts. In contrast, when they had a rich bonding layer they were less likely to rely on multiple contacts in a longer chain. Thus a deficient bonding layer compels Chinese job seekers to ask for help from multiple contacts, some of whom may not be familiar to them. It should also be noted that Chinese people had a significantly weaker bonding layer than Americans or the Taiwanese (refer to Table 5.22 and the description of the bonding layer measure on p. 81). Therefore both crossnational and within-country deficiency and unequal distribution of the bonding layer result in a significant disadvantage for Chinese workers, forcing them to look for help from multiple contacts in getting a job.

In addition, father's education is positively and significantly related to chain length in China and its effect is significantly greater than that in the United States (note that father's education is not related to chain length in the United States or Taiwan). The result is consistent with the previous finding on presence of contact; recall that father's education was significantly associated with presence of contact for adult children in China. Moreover, father's education was the strongest predictor of both presence of contact and chain length in China because its standardized coefficient was greater than any other coefficient, including accessed social capital; also note that both father's education and occupational status were significantly related to contact status (Table 7.11). These results signal that Chinese fathers of advantageous socioeconomic status exert effort in mobilizing multiple well-positioned contacts for their adult children's job searches. This indicates the plausible existence of intergenerational transfer of socioeconomic status in a socialist country. This is not surprising, however, since it is well known that not a few leading Communist Party cadres successfully turned their adult children into entrepreneurs in the transition to the market economy. In this particular regard, Lin recently explained vividly how and why the status transfer from party cadre fathers to economic elite children has taken advantage of the economic transition:

> This intertwining between the political and economic spheres also facilitates intergenerational inheritance among the leading cadres at the central and local governments. Instead of escorting their children through government bureaucracies and being accused of nepotism, they can now see their children promoted through corporations . . . Levin Zhu, son of Zhu Rongji . . . heads the China International Capital Corporation. China Development Bank is run by Chen Yuan, son of Chen Yun, one of the eight pioneering communists. Jiang Mianheng, son of former president Jiang Zemin . . . controls Shanghai Alliance Investment Limited, a government-owned investment company freely competing as a private equity firm.
>
> (Lin 2011: 75)

Thus it seems that one pathway of this intergenerational inheritance is the use of contacts, or social capital, for the status attainment of adult children. Even though father's job was consistently related to presence of contact, chain length, and contact status in Taiwan, the tests of parameter invariance did not find its effect to be significantly greater than that in the other two countries.

Before proceeding to the next variable, routine job information, I conclude that the findings thus far show that accessed social capital is most significantly related to the three indicators of activated social capital – presence of contact, chain length, and contact status – in China followed by Taiwan and the United States, and that the gaps between China and the United States are statistically significant.

ROUTINE JOB INFORMATION

The last indicator of activated social capital, routine job information, shows a different pattern of association among the three countries in Table 7.14. Accessed social capital was significantly related to receiving routine job information in all three countries, and no significant crossnational gap was found in the association.

In regard to structural layers, bonding did not matter in obtaining routine job information in the United States and Taiwan, while it was significantly and positively related to receiving routine job information in China. The gap between Taiwan and China was statistically significant, denoting that Chinese workers with a richer bonding layer received more routine job information; this effect was significantly different from that in Taiwan. Thus Chinese workers are more likely to instrumentally utilize their daily contact with social ties in order to get job-related information than Taiwanese workers. The belonging layer shows an interesting hierarchy among the three countries: the United States had the most significant effect of belonging (community participation) on routine job information, followed by China and Taiwan. This partially confirms that volunteerism in the United States is related to status attainment (e.g., Wilson and Musick 2003).

Age is also related to routine job information in China, and its effect was significantly greater than in the United States or Taiwan. In turn, the age-squared term was negatively related to routine job information in China, and the effect was statistically distinct compared to the other two countries. This means that Chinese workers get more routine job information as they age; however, when they get too old they are less likely to acquire the information. Father's job and education showed mixed results in China; father's job was negatively associated with routine job information, while father's education was positively related. Nonetheless, only the negative effect of father's job had a significant crossnational difference from Taiwan. In other words, father's occupational status is less likely to be related to routine job information; rather, as we saw above, it could work more directly in adult children's job searches by providing pertinent contacts.

Activated social capital to status attainment

It is of great interest to check if the effect of activated social capital on status attainment, a factor measure combining occupational class and annual

Table 7.14 Test of parameter invariance on activated social capital (routine job information)

Outcome: Activated social capital (routine job information)	US	Taiwan	China	Test of parameter invariance
Accessed social capital	0.23***	0.19***	0.19***	US=Taiwan=China
Structural layers				
Binding	−0.05	−0.06*	−0.01	US=Taiwan=China
Bonding	0.03	0.00	0.08**	China>Taiwan
Belonging	0.10***	0.05*	0.09**	US>China China>Taiwan
Age	−0.33*	−0.09	0.57**	China>US China>Taiwan
Age²	0.21	0.00	−0.53**	US>China Taiwan>China
Male	0.10***	0.09***	−0.04	US=Taiwan=China
Education	−0.00	0.04	0.00	US=Taiwan=China
Previous job	0.11***	0.03	0.07*	US=Taiwan=China
First job	0.07*	0.11***	0.09**	US=Taiwan=China
Father's job	0.00	0.01	−0.07**	Taiwan>China
Father's education	0.01	0.04	0.10**	US=Taiwan=China
Mother's education	0.02	0.03	0.03	US=Taiwan=China
R-squared	0.13	0.12	0.13	–
Model fit index				
CFI		1.00		–
TLI		1.00		–
RMSEA		0.00		–
N	2,415	2,578	2,684	–

Notes: Standardized structural coefficients are reported; the WLSMV (weighted least square parameter estimates using a diagonal weight matrix with standard errors and mean- and variance-adjusted chi-square test statistic) estimator is employed; * $p < 0.05$; ** $p < 0.01$; *** $p < 0.001$ (two-tailed test).

income, is significantly different across the three societies. Most of all, the top priority is analyzing how contact status, a representative indicator of activated social capital, is related to status attainment. Table 7.15 shows the test results, first presenting the process of the chi-squared difference test.

The second row of Table 7.15 shows the structural coefficients of contact status on status attainment in the three societies. The first test result of total invariance assumption indicates that the effect of contact status cannot be assumed to be the same across the three societies. It follows that the partial invariance assumption between the United States and Taiwan was supported, meaning that the gap between the two countries is not statistically significant. However, the next test of parameter partial invariance between the United States and China confirms that the structural coefficients of contact status cannot be assumed to be the same between these two countries; that is, there was a significantly greater effect of contact status on status attainment in the

Table 7.15 Test of parameter invariance on status attainment (presenting test procedure)

Outcome: Status attainment	US	Taiwan	China
Activated Social Capital	0.22***	0.20***	0.09**
Contact status			
Total invariance (US=TW=CH)			
χ^2 (df=2)		11.067	
p-value		0.004**	
Partial invariance (US=TW)			
χ^2 (df=1)		0.043	
p-value		0.836	
Partial invariance (US=CH)			
χ^2 (df=1)		7.230	
p-value		0.007**	
Partial invariance (TW=CH)			
χ^2 (df=1)		8.470	
p-value		0.004*	
Crossnational comparison		US>China	
		Taiwan>China	

Notes: Standardized structural coefficients are reported; the MLMV (maximum likelihood parameter estimates with standard errors and a mean- and variance-adjusted chi-square test statistic) estimator is employed. The structural coefficients are different from those reported in the path model (Figure 7.2) because the present model deals with a specific part of the path analysis; * $p < 0.05$; ** $p < 0.01$; *** $p < 0.001$ (two-tailed test).

United States than in China. The last test of parameter partial invariance verifies in the same way that this assumption was rejected between Taiwan and China; namely, the effect of contact status on status attainment was significantly greater in Taiwan than in China. Therefore the last row of Table 7.15 reports that the United States and Taiwan had significantly greater impact of contact status on status attainment than China. These test results do not imply that activated social capital measured by contact status was not significant in predicting status attainment in China; indeed, it was. Rather, the thrust of the test results is that the effect size of contact status on status attainment was smaller in China than in the United States or Taiwan. This seems remarkable, since in China accessed social capital was most strongly related to contact status (see Table 7.11), yet its effect of contact status on status attainment was the smallest among the three countries.

Table 7.16 presents the full results of parameter invariance tests on all covariates having status attainment as the final outcome variable. In regard to activated social capital measures, the effects of presence of contact and routine job information were neither significant nor differentiated across the three societies. However, chain length of contacts had a significantly disadvantageous return on status attainment in the United States and Taiwan compared to China, where chain length did not matter. If an American or Taiwanese job seeker had to call on multiple contacts to obtain a job, it may indicate how

Table 7.16 Test of parameter invariance on status attainment (full results)

Outcome: Status attainment	US	Taiwan	China	Test of parameter invariance
Activated social capital				
Contact status	0.22***	0.20***	0.09**	US>China Taiwan>China
Presence of contact	–0.02	–0.07	–0.08	US=Taiwan=China
Chain length	–0.17**	–0.12**	–0.01	China>US China>Taiwan
Routine job information	0.01	–0.02	–0.01	US=Taiwan=China
Accessed social capital	0.07***	0.08***	0.07***	US=Taiwan=China
Structural layers				
Binding	0.03	0.08***	0.02	Taiwan>US Taiwan>China
Bonding	0.03	0.06***	0.07***	US=Taiwan=China
Belonging	0.07**	0.05**	0.01	US=Taiwan=China
Age	0.01	0.10	0.14	US=Taiwan=China
Age^2	–0.08	–0.08	–0.10	US=Taiwan=China
Male	0.07***	0.16***	0.08***	Taiwan>US Taiwan>China
Education	0.47***	0.54***	0.46***	US=Taiwan=China
Previous job	0.18***	0.07***	0.10***	US>Taiwan
First job	0.02	0.12***	0.06**	Taiwan>US China>US
Father's job	0.04	0.05***	0.02	US=Taiwan=China
Father's education	0.04	0.03	0.02	US=Taiwan=China
Mother's education	–0.04	–0.07***	–0.01	US=Taiwan=China
R-squared	0.42	0.50	0.32	–
Model fit index				
CFI		1.00		–
TLI		1.00		–
RMSEA		0.00		–
N	1,810	2,545	2,613	–

Notes: Standardized structural coefficients are reported; the MLMV (maximum likelihood parameter estimates with standard errors and a mean- and variance-adjusted chi-square test statistic) estimator is employed. The structural coefficients are different from those reported in the path model (Figure 7.2) because the present model deals with a specific part of the path analysis; * $p < 0.05$; ** $p < 0.01$; *** $p < 0.001$ (two-tailed test).

poor the job candidate was because a competent candidate may contact an influential helper directly. It may be that chain length was not significant in China because the main purpose of having multiple contacts in a job search chain is to get a helper of higher status, the effect of which was already absorbed in contact status. In conclusion, contact status and chain length indicate significant crossnational differences between the capitalist (the United States and Taiwan) and socialist (China) regimes.

The effect of accessed social capital was significant in predicting status attainment in the three countries but statistically nondifferentiated among them, according to the test results of parameter invariance. Thus I conclude that the Chinese socialist regime could not constrain the effect of accessed social capital even though its tight institutional control was successful in reducing the efficacy of activated social capital on status attainment compared to the other two societies. Further, although accessed social capital was not related to three out of four indicators of activated social capital in the United States including contact status, both accessed social capital and contact status were significant predictors of status attainment. This implies that even though American job seekers can reach helpers of high status regardless of their own stock in accessed social capital, and it is true that high-status helpers are instrumental in bringing better jobs to job searchers, what also matters is that employers evaluate and treat job seekers differently by how much accessed social capital they possess.

Next, the parameter invariance tests on structural layers of social relations also report interesting differences in the binding layer among the societies. It is confirmed that Taiwan is the only country where binding, the innermost layer of social relations with and through spouses, worked significantly for status attainment. The family-oriented feature of Confucian social relations may be the reason for its significance. There was no significant gap found in the other two layers among the three societies – for instance, the belonging layer seemed to be strongest in its efficacy for status attainment in the United States; however, its effect was not differentiated from the other two societies according to the tests of parameter invariance.

In terms of demographic features, age showed no significant structural differences among the three societies. However, being male revealed another noticeable difference: being male was significantly more advantageous in Taiwan than in the United States and China, even though males in all three societies had significantly more return on their status attainment than females. I suspect that the male advantage in status attainment in Taiwan was largely due to the traditional Confucian constraint of gender equality that formed the male-dominant labor market structure. In terms of the lower efficacy of being male in China, another Confucian society, I infer that its socialist system suppressed the Confucian constraint on gender equality. Note that from the beginning the socialist government in China tried to subvert the feudalistic Confucian social order through socialist modernization by which the status and role of females was redefined to mobilize women in production (Croll 1983). Nonetheless, it is noteworthy that being female was still significantly worse than being male for obtaining better returns from the Chinese labor market (Shu and Bian 2003).

Among the socioeconomic covariates, first and previous jobs showed another striking difference between American and East Asian societies. First job status did not matter significantly in getting status attainment in the United States but it was significant in the two East Asian societies; and this difference between the United States and the two East Asian countries was confirmed to be significant. However, previous job status showed the opposite pattern. The impact was the greatest in the United States; its structural coefficient was thus significantly greater than that of Taiwan. I conclude that in order to get better returns from labor markets, people in East Asian societies should obtain a first job with high status. However, for Americans it is more important to grow their careers to reach high-status jobs, regardless of where they began in the occupational hierarchy. The other covariates such as education and origin status found no significant differences among the three societies.

Conclusion

Following the previous chapter in checking the pattern of association among the key variables in the status attainment model, in the first part of this chapter I presented how the indicators of accessed social capital, activated social capital, and status attainment are related. In the latter part of the chapter, using SEM models, I tested (1) if structural layers are related to accessed social capital; (2) whether accessed social capital predicts the four indicators of activated social capital; and (3) if activated and accessed social capital is associated with status attainment. To provide systematic comparison among the three societies, I employed SEM multigroup analysis and tests of parameter invariance based on a common set of covariates.

First, in regard to the relationship between structural layers and accessed social capital, the bonding and belonging layers are the main sources of accessed social capital. Even though there are no significant differences in the binding and belonging layers across societies, it was found that the effect of the bonding layer is significantly greater in China and Taiwan than in the United States. Also, the effects of age and being male in Taiwan and China respectively showed significant differences from the United States, indicating the efficacy of the Confucian cultural tradition favoring elderly males.

Second, I found that in general accessed social capital is more strongly associated with activated social capital in China and Taiwan than in the United States. Specifically, accessed social capital is not associated with contact status, presence of contact, and chain length in the United States, whereas they are strongly related in China; and the gaps between the United States and China are all statistically significant. The association between accessed and activated social capital measures in Taiwan is significant, but its strength lies midway between those of China and the United States. Routine job information is significantly related to accessed social capital, and this association is not differentiated among the three countries.

Third, at the next step of the SEM model where status attainment was employed as its final endogenous measure, the relative weakness of activated social capital (contact status) in China compared to the other two countries was confirmed by the tests of parameter invariance. In particular, the test results of contact status and chain length showed that a significant difference in the activating pattern of social capital exists between capitalist and socialist regimes in the process of status attainment.

The tests of parameter invariance also indicated that the effects of accessed social capital on status attainment are not differentiated across the three societies, which particularly denotes that accessed social capital is resilient to the socialist constraint in China. Therefore institutional constraint in China suppressed the activation process of social capital so that the effect of contact status is weaker than in the United States or Taiwan. In addition, a lengthy job search chain is considered normal in China. These results imply that the impact of the socialist control of the job assignment system continues to affect job search behaviors even after the actual constraint was abolished. In attempting to explain the direct effect of accessed social capital on status attainment it is plausible that employers in the three societies take into account the volume of accessed social capital that job seekers hold in the selection process of job candidates so that candidates with richer accessed social capital are more likely to obtain better jobs.

Further, the test results of the binding layer and gender showed that Taiwan stands out among the three societies in maintaining the efficacy of traditional family ties and male dominance in its process of status attainment in the labor market.

Now I turn to the conclusion of the study in the next chapter, checking if the hypotheses presented in Chapter 4 were supported. I also wrap up some findings that were not specifically hypothesized but have important implications.

8 Social capital and institutional constraints

The main purpose of this monograph was to identify whether crossnational structural differences in social capital, presumably formed by institutional constraints of political economy and culture, have made distinctive patterns of association with labor market outcomes in China, Taiwan, and the United States. To test the idea, I constructed a status attainment model in which the measures of structural layers of social relations and accessed and activated social capital were posited as the main explanatory mechanism of status attainment. I was able to conduct a series of empirical tests because the surveys administered in the three countries provided comparable data sets equipped with the core modules of accessed and activated social capital.

In this concluding chapter I first wrap up the findings from the empirical tests. The best way to do so is to go back to my earlier hypotheses and evaluate whether they were supported or rejected by the findings. All the findings are considered in this process; however, the most important criterion should be the test of parameter invariance, particularly in cases where the focal point of a hypothesis is related to comparison among the three sampled countries. Relying on robust and conservative test results of parameter invariance to tell if hypotheses are supported helps avoid premature conclusions based on ballpark estimates of seeming – and sometimes ostensible – differences in regression coefficients among the countries. After a thorough review of the hypotheses I also introduce some important findings, even though no hypotheses were proposed specifically for them. I then conclude the study by acknowledging several limitations and proposing future research.

Hypotheses revisited

Preparing for empirical tests, in Chapter 5 I introduced the three indices of accessed social capital – extensity, upper reachability, and range of prestige – and compared them across the three countries. I checked if the indicators of accessed social capital were differentially related to gender and race. Turning to the indicators of activated social capital, I checked how presence of contact, chain length, contact status, and routine job information were distributed in the three sampled countries. I then presented descriptive information regarding occupational class and annual income, the two indicators of status attainment. Among the explanatory measures, the three structural layers – binding, bonding, and belonging – were of main interest because I proposed that they are the sources of accessed social capital. Other covariates such as demographic and socioeconomic measures were also introduced.

Chapter 6 presented how the structural layers are related to accessed social capital in the three countries using multivariate regression analyses. The structural equation modeling (SEM) latent mean comparison was also conducted to check if accessed social capital had disparities in its distribution among the three countries. Chapter 7 then presented the remaining parts of regression analyses regarding the status attainment model from accessed and activated social capital to occupational class and annual income. Combining occupational class and income in a latent factor variable of status attainment, I proceeded to SEM multigroup (that is, multination) path analysis to show the general pattern of association among the key measures; in the model contact status was employed as the sole indicator of activated social capital. At the last stage the tests of parameter invariance were conducted on each step of the status attainment model based on SEM multigroup models; all four indicators of activated social capital were put back. In these tests all exogenous (or explanatory) measures were systematically compared among the three countries at each step of the SEM multigroup models, from structural layers to accessed and activated social capital to status attainment. Thus the test results of parameter invariance work as judgment calls for the hypotheses when necessary. I now specifically check if the proposed hypotheses of the study were supported, considering all the empirical results found at the univariate, bivariate, and multivariate levels of analyses.

There were two sets of hypotheses presented in Chapter 4; Hypotheses 1-i series was made up of causal arguments regarding the formation and composition of accessed social capital, while Hypotheses 2-i series was theoretical predictions on the effect of activated social capital on status attainment in the three societies. Each of the hypotheses is presented, with the decision of whether it was supported or rejected by relevant empirical tests.

> *Hypothesis 1-1*:   People in China have less upper reachability in terms of highest prestige score attached to the jobs of network alters than their capitalist counterparts in the United States and Taiwan.
> *Partially supported*

It was shown that Chinese people had lower mean upper reachability than their American counterparts, but they had greater mean upper reachability than the Taiwanese (see Table 5.3). The reason that I predicted that Chinese upper reachability would be less than that of the other two peoples was that China has been under the double constraints of the socialist control and Confucian models, and its economy and labor market have not developed as much as that of the other two countries. However, the hypothesis did not take the recent rapid economic development in China into account and thus missed the growing presence of market-oriented occupations such as CEO in the index of position generators. Nonetheless, it was verified that there were significant gaps between the United States and the two East Asian societies in terms of having higher upper reachability, according to t-tests.

> *Hypothesis 1-2*: People in China have a smaller range of prestige in terms of accessed social capital than their capitalist counterparts in the United States and Taiwan.
> *Supported*

The hypothesis regarding the inequality in range of prestige among the three societies was supported in the predicted direction (Table 5.4). It was shown that the Chinese had the smallest range of prestige than the other two peoples. American people had the greatest range of prestige, indicating that they have the most diverse composition in their social networks.

> *Hypothesis 1-3*: On average, people in China have a smaller number of ties in their accessed social capital compared to their capitalist counterparts in the United States and Taiwan.
> *Supported*

This hypothesis was also supported because it was verified that the Chinese had the lowest mean number of ties (extensity) in their social networks (Table 5.2). The American people again had the greatest extensity, followed by the Taiwanese.

Even though it was not specifically hypothesized, I also showed that the United States had the highest mean in the accessed social capital latent variable among the three societies; there was no significant gap in the means of latent measure of accessed social capital between Taiwan and China even though the Taiwanese mean was slightly higher than the Chinese mean (Table 6.5). Thus I conclude that the United States has the greatest accessed social capital among the target societies. It appears that Taiwan has greater accessed social capital than China, but the difference was not statistically significant.

> *Hypothesis 1-4*: Females in the three societies experience disadvantages compared to males in formulating accessed social capital (upper reachability, range of prestige, and extensity).
> *Partially supported*

This hypothesis addressing the general gender inequality in the three societies did not get full support from the empirical tests because American females did not experience deficiency in accessed social capital, while females in the two

East Asian societies were disadvantaged in terms of all three indices of accessed social capital compared to males (Tables 5.5–5.7). Thus it is found that females were equal to or better than males in accessing social resources in the United States, although this does not guarantee that the two genders are equal in the final outcome of status attainment.

> *Hypothesis 1-5*:   Chinese females are the most disadvantaged among the three female groups in obtaining accessed social capital due to the double constraints of state socialist and Confucian models. American females are the least disadvantaged among the females in the three societies since they suffer only a baseline gender inequality and no additional institutional constraints. Taiwanese females, affected by the Confucian cultural disadvantage in addition to baseline gender inequality, fall somewhere in between the most (China) and least (United States) disadvantaged female groups.
> *Partially supported*

The differences between male and female means of extensity, upper reachability, and range of prestige show that the largest gaps were consistently found in China in all three indices of accessed social capital (Tables 5.5–5.7). However, as discussed above, American females are not a disadvantaged gender group because they are actually better in achieving higher or undifferentiated means in those indices.

> *Hypothesis 1-6*:   When racial inequality in the United States is identified by the analysis of social capital composition, whites have greater accessed social capital (upper reachability, range of prestige, and extensity) than nonwhites.
> *Supported*

The hypothesis was supported; whites had greater mean scores in all three accessed social capital indices than nonwhites (Table 5.8). However, when specifically compared to African-Americans, whites had a higher mean of upper reachability but not in the other two indicators of accessed social capital (Table 5.9). Further, I found that within-minority inequality in accessing social capital existed between African-Americans and Latinos (Table 5.10).

> *Hypothesis 1-7*:   Among the three structural layers of social relations, the outermost layer of belonging is the main source of accessed social capital because memberships in voluntary associations increase the probability of contacting diverse social ties.
> *Partially supported*

Multivariate analyses showed that belonging was a strong source of the three indicators of accessed social capital in the three countries (Tables 6.1–6.3). However, according to the standardized coefficients based on the regression model in which accessed social capital factor was employed, belonging had the greatest impact on accessed social capital only in the United States (see Table 6.4; note that the table presents unstandardized coefficients). Bonding was the strongest predictor of accessed social capital in China and Taiwan, although belonging was significantly related to accessed social capital in the two countries as well. This is understandable since volunteerism has been regarded as a unique product of American exceptionalism and its participatory democracy (Curtis, Grabb, and Baer 1992; Curtis, Baer, Grabb 2001), whereas the volunteering culture is not as widespread in the two East Asian countries. Thus it seems that the belonging layer based on volunteerism is most strongly related to expansion of social relations in the United States.

> *Hypothesis 1-8*:   Among the three structural layers of social relations, the innermost layer of binding is a significant source of accessed social capital in the two East Asian societies, but not in the United States.
> *Partially supported*

This hypothesis did not get full support from empirical tests (Tables 6.1–6.4). First, in China, one of the two East Asian societies, binding was not a significant source of accessed social capital, as shown in the regression analyses on all three indices of accessed social capital and its latent factor. Second, the binding layer was a significant source of accessed social capital in Taiwan when extensity, one of the three indices of accessed social capital, and the factor score of accessed social capital were the outcome variables. In other words, it was not significant when upper reachability and range of prestige were the outcome variables. Still, the binding layer based on family ties is a significant predictor of accessed social capital in Taiwan. This result seems to reflect the fact that small- and medium-sized family enterprises (SMEs) are the backbone of the Taiwanese economy and its labor market. As expected, the binding layer was not significantly related to accessed social capital in the United States.

Let us now turn to Hypotheses 2-i series on the relationships between status attainment and social capital measures.

> *Hypothesis 2-1*:   The higher the status of the contact person, the better the attained status of ego in China, Taiwan, and the United States.
> *Supported*

The hypothesis was confirmed in the three societies (Tables 7.15 and 7.16). In China contact status was related to occupational class but not to annual income; nonetheless, contact status was a predictor of the latent factor of occupational class and income (Tables 7.6 and 7.7; Figure 7.2). To test if the effects of contact status and other measures of social capital were consistent for job seekers under the job assignment system under the command economy, I ran regression analysis on the two subsamples of those who obtained their current/last jobs before and after the year of 1990, an arbitrary time-point indicating the abolition of the compulsory job assignment system, and found that activated and accessed social capital were consistently related to status attainment outcomes in general (Table 7.8). This indicates that the effects of contact status and accessed social capital were applied similarly to job seekers with or without the institutional constraint of job assignment. The effect of compulsory job assignment for about four decades seems to have solidified the pattern of association among accessed and activated social capital and status attainment. I thus conclude that the effect of activated social capital is generally applied to all three target societies, even though China experienced a structural transition from job assignment to labor marketization.

> *Hypothesis 2-2*:   The magnitude of the effect of activated social capital
>   (contact status) is greatest in the United States and
>   smallest in China, with that in Taiwan lying between
>   these two societies.
>   *Partially supported*

Even though contact status, the main indicator of activated social capital, was significant in China, its magnitude was smaller than in the other two societies mainly because the socialist control model in China reduced the efficacy of activated social capital in its job market. The job assignment system that was in place until the early 1990s may be the greatest reason for the significantly diminished impact of contact status in the Chinese job market compared to those in the United States and Taiwan.

   However, the hypothesis was partially supported by the SEM tests of parameter invariance (Table 7.15) because the difference in magnitudes of contact status coefficients between the United States and Taiwan was not statistically significant. In other words, there was no significant difference in the effect of contact status between American and Taiwanese societies, whereas there was a significantly greater impact of contact status on status attainment in these two societies than in China, as hypothesized.

> *Hypothesis 2-3*:   The chain of activated contacts for getting a job is
>   longer for Chinese than for Taiwanese or Americans.
>   *Supported*

The mean length of helpers' chain for Chinese job seekers was significantly longer than those of the other two peoples (Table 5.14). In addition, there was no significant difference in the mean chain length between the United States and Taiwan. This implies that the socialist control model in China forced its people to use longer chains through trustable ties that would not reveal informal job search behavior to the government (Bian 1997). According to Table 7.13, the SEM tests of parameter invariance found that accessed social capital was strongly related to the length of contact chain in China but was unrelated to chain length in the United States; this crossnational gap was significant. In other words, the more accessed social capital Chinese people retained, the more likely that they utilized multiple contacts in the job search process; however, this does not apply to American job seekers.

> *Hypothesis 2-4*: Chinese people tend to activate more family ties than nonfamily ties in the job search process, whereas Taiwanese and American people utilize more nonfamily ties than family ties.
> *Supported*

It was confirmed that the majority of Chinese job seekers (58 percent) used family ties when they utilized direct ties in their job search, whereas 21 and 39 percent of American and Taiwanese people respectively used family ties; and the gaps between China and the other two countries were statistically significant (Table 5.15). It is still notable that the difference between the United States and Taiwan was also significant; that is, Americans were the least dependent on family ties in their job search even though it was not hypothesized. This speaks to the fact that the two East Asian societies maintain family cohesiveness due to the Confucian culture and utilize it for instrumental purposes such as a job search.

> *Hypothesis 2-5*: In all three societies males are more likely than females to achieve better status attainment through activated social capital. The gap between males and females in returns of activated social capital from the labor market is largest in China. The smallest gap between gender groups occurs in the United States.
> *Partially supported*

The SEM multigroup model supported the first part of the hypothesis (Table 7.16), showing that in general males had better socioeconomic status than females in the three societies. Recall that it was earlier reported by regression analyses that males had lower occupational class than females in the United States and China (Table 7.6), while males earned more annual income than females in the three societies (Table 7.7). As explained earlier, occupational class may not have been sensitive enough to capture gender inequality to its full extent because it aggregated hundreds of occupations into a limited number of categories. It should also be considered that females are usually excluded from manual labor and tend to be employed in service and administrative positions.

Thus when occupational class and income were merged in a latent factor of status attainment, it became clear that gender inequality exists in the sampled countries.

However, the latter part of the hypothesis was not supported because the greatest gender gap in status attainment was identified in Taiwan rather than in China (again, see Table 7.16). I infer that the socialist control model in China was effective in refuting the Confucian doctrine of male dominance and reducing gender inequality in the job market to some extent by assigning jobs equally to females and males. However, Taiwanese females were most disadvantaged among the three societies in terms of getting returns in the labor market because the Taiwanese society still operates on the Confucian social organization that practically prevents equal relationships between gender groups in the labor market.

> *Hypothesis 2-6*:   In the United States whites obtain greater returns in the labor market from their activated social capital than nonwhites.
> *Rejected*

Tables 7.6 and 7.7 showed that belonging to a racial minority is negatively associated with higher occupational class and annual income; in particular, African-American deficits in both occupational class and income were identified as statistically significant compared to whites. Nevertheless, these are far from being a direct test of whether the effect of contact status is greater for whites. Thus to test the hypothesis, two steps should be taken. First, it is necessary to see if whites get more benefit in status attainment than nonwhites, controlling for other covariates. Second, an interaction effect between being white and contact status should be tested. If the interaction term turns out to be significant in a positive direction, then it is plausible to conclude that whites get more return in status attainment by the use of better contact status compared to nonwhites. In the following regression analysis I employ the latent factor of status attainment, combining occupational class and income as the outcome measure.

Table 8.1 shows that being white was positively and significantly related to status attainment in model 1. However, when the interaction term between being white and contact status was added in model 2, it was not significant. Therefore the hypothesis is not supported. Also note that the interaction term was in a negative direction, signaling that nonwhites may see the benefit of contact status. I thus checked if any of the minority groups (i.e., African-Americans, Latinos, or others) had significant returns from using contacts of high status (not tabled). The interaction effect was not significant for any of the minorities. Nonetheless, the interaction terms for nonwhites were all in a positive direction. Based on these relevant findings, I thus conclude that minorities tend to utilize contacts of high status to advance in the occupational hierarchy.

Table 8.1 Standardized robust OLS regression of status attainment in the United States

	Model 1	Model 2
Activated social capital		
Contact status	0.19***	0.25**
Presence of contact	−0.02	−0.02
Chain length	−0.16**	−0.16**
Routine job information	0.03	0.03
Accessed social capital	0.06**	0.06**
Structural layers		
Binding	−0.01	−0.01
Bonding	0.02	0.04
Belonging	0.05*	0.05*
Controls		
Age	0.29*	0.29*
Age^2	−0.36**	−0.37**
Male	0.07***	0.08***
White	0.05*	0.08**
White*contact status	–	−0.06
Education	0.41***	0.41***
Previous job	0.16***	0.17***
First job	0.00	0.00
Father's job	0.05*	0.05*
Father's education	−0.01	−0.01
Mother's education	−0.03	−0.03
Quota	0.02	0.03
Intercept	2.81***	−2.87***
R-squared	0.32	0.32
N	2,004	2,004

* $p < 0.05$; ** $p < 0.01$; *** $p < 0.001$ (two-tailed test).

Hypothesis 2-7:   Among the three structural layers of social relations, the outermost layer of belonging has the greatest effect on status attainment in the three societies.
Rejected

This hypothesis was not supported according to Table 7.16, in which there was no consistent hierarchical pattern of association between structural layers and status attainment across the three countries. It appears that belonging is the strongest structural layer in its effect on status attainment in the United States, whereas binding is the strongest layer in Taiwan. In China only the bonding layer kept its significance in its association with status attainment. Also note that the effect of belonging is negligible in China, where free formation of and participation in voluntary associations have been strictly controlled by government. Today this governmental control has also been extended to Internet space; it is well known that the Chinese government has limited access to globally popular websites such as Facebook, Twitter, Blogspot, or

Youtube, most of which are related to social networking services and sharing information.

Given that belonging is close to the concept of weak ties, this implies that the strength-of-weak-ties argument may not be applied in a universal fashion to varied societies. Thus the political and cultural conditions of target societies in comparison should be fully considered before assuming universal principles originating from the West. It should also be noted that the effect of belonging is not significantly greater in the United States than in the two East Asian countries, according to the tests of parameter invariance.

> *Hypothesis 2-8*:   Among the three structural layers of social relations, the innermost layer of binding has a significant effect on status attainment in the two East Asian societies, but not in the United States.
> *Partially supported*

The effect of the binding layer was the most significant among the three layers in Taiwan, while it was insignificant in China and the United States; the hypothesis is thus partially supported (Table 7.16). It may be the Confucian influence that makes binding (family-related ties) a significant predictor of status attainment in Taiwan. Further, this unique effect of the binding layer also seems to arise from the fact that family enterprises serve as the main engine of the Taiwanese economy. Note that Taiwan was the only country that had a significant effect of the binding layer on accessed social capital, although this effect was not confirmed to be significantly greater than in the other two countries (Tables 6.4, 7.10). Thus in Taiwan the effect of the binding layer has both direct and indirect pathways to status attainment via accessed social capital. However, it affected neither accessed social capital nor status attainment in China.

Important but nonhypothesized findings

There are a few more findings worth summarizing, although they were not specifically hypothesized. First, the effect of accessed social capital on contact status, a major indicator of activated social capital, was strongest in China and its effect was significantly greater than in the United States (Table 7.11). The same pattern was also evident in presence of contact and chain length (Tables 7.12 and 7.13); that is, the linkage between accessed and activated social capital was strongest in China and the gap between China and the United States was confirmed to be statistically significant according to the tests of parameter invariance. In addition, there was no significant difference among the countries in the effect of accessed social capital on routine job information, another indicator of activated social capital (Table 7.14). Nonetheless, as we observed while testing Hypothesis 2-2, the effect of contact status on status attainment was the weakest in China, and the other three measures of activated social capital were not related to status attainment. Thus Chinese people are better at turning their social relations into instrumental contacts for job searches, particularly more than Americans, but the effect of utilized contacts is worst among the three peoples. Thus the instrumental orientation of Chinese social relations has been suppressed by the socialist institutional control of job assignment and its legacy effect even in the labor marketization era. Still, it should not be overlooked that the effect of contact status on occupational class was significant even when the job assignment system was in place (see Table 7.8).

Second, it was found that father's education was significantly and positively related to presence of contact and job search chain length in China (Tables 7.12 and 7.13). Specifically, the effect of father's education on presence of contact in China was significantly greater than in either Taiwan or the United States, and the effect on chain length was greater than in the United States. These findings hint at a tendency toward intergenerational inheritance of socioeconomic status in China, a socialist regime.

Third, the belonging layer was strongest in its effect on generating routine job information in the United States, followed by China and Taiwan (Table 7.14). This finding confirms that volunteerism is a significant source of job-related information in the three countries, but more so in the United States. In addition, it was also confirmed that in China the older the worker the more routine job information they received; this advantage of seniority was significantly greater than in the other two countries.

Lastly, in terms of status attainment, the effect of first job in Taiwan and China was significant but did not matter in the United States, and the gap between the two East Asian countries and the United States was confirmed to be significant (Table 7.16). In turn, however, the effect of previous job on status attainment was greatest in the United States and the gap between the United States and Taiwan was statistically significant. These findings show that initial position in the labor market is important in predicting future prospects for status attainment in the two East Asian societies, whereas in the United States what matters more is how well a worker develops his/her career across time, regardless of how high or low the starting point is in the occupational hierarchy.

Conclusion

The key findings by countries are summarized as follows. In China the effect of activated social capital on status attainment was the smallest, even though the linkage between accessed and activated social capital (contact status) was the strongest among the three countries. I thus suspect that the influence of governmental control through job assignment had a long-lasting effect in suppressing activated social capital even after the job assignment era (Table 7.8). Nonetheless, the direct effect of accessed social capital on status attainment in China was comparable to the other two countries (Table 7.16).

In Taiwan the effects of accessed and activated social capital on status attainment were as strong as in the United States (Table 7.16). In terms of the linkage between the two types of social capital, accessed social capital was significantly related to activated social capital (contact status) in Taiwan (Table 7.11). I therefore conclude that the tripartite mediatory paths among accessed and activated social capital and status attainment were most stable and balanced in Taiwan. However, Taiwan had less accessed social capital than the United States (Table 6.5). Also, female deficit in status attainment was the greatest in Taiwan after controlling for the effects of social capital and other covariates (Table 7.16).

In the United States the impact of activated social capital on status attainment was the greatest, even though it was not statistically differentiated from that in Taiwan (Table 7.15). Also, its amount of accessed social capital was the greatest among the three countries (Table 6.5). However, the linkage of accessed social capital to activated social capital was the weakest of the three countries (Tables 7.11–7.13). In other words, in the United States the effect of accessed social capital is not channeled through activated social capital in the status attainment process.

Having examined the main findings, I now turn to general discussion of the comparative study of social capital and status attainment in the labor markets in China, Taiwan, and the United States. The first thing to note is that the effect of activated social capital on status attainment was significant in the three countries in varying degrees. Activated social capital is an individual choice to maximize returns from the labor market through the influence and/ or resources of social contacts. In general activated social capital as an individual choice is legitimately included in the institutional rules, norms, and rituals of labor markets. The capacity to activate social resources is itself an asset of a job seeker that signals his/her ability and credentials endorsed by contact persons and possibly acknowledged by employers. Thus many societies institutionalize it in that employers, schools, and other organizations ask their candidates to provide references. Part of the reason may be that they want to check candidates' performance in prior stages of life through this institutionalized means. It also follows that companies and organizations want new members with better connections to diverse and resourceful social ties outside their own boundaries.

However, if activating social capital in the job search process goes against institutional rules and norms in certain societies, this complicates how people socialize and interact and to what extent they can exchange favors with one another. It thus eventually generates tension between instrumental use of social relations and legal enforcement banning it. Basically, obtaining and maintaining access to diverse and rich social resources is mostly valued in any social context. However, when instrumental utilization of social resources is defined as illegal, individual choices to utilize accessed social capital are constrained. There could then be two kinds of reactions from individuals. First, they refrain from using social contacts, afraid of possible legal punishment and communal denigration. It is also possible that some accept the illegalization of using private contacts as a way to institutionalize meritocracy. In this case institutional constraint weakens the power of agency. This was empirically proven by the finding in the present study that activated social capital was least effective on status attainment in China compared to the other two sampled countries. Second, individuals secretively activate trustable contacts and continue to exchange favors. In this case they are more likely to share particularistic ties among themselves that can offset the hazard of being reported to the regulatory authorities. This secretive activation of social capital creates dissonance between institutional norms and actual practice. The degree of dissonance indicates how resilient agency can be to the governance of institutional constraint. The study found that the linkage between accessed and activated social capital was strongest in China, which indicates that Chinese people – including those who got their jobs under the job assignment system – were eager to utilize their social ties for instrumental purposes; some were indeed activated even though the activation rate and effect were reported to be the lowest among the three countries.

These findings may also be applied to non-Chinese social contexts. For instance, activation of social capital was illegal not only in China, as shown in the present study, but also under the military regime in South Korea in the 1980s. At that time it was common to find plates inscribed "Do not Ask for Favors" next to officials' nameplates in governmental offices. The military regime believed that particularistic connections such as school ties, regional ties, and blood ties were being rampantly utilized as channels of corruptive transactions. The regime thus frequently convened government employees in assembly halls, publicly warning them that they would face maximum penalties if they were caught in bribery or corruption. Nonetheless, despite strong governmental control, more than a few large financial and political scandals occurred involving high-ranking officials who could not resist the influence of particularistic social relations. The irony is that at the center of those scandals were close family members of the then president, who had pushed the campaign illegalizing the use of personal connections. The social problem related to the use of personal contacts is not contained in the East Asian region. It was recently reported by *TIME* magazine that in Hamas-controlled Gaza the use of *wasta* (connections) is still prevalent, even though Hamas had promised in elections that it would eliminate *wasta* (Vick 2011). It is also well known that the old Soviet Union suffered from *Blat*, nepotistic connections frequently involving Communist Party members and influential politicians. Even the United States and the United Kingdom are not exceptions – personal connections called the "old boys network" take place; this is probably part of the reason that we observed the strong effect of activated social capital on status attainment in the United States in this study. Sometimes network closure is based on racialized occupational interests. For instance in her in-depth interviews with graduates of a vocational high school, Royster (2003) shows how white, male, unionized manual workers passed their jobs to young white males excluding comparably educated African-American youth.

In light of this study's findings, I argue that sociological research on the labor market and social capital has not considered well the interaction between institutions and individual choices, assuming an impractically universal utility of individual choices regardless of diverse institutional arrangements. As shown thus far, agency did not get the same returns among the three societies by utilizing contacts; rather, there was variation in the effects of choices across countries. Another notable example that negates the assumption of universality is the proposition of strength-of-weak-ties. Even though the proposition is widely accepted among social network researchers, the present study reports that the binding structural layer – simply put, strong ties – was more efficacious in affecting status attainment than the belonging layer, an indicator of weak ties, in Taiwan; the belonging layer did not matter in China (Table 7.16).

Nevertheless, the study also identified a counterreaction by agency against the institutional constraints reflected in the significant effect of accessed social capital on status attainment in all three societies. Specifically, accessed social capital in China did not lose its significant power on status attainment, even though activated social capital had the smallest (but significant) impact among the three societies. I argue that this manifests the resilience of individual choices in the sense that the latent effect of accessed social capital on instrumental gains was not eliminated by socialist control. It is thus certain that access to more diverse and richer social ties significantly increased the chance of getting better returns from the labor market, even when tight control reduced the effect of activated social capital. Still, it remains unclear how accessed social capital finds its direct pathway to status attainment. There could be unmeasured mediating mechanisms linking the two, the so-called invisible hand of social capital.

In spite of some new findings in this monograph it has limitations, mainly due to the complexity of the macrocomparative research design. Given that the efficacy of social capital was examined in the labor markets of the three societies, analyses of the labor market structure and government policies over time in each society could increase the explanatory power of the study. For instance, macrolevel indices such as female labor participation rates in the three societies could have explained more variations of the gender inequality embedded in the labor market structures. In 2004 when the surveys were conducted it was reported that female workers held 46 percent of the US labor force, 45 percent of the Chinese labor force, and 41 percent of the Taiwanese labor force (United States and China: http://go.worldbank.org/006SWP3YU0, Taiwan: http://eng.dgbas.gov.tw/public/data/dgbas03/bs2/yearbook_eng/y021.pdf). It may be that the relatively lower participation rate of Taiwanese females indicates their comparative disadvantage in the status attainment process found in the present study compared to females in the other two societies – of course, it is plausible that the lower labor force participation rate itself was affected by the Confucian social order. Also, the use of cross-sectional data from the three countries did not allow a longitudinal track of the size of accessed social capital, the activation rates of social resources, and the effects of social capital on status attainment within each country. In terms of structural features related to position generator items, size differentials of each occupation in the three societies could work as controls in teasing out the effect of accessed social capital. However, such specific information or data were not available.

Next, in order to avoid excessively complicated models across the three societies, I did not include interaction terms among the variables of interest. Rather, I aimed to straightforwardly examine structural differences of key covariates through their main effects. For instance, gender inequality in activated social capital in the status attainment process was not checked through an interaction term between gender and activated social capital – note, though, that the interaction term was not significant according to supplementary analysis (not tabled). Nonetheless, the main effects of some key variables did report major differences among the societies.

I conducted another supplementary analysis of the status attainment model on a subsample of respondents from Beijing and Shanghai (not tabled), and found that activated social capital in these urbanized cities had similar pattern and strength of association with status attainment measures (occupational class and annual income) to those identified in the whole sample. Thus regional differences in China in terms of economic development and urbanization do not weaken the findings from the sample. Nonetheless, further mid-ranged comparisons between certain types of regional units are worth doing in future comparative research. It should also be checked, using hierarchical modeling, whether regional or contextual variables have any impact on social capital formation and its efficacy on status attainment.

In addition, I acknowledge that each selected country in the present study is only a case within its ideal typical category; for instance, China is a case of the "socialist control model" within which there are not a few old socialist nation-states in market transition. Thus the crossnational differences I found in the present study, for instance between the United States and China, might not be generalizable differences between market-dominant and socialist-control models. To overcome such limitations, more cases should be added into the comparative schema in future studies.

In regard to the Chinese sample, I acknowledge that it was not possible to know if a Chinese respondent got his/her current job by state assignment. The survey did not ask the question directly. Further, this is difficult to identify because the time points of abolishing the job allocation system varied by province and region. However, I found that the general pattern of association between final outcome measures and explanatory variables stayed similar when a supplementary analysis was conducted based on the two subsamples of those who got their current/last jobs before and after the year of 1990, an approximate time point when the job assignment system lost its effect and labor marketization began (Table 7.8).

Even though it has some critical limitations, the present study showed how the institutional constraints of socialist control and the Confucian culture limited individual choices and the efficacy of social capital. However, the relationship between institution and agency is not unidirectional in the sense that we also observed through empirical tests the resilience of individual social capital to institutional constraints. If institutions held complete sway over individual choices, it would indicate absolute totalitarianism. In contrast, if individual choices were the only thing that mattered in status attainment, it would denote an anomic Hobbesian chaos. The findings we have observed demonstrate that the three sampled countries are located between these two extremes, that is, we saw that with more constraints the effect of social capital is reduced accordingly. In other words, this comparative study provides empirical support for an integrative theoretical perspective between social networks and new institutionalism that proposes choices within institutional constraints (Nee and Ingram 1998).

It is thus the future task of comparative researchers to identify to what extent and how systematically the interaction between choices and institutions can vary – indeed, this has been one of the main themes of sociology from the beginning of the discipline. Having scrutinized the composition of social capital and its effect on status attainment in the three case countries, I conclude that social capital is a valid and useful tool for measuring crossnational and crosscultural variation of individual choices moderated by institutional constraints.

Appendix A   Identical module of position generators in the three societies

Position generator items
1. Nurse (54)
2. Writer (57)
3. Farmer (47)
4. Lawyer (73)
5. Middle school teacher (60)
6. Fulltime babysitter (23)
7. Janitor (25)
8. Personnel manager (60)
9. Administrative assistant in a large company (53)
10. Hairdresser (32)
11. Bookkeeper (49)
12. Security guard (30)
13. Production manager (60)
14. Operator in a factory (34)
15. Computer programmer (51)
16. Receptionist (38)
17. Taxi driver (31)
18. Professor (78)
19. Hotel bellboy (22)
20. Policeman (40)
21. CEO of a big company (70)

*Note: The occupational prestige scores of Treiman's Standard Industrial Occupational Prestige Scale (SIOPS) are in parentheses (Ganzeboom and Treiman 1996).

Appendix B   Survey questions of a position generator (nurse)

C. Position Generator

Next, I am going to ask some general questions about jobs some people you know may now have. These people include your relatives, friends and acquaintances (acquaintances are people who know each other by face and name). If there are several people you know who have that kind of job, please tell me the one that occurs to you first.

C1-NURSE.

C1_1.   Is there anyone you know who is a NURSE?
      (1) Yes   (0) No *[If no, ask the next position]*

C2_1.   If yes, what is his/her relationship to you? *[Choose only one relationship the respondent considers as the most important.]*

      (1)   Spouse (current or previous)
      (2)   Parents
      (3)   Father-in-law/mother-in-law
      (4)   Children
      (5)   Sibling
      (6)   Daughter-in-law
      (7)   Son-in-law
      (8)   Other relative
      (9)   Old neighbor
      (10)   Current neighbor
      (11)   School/class mate
      (12)   Compatriot
      (13)   Teacher
      (14)   Student
      (15)   Current co-worker
      (16)   Current boss/superior
      (17)   Current subordinate
      (18)   Co-worker, boss/superior, or subordinate from a previous firm

(19) Client
(20) Person working for another firm, but known through work relations
(21) Someone from the same religious group
(22) Someone from the same association, club or group
(23) Close friend
(24) Ordinary friend
(25) Someone known because he/she provides a service to me or my family
(26) Someone know from the Internet
(27) An acquaintance
(28) Indirect relationship (known via someone else)
(29) Else_____C2_1a

C3_1. Did you get to know him/her through your spouse or partner? *[For those who are single or do not have partners: skip to C4_1]*
(1) Yes   (0) No

C4_1. Is the NURSE male or female?
(1) Male   (0) Female

C5_1. How long have you known each other? _____ Years

C6_1. How close are you to him/her?
(1) Very close
(2) Close
(3) So, so
(4) Not close
(5) Not close at all

C7_1. What is the racial/ethnic background of this person?
(1) White (non-Latino)
(2) African-American
(3) Latino (specify: _____ C7_1a)
(4) Asian (specify: _____C7_1a)
(5) Native American
(6) Other (specify_____C7_1a)

Appendix C Types of community organizations in the three societies

US	Taiwan	China
• Political parties	• Political parties	–
• Labor unions	• Labor unions	–
• Religious groups	• Religious groups	• Religious groups
• Leisure, sports, or culture groups	• Leisure, sports, or culture groups	• Sports groups
• Professional organizations	–	• Professional organizations
• Charities	–	• Charities
• Neighborhood organizations	–	–
• School and PTA	–	• Alumni organization
• Ethnic or civil rights organizations	–	–
• Other organizations	• Other organizations	• Other organizations
		• Academic organization, culture groups
		• Medical and health organization
		• International organization
		• Economic organization
		• Clan organization
N=10	N=5	N=11

References

Acemoglu, D., Autor, D.H., and Lyle, D. (2004) 'Women, War, and Wage: The Effect of Female Labor Supply on the Wage Structure at Midcentury', *Journal of Political Economy*, 112: 497–551.

ACNielsen (2005) *Consumers in Asia Pacific – Car Ownership and Purchase Intentions.* HTTP: <http://jp.nielsen.com/news/documents/AP_Automotive_Report_April2005.pdf> (accessed 28 September 2011).

Adler, P.S. and Kwon, S-W. (2002) 'Social Capital: Prospects for a New Concept', *Academy of Management Review* 27: 17–40.

Aguilera, M.B. and Massey, D.S. (2003) 'Social Capital and the Wages of Mexican Migrants: New Hypotheses and Tests', *Social Forces* 82: 671–702.

Allmendinger, J. (1989) *Career Mobility Dynamics: A Comparative Analysis of the United States, Norway, and West Germany*, Studien and Berichte 49, Berlin: Max-Planck-Institut fur Bildungsforschung.

Amsden, A.H. (1992) *Asia's Next Giant*, New York: Oxford University Press.

Amsden, A.H. and Chu, W. (2003) *Beyond Late Development: Taiwan's Upgrading Policies*, Cambridge, MA: The MIT Press.

Angelusz, R. and Tardos, R. (2001) 'Change and Stability in Social Network Resources: The Case of Hungary under Transformation', in N. Lin, K. Cook, and R.S. Burt (eds) *Social Capital: Theory and Research*, New York: Aldine De Gruyter.

Appleby, J.O. (1984) *Capitalism and a New Social Order: The Republican Vision of the 1790s*, New York: New York University Press.

Arrow, K.J. and Borzekowski, R. (2004) 'Limited Network Connections and the Distribution of Wages', *Finance and Economics Discussion Series* 2004-41, Board of Governors of the Federal Reserve System (United States).

Baker, H.D.R. (1979) *Chinese Family and Kinship*, New York: Columbia University Press.

Bebbington, A. and Perreault, T. (1999) 'Social Capital, Development, and Access to Resources in Highland Ecuador', *Economic Geography*, 75: 395–418.

Beckert, J. (2002) *Beyond the Market: The Social Foundations of Economic Efficiency*, Princeton, NJ: Princeton University Press.

Bellah, R.N., Madsen, R., Sullivan, W.M., Swidler, A., and Tipton, S.M. (1985) *Habits of Heart: Individualism and Commitment in American Life*, Berkeley: University of California Press.

Bertrand, M. and Mullainathan, S. (2004) 'Are Emily and Greg More Employable than Lakisha and Jamal? A Field Experiment on Labor Market Discrimination', *American Economic Review*, 94: 991–1013.

Bian, Y. (1994) 'Guanxi and the Allocation of Urban Jobs in China', *The China Quarterly*, 140: 971–999.

—— (1997) 'Bringing Strong Ties Back In: Indirect Connection, Bridges, and Job Search in China', *American Sociological Review*, 62: 366–385.

Bian, Y. and Ang, S. (1997) '*Guanxi* Networks and Job Mobility in China and Singapore', *Social Forces*, 75: 981–1005.

Bielby, W.T. and Bielby, D. (1994) 'She Works Hard for the Money: Household Responsibilities and the Allocation of Work Effect', *American Journal of Sociology*, 93: 1031–1059.

Blau, P. and Duncan, O.D. (1967) *The American Occupational Structure*, New York: Wiley.

Blau, P.M., Ruan, D., and Ardelt, M. (1991) 'Interpersonal Choice and Networks in China', *Social Forces*, 69: 1037–1062.

Block, F. (1990) *Postindustrial Possibilities: A Critique of Economic Discourse*, Berkeley: University of California Press.

Bobo, L. (1991) 'Social Responsibility, Individualism, and Redistributive Policies', *Sociological Forum*, 6: 71–92.

Bollen, K.A. (1989) *Structural Equations with Latent Variables*, New York: Wiley.

Bonacich, E. (1972) 'A Theory of Ethnic Antagonism: The Split Labor Market', *American Sociological Review*, 37: 547–559.

Bonilla-Silva, E. (2006) *Racism without Racists: Color-blind Racism and the Persistence of Racial Inequality in the United States*, Lanham: Rowman & Littlefield Publishers.

Boris, E.T. (1999) 'The Nonprofit Sector in the 1990s', in C. Clotfelter and T. Ehrlich (eds) *Philanthropy and the Nonprofit Sector in a Changing America*, Bloomington: Indiana University Press.

Bourdieu, P. (1986) 'The Forms of Capital', in J.G. Richardson (ed.) *Handbook of Theory and Research for the Sociology of Education*, Westport, CT: Greenwood Press.

Boxman, E.A.W., De Graaf, P.M., and Flap, H.D. (1991) 'The Impact of Social and Human Capital on the Income Attainment of Dutch Managers', *Social Networks*, 13: 51–73.

Braude, L. (1975) *Work and Workers: A Sociological Analysis*, New York: Praeger Publishers.

Breiger, R.L. (2004) 'The Analysis of Social Networks', in M. Hardy and A. Bryman (eds) *Handbook of Data Analysis*, London: Sage Publications.

Bridges, W.P. and Villemez, W.J. (1986) 'Informal Hiring and Income in the Labor Market', *American Sociological Review*, 51: 574–582.

Briggs, X. (1998) 'Brown Kids in White Suburbs', *Housing Policy Debate*, 9: 177–221.

—— (2007) ' "Some of My Best Friends Are. . .": Interracial Friendships, Class, and Segregation in America', *City & Community*, 6: 263–290.

Brouthers, L.E., O'Donnell, E., and Hadjimarcou, J. (2005) 'Generic Product Strategies for Emerging Market Exports into Triad Nation Markets: A Mimetic Isomorphism Approach', *Journal of Management Studies*, 42: 225–245.

Burt, R.S. (1992) *Structural Holes: The Social Structure of Competition*, Cambridge, MA: Harvard University Press.

Campbell, K.E., Marsden, P.V., and Hurlbert, J.S. (1986) 'Social Resources and Socioeconomic Status', *Social Networks*, 8: 97–117.

Candland, C. (2001) 'Faith as Social Capital: Religion and Community Development in Southern Asia', *Policy Sciences*, 33: 355–374.

Chan, A.L. (2001) *Mao's Crusade: Politics and Policy Implementation in China's Great Leap Forward*, New York: Oxford University Press.

Chang, H. (2002) *Kicking Away the Ladder: Development Strategy in Historical Perspective*, London: Anthem Press.

—— (2007) *Bad Samaritans: Rich Nations, Poor Policies, and the Threat to the Developing World*, London: Random House.

—— (2010) *23 Things They Don't Tell You About Capitalism*, New York: Penguin Books Ltd.

Charney, J.I. and Prescott, J.R.V. (2000) 'Resolving Cross-strait Relations between China and Taiwan', *American Journal of International Law*, 94: 453–477.

Chen, J. and Deng, P. (1995) *China since the Cultural Revolution: From Totalitarianism to Authoritarianism*, Westport, CT: Praeger.

Coleman, J.S. (1987) 'Norms as Social Capital', in G. Radnitzky and P. Bernholz (eds) *Economic Imperialism: The Economic Method Applied Outside the Field of Economics*, New York: Paragon House Publishers.

—— (1988) 'Social Capital in the Creation of Human Capital', *American Journal of Sociology* 94: S95–S120.

—— (1990) 'Social Capital', in *Foundations of Social Theory*, Cambridge, MA: Harvard University Press.

Collins, L.M. and Wulgalter, S.E. (1992) 'Latent Class Models for Stage-Sequential Dynamic Latent Variables', *Multivariate Behavioral Research* 27: 131–157.

Commons, J.R., Saposs, D.J., Sumner, H.L., Mittelman, E.B., Hoagland, H.E., Andrews, J.B., Perlman, S., Raushenbach, E.B., Taft, P., and Lescohier, D.D. (1918) *History of Labour in the United States*, New York: Macmillan Company.

Croll, E. (1983) *Chinese Women since Mao*, New York: M.E. Sharpe.

Curtis, J.E., Grabb, E.G., and Baer, D.E. (1992) 'Voluntary Association Membership in Fifteen Countries: A Comparative Analysis', *American Sociological Review*, 57: 139–152.

Curtis, J.E., Baer, D.E., and Grabb, E.G. (2001) 'Nations of Joiners: Explaining Voluntary Association Membership in Democratic Societies', *American Sociological Review*, 66: 783–805.

De Graaf, N.D. and Flap, H.D. (1988) 'With a Little Help from My Friends', *Social Forces*, 67: 452–472.

Deng, Z. and Treiman, D.J. (1997) 'The Impact of the Cultural Revolution on Trends in Educational Attainment in the People's Republic of China', *American Journal of Sociology*, 103: 391–428.

Dietz, T., Frey, R.S., and Kalof, L. (1987) 'Estimation with Cross-National Data: Robust and Nonparametric Methods', *American Sociological Review*, 52: 380–390.

DiMaggio, P.J. and Powell W.W. (1983) 'The Iron Cage Revisited: Institutional Isomorphism and Collective Rationality in Organizational Fields', *American Sociological Review*, 48: 147–160.

Dobbin, F. (2004) *The New Economic Sociology*, Princeton, NJ: Princeton University Press.

Douglas, M. (1986) *How Institutions Think*, Syracuse, NY: Syracuse University Press.

Duesenberry, J. (1960) 'Comment' (on 'An Economic Analysis of Fertility' by G.S. Becker), in NBER (ed.) *Demographic and Economic Change in Developed Countries*, New York: Columbia University Press.

Durkheim, E. [1893] (1984) *The Division of Labor in Society*, trans. W.D. Halls, Hong Kong: Macmillan Education.

—— [1895] (1964) *The Rules of Sociological Method*, trans. S.A. Colovay and J.H. Mueller, New York: The Free Press.

—— [1897] (1951) *Suicide*, trans. J.A. Spaulding and G. Simpson, New York: Free Press.

Eagle, N., Macy, M., and Claxton, R. (2010) 'Network Diversity and Economic Development', *Science*, 328: 1029–1031.

Erickson, B.H. (1996) 'Culture, Class, and Connections', *American Journal of Sociology*, 102: 217–251.

Evans, P. (1995) *Embedded Autonomy: States and Industrial Transformation*, Princeton, NJ: Princeton University Press.

—— (1996) 'Government Action, Social Capital and Development: Reviewing the Evidence on Synergy', *World Development*, 24: 1119–1132.

Feagin, J.R. (2000) *Racist America: Roots, Current Realities, and Future Reparations*, New York: Routledge.

Feenstra, R.C. and Hamilton, G.G. (2006) *Emergent Economies, Divergent Paths: Economic Organization and International Trade in South Korea and Taiwan*, New York: Cambridge University Press.

Fell, D. (2011) *Government and Politics in Taiwan*, New York: Routledge.

Fernandez, J.A. and Underwood, L. (2006) *China CEO: Voices of Experience from 20 International Business Leaders*, Singapore: Wiley.

Fernandez, R.M. and Weinberg, N. (1997) 'Sifting and Sorting: Personal Contacts and Hiring in a Retail Bank', *American Sociological Review*, 62: 883–902.

Fernandez, R.M., Castilla, E.J., and Moore, P. (2000) 'Social Capital at Work: Networks and Employment at a Phone Center', *American Journal of Sociology*, 105: 1288–1356.

Fields, G.S. (1992) 'Living Standards, Labour Markets and Human Resources in Taiwan', in G. Ranis (ed.) *Taiwan: From Developing to Mature Economy*, Boulder, CO: Westview Press.

Fields, G.S. and Kraus, A.N. (2007) *Education and Taiwan's Changing Employment and Earning Structure (Articles & Chapters, Paper 469)*. HTTP: <http://digitalcommons.ilr.cornell.edu/articles/469> (accessed 17 October 2011).

Flap, H.D. (2002) 'No Man is an Island', in O. Favereau and E. Lazega (eds) *Conventions and Structures in Economic Organization: Markets, Networks, and Hierarchies*, Cheltenham: Edward Elgar.

Forsythe, N., Korzeniewicz, R.P., and Durrant, V. (2000) 'Gender Inequality and Economic Development: A Longitudinal Evaluation', *Economic Development and Cultural Change*, 48: 573–671.

Franklin, J.H. and Moss, A.A., Jr. (1994) *From Slavery to Freedom: A History of African Americans*, New York: McGraw-Hill.

Freund, J. (1968) *The Sociology of Max Weber*, New York: Pantheon Books.

Fukuyama, F. (2001) 'Social Capital, Civil Society and Development', *Third World Quarterly*, 22: 7–20.

Gans, H.J. (1988) *Middle American Individualism: The Future of Liberal Democracy*, New York: Free Press.

Ganzeboom, H.B.G. and Treiman, D.J. (1996) 'Internationally Comparable Measures of Occupational Status for the 1988 International Standard Classification of Occupations', *Social Science Research*, 25: 201–239.

Geertz, C. (1973) *The Interpretation of Cultures: Selected Essays*, New York: Basic Books.

Goerzen, A. and Beamish, P.W. (2005) 'The Effect of Alliance Network Diversity on Multinational Enterprise Performance', *Strategic Management Journal*, 26: 333–354.

Gold, T.B. (1991) 'Civil Society in Taiwan: The Confucian Dimension', paper presented at the Conference on the Confucian Dimension of Dynamics of Industrial East Asia, American Academy of Arts and Sciences, Cambridge, MA, 1991.

Goldin, C. (1990) *Understanding the Gender Gap*, New York: Oxford University Press.

Goldman, M. (1994) *Sowing the Seeds of Democracy in China: Political Reform in the Deng Xiaoping Era*, Cambridge, MA: Harvard University Press.

Grafstein, R. (1998) 'The Problem of Institutional Constraint', *Journal of Politics*, 50: 577–599.

Granovetter, M. (1973) 'The Strength of Weak Ties', *American Journal of Sociology*, 78: 1360–1380.

—— [1974] (1995) *Getting a Job: A Study of Contacts and Careers*, Chicago, IL: University of Chicago Press.

Granovetter, M. and Swedberg, R. (2001) *The Sociology of Economic Life*, Boulder, CO: Westview Press.

Greely, A. (1997) 'The Other Civic America: Religion and Social Capital', *American Prospect*, 32: 68–73.

Guzda, H.P. (1983) 'The U.S. Employment Service at 50: It Too Had To Wait Its Turn', *Monthly Labor Review*, 106: 12–19.

Hall, P.A. and Soskice, D.W. (eds) (2001) *Varieties of Capitalism: The Institutional Foundations of Comparative Advantage*, Oxford: Oxford University Press.

Hamilton, G.G. (1990) 'Patriarchy, Patrimonialism, and Filial Piety: A Comparison of China and Western Europe', *British Journal of Sociology*, 41: 77–104.

Hamilton, G.G. and Biggart, N.W. (1991) 'The Organization of Business in Taiwan: Reply to Numazak', *American Journal of Sociology*, 96: 999–1006.

Hamilton, G.G., Feenstra, R., Choe, W., Kim, C.K., and Lim, E.M. (2000) 'The Role of Economic Organization in Asian Development', *International Sociology*, 15: 288–305.

Han, S-K. (1994) 'Mimetic Isomorphism and Its Effect on the Audit Services Market', *Social Forces*, 73: 637–664.

Hauser, R.M. and Warren, J.R. (1997) 'Socioeconomic Indexes for Occupations: A Review, Update, and Critique', *Sociological Methodology*, 27: 177–298.

Haveman, H.A. (1993) 'Follow the Leader: Mimetic Isomorphism and Entry into New Markets', *Administrative Science Quarterly*, 38: 593–627.

Henderson, J. (2011) *East Asian Transformation: On the Political Economy of Dynamism, Governance and Crisis*, New York: Routledge.

Hirshman, C. and Wong, M.G. (1984) 'Socioeconomic Gains of Asian Americans, Blacks and Hispanics: 190–1976', *American Journal of Sociology*, 90: 584–607.

Homans, G.C. (1950) *The Human Groups*, New York: Harcourt, Brace.

Houn, F.W. (1958) 'Chinese Communist Control of the Press', *The Public Opinion Quarterly*, 22: 435–448.

Huffman, M.L. and Torres, L. (2002) 'It's Not Only Who You Know That Matters : Gender, Personal Contacts and Job Lead Quality', *Gender and Society*, 16: 793–813.

Huntington, S.P. (1996) *The Clash of Civilizations and the Remaking of World Order*, New York: Simon & Schuster.

Jenkins, R.M. (2001) 'Labor Markets and Economic transformation in Postcommunist Europe', in I. Berg and A.L. Kalleberg (eds) *Sourcebook of Labor Markets: Evolving Structures and Processes*, New York: Kluwer Academic/Plenum Publishers.

Johnston, J. (1984) *Econometric Methods*, New York: McGraw-Hill.

Kawachi, I., Kennedy, B.P., Lochner, K., and Prothrow-Stith, D. (1997) 'Social Capital, Income Inequality, and Mortality', *American Journal of Public Health*, 87: 1491–1498.

Kääriäinen, J. and Lehtonen, K. (2006) 'The Variety of Social Capital in Welfare State Regimes – A Comparative Study of 21 Countries', *European Societies*, 8: 27–57.

Keeter, S., Miller, C., Kohut, A., Groves, R.M., and Presser, S. (2000) 'Consequences of Reducing Nonresponse in a National Telephone Survey', *Public Opinion Quarterly*, 64: 125–148.

Keeter, S., Kennedy, C., Dimock, M., Best, J., and Craighill, P. (2006) 'Gauging the Impact of Growing Nonresponse on Estimates from A National RDD Telephone Survey', *Public Opinion Quarterly*, 70: 759–779.

Kim, L. (1997) *Imitation to Innovation: The Dynamics of Korea's Technological Learning*, Cambridge, MA: Harvard Business School Press.

Klein, A. and Moosbrugger, H. (2000) Maximum Likelihood Estimation of Latent Interaction Effects with the LMS Method', *Psychometrika*, 65: 457–474.

Kline, R.B. (2005) *Principles and Practice of Structural Equation Modeling*, New York: Guilford Press.

Knack, S. (2002) 'Social Capital and the Quality of Government: Evidence from the States', *American Journal of Political Science*, 46: 772–785.

Knack, S. and Keefer, P. (1997) 'Does Social Capital Have an Economic Payoff? A Cross-Country Investigation', *Quarterly Journal of Economics*, 112: 1251–1288.

Knight, J. and Song, L. (2005) *Towards a Labour Market in China*, New York: Oxford University Press.

Ladd, E. (1999) *The Ladd Report*, New York: Free Press.

Lam, P-Y. (2006) 'Religion and Civic Culture: A Cross-National Study of Voluntary Association Membership', *Journal for the Scientific Study of Religion*, 45: 177–193.

Lancee, B. (2010) 'The Economic Returns of Immigrants' Bonding and Bridging Social Capital: The Case of the Netherlands', *International Migration Review*, 44: 202–226.

Lazarsfeld, P.F. and Merton, R.K. (1954) 'Friendship as Social Process: A Substantive and Methodological Analysis', in P.L. Kendall (ed.) *The Varied Sociology of Paul F. Lazarsfeld*, New York: Columbia University Press.

Lee, A. (2004) *In the Name of Harmony and Prosperity: Labour and Gender Politics in Taiwan's Economic Restructuring*, New York: State University of New York Press, Albany.

Lee, J.S. (1995) 'Economic Development and the Evolution of Industrial Relations in Taiwan, 1950–1993', in A. Verma, T.A. Kochan, and R.D. Landsbury (eds) *Employment Relations in the Growing Asian Economies*, New York: Routledge.

—— (2007) 'Labour Market Flexibility and Employment: An Overview', in J.S. Lee (ed.) *The Labour Market and Economic Development of Taiwan*, Northhampton, MA: Edward Elgar Publishing Limited.

Lee, R.P.L, Ruan, D., and Lai, G. (2005) 'Social Structure and Support Networks in Beijing and Hong Kong', *Social Networks*, 27: 249–274.

Lee, W. (2009) 'Private Deception and the Rise of Public Employment Offices in the United States, 1890–1930' in *Studies of Labor Market Intermediation (A National*

Bureau of Economic Research conference report), Chicago, IL: University of Chicago Press.

Levenson, J.R. (1962) 'The Place of Confucius in Communist China', *China Quarterly*, 1962: 1–18.

Li, C. (2000a) 'Introduction: Can Confucianism Come to Terms with Feminism?' in C. Li (ed.) *The Sage and the Second Sex: Confucianism, Ethics, and Gender*, Chicago, IL: Open Court.

—— (2000b) 'Confucianism and Feminist Concerns: Overcoming the Confucian "Gender Complex" ', *Journal of Chinese Philosophy*, 27: 187–199.

Li, C.Y., Chang, K.H., Feng, C.K., and Wu, S.C. (1999) 'Inter-rater Agreement on the Classification of Job Titles', *Chinese Journal of Public Health*, 18: 255–261.

Li, W. (1992) *China's Wage System*, Beijing: China Labour Publishing House [in Chinese].

Lichtenstein, N. (2002) *State of the Union: A Century of American Labor*, Princeton, NJ: Princeton University Press.

Lieberthal, K.G. and Lampton, D.M. (1992) *Bureaucracy, Politics, and Decision Making in Post-Mao China*, Berkeley, CA: University of California Press.

Lin, J.Y., Cai, F., and Li, Z. (2003) *The China Miracle: Development Strategy and Economic Reform*, Hong Kong: The Chinese University Press.

Lin, N. (1999) 'Social Networks and Status Attainment', *Annual Review of Sociology*, 25: 467–487.

—— (2001) *Social Capital: A Theory of Social Structure and Action*, New York: Cambridge University Press.

—— (2006) 'Social Capital', in J. Beckert and M. Zagiroski (eds) *Encyclopedia of Economic Sociology*, London: Routledge.

—— (2011) 'Capitalism in China: A Centrally Managed Capitalism (CMC) and Its Future', *Management and Organization Review*, 7: 63–96.

Lin, N. and Ao, D. (2008) 'The Invisible Hand of Social Capital', in N. Lin and B. Erickson (eds) *Social Capital: An International Research Program*, Oxford: Oxford University Press.

Lin, N. and Dumin, M. (1986) 'Access to Occupations Through Social Ties', *Social Networks*, 8: 365–385.

Lin, N. and Bian, Y. (1991) 'Getting Ahead in Urban China', *American Journal of Sociology*, 97: 657–688.

Lin, N., Dayton, P., and Greenwald, P. (1978) 'Analyzing the Instrumental Use of Relations in the Context of Social Structure', *Sociological Methods and Research*, 7: 149–166.

Lin, N., Ensel, W.M., and Vaughn, J.C. (1981) 'Social Resources and Strength of Ties: Structural Factors in Occupational Status Attainment', *American Sociological Review*, 46: 393–405.

Lin, N., Ye, X., and Ensel, W.M. (1999) 'Social Support and Depressed Mood: A Structural Analysis', *Journal of Health and Social Behavior*, 40: 344–359.

Lin, N., Fu, Y., and Hsung, R-M. (2001) 'The Position Generator: Measurement Techniques for Investigations of Social Capital', in N. Lin, K. Cook, and R.S. Burt (eds) *Social Capital: Theory and Research*, New York: Aldine de Gruyter.

Lin, N., Zhang, Y., Chen, W., Ao, D., and Song, L. (2009) 'Recruiting and Deploying Social Capital in Organizations: Theory and Evidence', in Lisa Keister (ed.) *Work and Organizations in China After Thirty Years of Transition (Research in the Sociology of Work, Volume 19)*, Bingley, UK: Emerald Group Publishing Limited.

Ling, L.H.M. and Shih, C. (1998) 'Confucianism with a Liberal Face: The Meaning of Democratic Politics in Postcolonial Taiwan' *Review of Politics*, 60: 55–82.

Long, J.S. and Freese, J. (2006) *Regression Models for Categorical Dependent Variables Using Stata*, College Station, TX: Stata Press.

Maguire, K. (1998) *The Rise of Modern Taiwan*, Brookfield, VT: Ashgate Publishing Company.

—— (1999) 'Taiwan: From Subcontractor to Regional Operations Centre', *European Business Review*, 99: 162–169.

Marsden, P.V. (1987) 'Core Discussion Networks of Americans', *American Sociological Review*, 52: 122–131.

Marsden, P.V. and Hurlbert, J.S. (1988) 'Social Resources and Mobility Outcomes: A Replication and Extension', *Social Forces*, 66: 1038–1059.

Marx, K. [1857] (1956) *Karl Marx: Selected Writings in Sociology & Social Philosophy*, trans. T.B. Bottomore, New York: McGraw-Hill.

—— [1859] (1970) *A Contribution to the Critique of Political Economy*, Maurice Dobb (ed.), trans. S.W. Ryazanskaya, Moscow: Progress Publishers.

—— (1994) 'Classes in Capitalism and Pre-capitalism', in David Grusky (ed.) *Social Stratification: Class, Race and Gender in Sociological Perspective*, Boulder, CO: Westview.

McClenaghan, P. (2000) 'Social Capital: Exploring the Theoretical Foundations of Community Development Education', *British Educational Research Journal*, 26: 565–582.

McDonald, S. (2005) 'Patterns of Informal Job Matching across the Work Career: Entry-Level, Reentry-Level, and Elite Non-Searching', *Sociological Inquiry*, 75: 403–428.

McDonald, S. and Elder, G.H., Jr. (2006) 'When Does Social Capital Matter? Non-Searching for Jobs across the Life Course', *Social Forces*, 85: 521–550.

McDonald, S. and Day, J.C. (2010) 'Race, Gender, and the Invisible Hand of Social Capital', *Sociology Compass*, 4: 532–543.

McPherson, J.M. and Smith-Lovin, L. (1986) 'Sex Segregation in Voluntary Associations', *American Sociological Review*, 51: 61–79.

—— (1987) 'Homophily in Voluntary Organizations: Status Distance and the Composition of Face-to-Face Groups', *American Sociological Review*, 52: 370–379.

McPherson, J.M., Smith-Lovin, L., and Brashears, M.E. (2006) 'Social Isolation in America: Changes in Core Discussion Networks over Two Decades', *American Sociological Review*, 71: 353–375.

Meyer, J.W. and Rowan, B. (1977) 'Institutionalized Organizations: Formal Structure as Myth and Ceremony', *American Journal of Sociology*, 83: 340–363.

Migdal, J.S. (1988) *Strong Societies and Weak States: State-Society Relations and State Capabilities in the Third World*, Princeton, NJ: Princeton University Press.

Moody, J. (2001) 'Race, School Integration, and Friendship Segregation in America', *American Journal of Sociology*, 107: 679–716.

Mosey, S. and Wright, M. (2007) 'From Human Capital to Social Capital: A Longitudinal Study of Technology-Based Academic Entrepreneurs', *Entrepreneurship Theory and Practice*, 31: 909–935.

Mouw, T. (2003) 'Social Capital and Finding a Job: Do Contacts Matter?' *American Sociological Review*, 68: 868–898.

—— (2006) 'Estimating the Causal Effect of Social Capital: A Review of Recent Research', *Annual Review of Sociology*, 32: 79–102.

Musick, M.A. and Wilson, J. (2008) *Volunteers: A Social Profile*, Bloomington: Indiana University Press.

Muthén, L.K. and Muthén, B.O. (2010) *Mplus User's Guide*, Los Angeles: Muthén & Muthén.

Nahapiet, J. and Ghoshal, S. (1998) 'Social Capital, Intellectual Capital, and the Organizational Advantage', *Academy of Management Review*, 23: 242–266.

Nee, V. and Ingram, P. (1998) 'Embeddedness and Beyond: Institutions, Exchange, and Social Structure', in Mary C. Brinton and Victor Nee (eds) *The New Institutionalism in Sociology*, Stanford, CA: Stanford University Press.

Naughton, B. (1995) *Growing Out of the Plan: Chinese Economic Reform, 1978–1993*, New York: Oxford University Press.

Norris, F.H. and Kaniasty, K. (1996) 'Received and Perceived Social Support in Times of Stress: A Test of the Social Support Deterioration Deterrence Model,' *Journal of Personality and Social Psychology*, 71: 498–511.

Ordeshook, P.C. (1986) *Game Theory and Political Theory*, Cambridge: Cambridge University Press.

Palmer, M. (1995) 'The Re-emergence of Family Law in Post-Mao China: Marriage, Divorce and Reproduction', *China Quarterly*, 141: 110–134.

Parkin, F. (1979) *Marxism and Class Theory: A Bourgeois Critique*, New York: Columbia University Press.

Paxton, P. (2002) 'Social Capital and Democracy: An Interdependent Relationship', *American Sociological Review*, 67: 254–277.

Phan-Thuy, N. (2001) *The Public Employment Service in a Changing Labour Market*, Geneva: International Labour Office.

Portes, A. (1998) 'Social Capital: Its Origins and Applications in Modern Sociology', *Annual Review of Sociology*, 24: 1–24.

Portes, A. and Truelove, C. (1987) 'Making Sense of Diversity: Recent Research on Hispanic Minorities in the United States', *Annual Review of Sociology*, 13: 359–385.

Przeworski, A. (1985) *Capitalism and Social Democracy*, Cambridge: Cambridge University Press.

Putnam, R.D. (1993) 'The Prosperous Community: Social Capital and Public Life', *American Prospect*, 13: 35–42.

—— (2000) *Bowling Alone: The Collapse and Revival of American Community*, New York: Simon & Schuster.

Putnam, R.D., Leonardi, R., and Nanetti, R.Y. (1993) *Making Democracy Work: Civic Traditions in Modern Italy*, Princeton, NJ: Princeton University Press.

Ralston, D.A., Egri, C.P., Stewart, S., Terpstra, R.H., and Kaicheng, Y. (1999) 'Doing Business in the 21st Century with the New Generation of Chinese Managers: A Study of Generational Shifts in Work Values in China', *Journal of International Business Studies*, 30: 415–427.

Ranis, G. (1994) 'From Developing to Mature Economy: An Overview', in G. Ranis (ed.) *Taiwan: From Developing to Mature Economy*, Boulder, CO: Westview Press.

—— (1995) 'Another Look at the East Asian Miracle', *World Bank Economic Review*, 9: 509–534.

Rees, A. (1966) 'Information Networks in Labor Markets', *American Economic Review*, 56: 559–566.

Reskin, B.F. and McBrier, D.B. (2000) 'Why Not Ascription? Organizations' Employment of Male and Female Managers', *American Sociological Review*, 65: 210–233.

Robbins, W.G. (1994) *Colony and Empire: The Capitalist Transformation of the American West*, Lawrence: University Press of Kansas.

Ross, C.E. and Mirowsky, J. (1989) 'Explaining the Social Patterns of Depression: Control and Problem Solving – or Support and Talking?' *Journal of Health and Social Behavior*, 30: 206–219.

Roy, D. (2003) *Taiwan: A Political History*, New York: Cornell University Press.

Royster, D.A. (2003) *Race and the Invisible Hand: How White Networks Exclude Black Men From Blue-collar Jobs*, Berkeley: University of California Press.

Ruan, D., Freeman, L.C., Dai, X., Pan, Y., and Zhang, W. (1997) 'On the Changing Structure of Social Networks in Urban China', *Social Networks*, 19: 75–89.

Ruiter, S. and De Graaf, N.D. (2009) 'Socio-economic Payoffs of Voluntary Association Involvement: A Dutch Life Course Study', *European Sociological Review*, 25: 425–442.

Ruskola, T. (1994) 'Law, Sexual Morality, and Gender Equality in Qing and Communist China', *Yale Law Journal*, 103: 2531–2565.

Ryan, L., Sales, R., Tilki, M., and Siara, B. (2008) 'Social Networks, Social Support and Social Capital: The Experiences of Recent Polish Migrants in London', *Sociology*, 42: 672–690.

Schafft, K.A. and Brown, D.L. (2000) 'Social Capital and Grassroots Development: The Case of Roma Self-Governance in Hungary', *Social Problems*, 47: 201–219.

Schofer, E. and Fourcade-Gourinchas, M. (2001) 'The Structural Contexts of Civic Engagement: Voluntary Association Membership in Comparative Perspective', *American Sociological Review*, 66: 806–828.

Schotter, A. (1981) *The Economic Theory of Social Institutions*, Cambridge: Cambridge University Press.

Sewell, W.H. and Hauser, R.M. (1975) *Education, Occupation and Earnings*, New York: Academic Press.

Sewell, W.H., Haller, A.O., and Portes, A. (1969) 'The Educational and Early Occupational Attainment Process', *American Sociological Review*, 34: 82–92.

Shaw, V.N. (1996) *Social Control in China: A Study of Chinese Work Units*, Westport, CT: Praeger.

Shu, X. and Bian, Y. (2003) 'Market Transition and Gender Gap in Earnings in Urban China', *Social Forces*, 81: 1107–1145.

Simmel, G. [1922] (1955) *Conflict and Web of Group Affiliations*, trans. K. Wolff and R. Bendix, New York: Free Press.

Smith, S.S. (2000) 'Mobilizing Social Resources: Race, Ethnic and Gender Differences in Social Capital and Persisting Wage Inequalities', *Sociological Quarterly*, 41: 509–537.

—— (2005) ' "Don't Put My Name on It": Social Capital Activation and Job-Finding Assistance among the Black Urban Poor', *American Journal of Sociology*, 111: 1–57.

Son, J., Lin, N., and George, L.K. (2008) 'Cross-National Comparison of Social Support Structures between Taiwan and the United States', *Journal of Health and Social Behavior*, 49: 104–117.

Song, L., Son, J., and Lin, N. (2010) 'Social Capital and Health', in W.C. Cockerham (ed.) *The New Blackwell Companion to Medical Sociology*, Malden, MA: Wiley-Blackwell.

Sprengers, M., Tazelaar, F., and Flap, H.D. (1988) 'Social Resources, Situational Constraints, and Reemployment', *Netherlands Journal of Sociology*, 24: 98–116.

Sun, Y. (1981) *Three Principles of the People*, trans. F.W. Price, Taipei: China Publishing Company.

Swedberg, R. (2003) *Principles of Economic Sociology*, Princeton, NJ: Princeton University Press.

Takeshi, A. (1973) 'Regression Analysis When the Dependent Variable is Truncated Normal', *Econometrica*, 41: 997–1016.

Tilly, C. (1998) *Durable Inequality*, Berkeley: University of California Press.

Tomaskovic-Devey, D. (1993) *Gender and Racial Inequality at Work: The Sources and Consequences of Job Segregation*, Ithaca, NY: ILR Press.

Tiryakian, E.A. (2008) *For Durkheim: Essays in Historical and Cultural Sociology*, Surrey: Ashgate.

Tocqueville, A. de [1840] (2003) *Democracy in America*, trans. G.E. Bevan, London: Penguin Books.

Treiman, D.J. (1977) *Occupational Prestige in Comparative Perspective*, New York: Academic Press.

Tu, W. (1991) 'The Search for Roots in Industrial East Asia: The Case of the Confucian Revival', in M. Marty and S. Appleby (eds) *Fundamentalisms Observed*, Chicago, IL: University of Chicago Press.

—— (1993) 'The Confucian Dimension in the East Asian Development Model', in Y. Tzong-shian and J.S. Lee (eds) *Confucianism and Economic Development*, Taipei,Taiwan: Chung-Hua Institution for Economic Research.

Van der Gaag, M.P.J. (2005) 'Measurement of Individual Social Capital', Ph.D. dissertation, Department of Sociology, University of Groningen, Groningen, Netherlands.

Van der Gaag, T., Snijders, A.B., and Flap, H.D. (2007) 'Position Generator Measures and Their Relationship to Other Social Capital Measures', in N. Lin and B. Erickson (eds) *Social Capital: Advances in Research*, Oxford: Oxford University Press.

Vick, K. (24 Oct. 2011) 'Why Hamas is losing Gaza', *TIME*, 178: 40–42.

Völker, B. and Flap, H.D. (1995) 'The Effects of Institutional Transformation on Personal Networks: East Germany, Four Years Later', *The Netherlands Journal of Social Sciences*, 31: 87–110.

—— (1999) 'Getting Ahead in the GDR: Human Capital and Social Capital in the Status Attainment Process Under Communism', *Acta Sociologica*, 42: 17–34.

Walder, A.G. (1983) 'Organized Dependency and Cultures of Authority in Chinese Industry', *Journal of Asian Studies*, 43: 51–76.

—— (1989) 'Social Change in Post-Revolution China', *Annual Review of Sociology*, 15: 405–24.

—— (1995) 'Local Governments as Industrial Firms: An Organizational Analysis of China's Transitional Economy', *American Journal of Sociology*, 101: 263–301.

Weber, M. [1905] (1998) *The Protestant Ethic and the Spirit of Capitalism*, trans. T. Parsons, Los Angeles: Roxbury Publication.

—— (1958) 'Class, Status, Party', in H. H. Gerth and C. Wright Mills (eds) *From Max Weber Essays in Sociology*, New York: Oxford University Press.

Wegener, B. (1991) 'Job Mobility and Social Ties: Social Resources, Prior Job and Status Attainment', *American Sociological Review*, 56: 1–12.

Wethington, E. and Kessler, R.C. (1986) 'Perceived Support, Received Support, and Adjustment to Stressful Life Events', *Journal of Health and Social Behavior*, 27: 78–89.

Whyte, M.K. and Parish, W.L. (1984) *Urban Life in Contemporary China*, Chicago, IL: University of Chicago Press.

Wilson, J. and Musick, M. (1998) 'The Contribution of Social Resources to Volunteering', *Social Science Quarterly*, 79: 799–814.

—— (2003) 'Doing Well by Doing Good: Volunteering and Occupational Achievement among American Women', *Sociological Quarterly*, 44: 433–450.

Wilson, W.J. (1987) *The Truly Disadvantaged: The Inner City, the Underclass, and Public Policy*, Chicago, IL: University of Chicago Press.

Wolf, M. (1985) *Revolution Postponed: Women in Contemporary China*, Stanford, C A: Stanford University Press.

Wong, Y. (2005) *From Deng Xiaoping to Jiang Zemin: Two Decades of Political Reform in the People's Republic of China*, Lanham, MD: University Press of America.

Wonnacott, R.J. and Wonnacott, T.H. (1981) *Regression: A Second Course in Statistics*, New York: Wiley.

Woolcock, M. (1998) 'Social Capital and Economic Development: Toward a Theoretical Synthesis and Policy Framework', *Theory and Society*, 27: 151–208.

Woolley, F. (2003) 'Social Cohesion and Voluntary Activity: Making Connections', in L. Osberg (ed.) *The Economic Implications of Social Cohesion*, Toronto: University of Toronto Press.

WuDunn, S. (1993) 'Wuhan Journal; Layoffs in China: A Dirty Word, but All Too Real', *New York Times*, May 11. HTTP: <http://www.nytimes.com/1993/05/11/world/wuhan-journal-layoffs-in-china-a-dirty-word-but-all-too-real.html> (accessed 10 October 2011).

Wuthnow, R. (1991) 'Tocqueville's Question Revisited: Volunteerism and Public Discourse in Advanced Industrial Societies', in R. Wuthnow (ed.) *Between States and Markets: The Voluntary Sector in Comparative Perspective*, Princeton, NJ: Princeton University Press.

—— (1999) 'Mobilizing Civic Engagement: The Changing Impact of Religious Involvement', in T. Skocpol and M.P. Fiorina (eds) *Civic Engagement in American Democracy*, Washington, DC: Brookings Institution Press.

Xinhua News Agency (2008) 'Employment of College Graduates after Thirty Years of the Open Door Policy: From Job Assignment to Independent Choice' (改革开放30年大学生就业: 从分配工作到自主选择). HTTP: <http://news.xinhuanet.com/edu/2008-12/05/content_10458476.htm> (accessed 23 September 2011).

Yao, S. (2002) *Confucian Capitalism: Discourse, Practice and the Myth of Chinese Enterprise*, London: RoutledgeCurzon.

Yu, L.C., Yu, Y., and Mansfield, P.K. (1990) 'Gender and Changes in Support of Parents in China: Implications for the One-Child Policy', *Gender and Society*, 4: 83–89.

Zang, X. (2000) *Children of the Cultural Revolution: Family Life and Political Behavior in Mao's China*, Boulder, CO: Westview Press.

Zhang, W-W. (1996) *Ideology and Economic Reform under Deng Xiaoping, 1978–1993*, New York: Columbia University Press.

Zhou, J. (2006) *Remaking China's Public Philosophy and Chinese Women's Liberation: The Volatile Mixing of Confucianism, Marxism, and Feminism*, Lewiston, NY: Edwin Mellen Press.

Zhou, X. (1995) 'Partial Reform and the Chinese Bureaucracy in the Post-Mao Era', *Comparative Political Studies*, 28: 440–468.

Zhou, X., Tuma, N.B., and Moen, P. (1996) 'Stratification Dynamics under State Socialism: The Case of Urban China, 1949–1993', *Social Forces*, 74: 759–796.

Index

1:38

Can Clark Sewed 2411
604 - 580 - 3673
1 - 604 - 985 3673

Printed by Publishers' Graphics Kentucky